THE BEDFORD SERIES IN HISTORY AND CULTURE

Utopia

by Sir Thomas More

TRANSLATED BY RALPH ROBYNSON, 1556

Related Titles in
THE BEDFORD SERIES IN HISTORY AND CULTURE
Advisory Editors: Natalie Zemon Davis, Princeton University
Ernest R. May, Harvard University

THE BEDFORD SERIES IN HISTORY AND CULTURE

Utopia

by Sir Thomas More

TRANSLATED BY RALPH ROBYNSON, 1556

Edited with an Introduction by

David Harris Sacks

Reed College

BEDFORD/ST. MARTIN'S   Boston   New York

For Bedford/St. Martin's
History Editor: Katherine E. Kurzman
Developmental Editor: Louise Townsend
Editorial Assistant: Molly Kalkstein
Production Supervisor: Dennis Conroy
Project Management: Books By Design, Inc.
Marketing Manager: Charles Cavaliere
Text Design: Claire Seng-Niemoeller
Index: Books By Design, Inc.
Cover Design: Richard Emery Design, Inc.
Cover Art: Hans Holbein the Younger, *Sir Thomas More* (detail). Copyright The Frick
   Collection, New York.
Composition: G & S Typesetters, Inc.
Printing and Binding: Haddon Craftsmen, an R. R. Donnelley & Sons Company

President: Charles H. Christensen
Editorial Director: Joan E. Feinberg
Director of Editing, Design, and Production: Marcia Cohen
Manager, Publishing Services: Emily Berleth

Library of Congress Catalog Card Number: 98-87540

For information, write: Bedford/St. Martin's, 75 Arlington Street, Boston, MA 02116
(617–426–7440)

ISBN: 0–312–10145–7 (paperback)
ISBN: 0–312–12256–X (hardcover)

DEDICATED TO

Richard Marius
and the Memory of
Jack Hexter

Amicorum communia omnia
Amicus alter ipse

Foreword

The Bedford Series in History and Culture is designed so that readers can study the past as historians do.

The historian's first task is finding the evidence. Documents, letters, memoirs, interviews, pictures, movies, novels, or poems can provide facts and clues. Then the historian questions and compares the sources. There is more to do than in a courtroom, for hearsay evidence is welcome, and the historian is usually looking for answers beyond act and motive. Different views of an event may be as important as a single verdict. How a story is told may yield as much information as what it says.

Along the way the historian seeks help from other historians and perhaps from specialists in other disciplines. Finally, it is time to write, to decide on an interpretation and how to arrange the evidence for readers.

Each book in this series contains an important historical document or group of documents, each document a witness from the past and open to interpretation in different ways. The documents are combined with some element of historical narrative — an introduction or a biographical essay, for example — that provides students with an analysis of the primary source material and important background information about the world in which it was produced.

Each book in the series focuses on a specific topic within a specific historical period. Each provides a basis for lively thought and discussion about several aspects of the topic and the historian's role. Each is short enough (and inexpensive enough) to be a reasonable one-week assignment in a college course. Whether as classroom or personal reading, each book in the series provides firsthand experience of the challenge — and fun — of discovering, recreating, and interpreting the past.

Natalie Zemon Davis
Ernest R. May

Preface

Thomas More's *Utopia* is a book of serious thought, considerable wit, genuine literary imagination, and profound ambiguity. To its author's credit, it has become one of the most frequently studied works in European literature. Discussions of its true meaning started in More's own day and have continued unabated into the present.

It was first published in Latin at Louvain in 1516 and had an early success. Another Latin edition was published in Paris in 1517, two more in Basel in 1518, another in Florence in 1519, and subsequent Latin editions in 1548, 1555, 1563, 1565–66, 1601, 1613, 1629, 1663, 1668, 1672, and 1777. Unlike many other literary works produced in the Renaissance, it has survived in Latin into the modern era and still remains in print in that language.[1] Almost from the start, there was a significant demand for it in modern languages as well. It first appeared in German in 1524, in Italian in 1548, in French in 1550, and in Dutch in 1553. It appeared in English for the first time in 1551, in a version by Ralph Robynson, which was published four more times before 1640 (1556, 1597, 1624, and 1639) and twice more in the Restoration era (1684 and 1685).[2]

---

[1] Thomas More, *Utopia,* vol. 4 of *The Yale Edition of the Complete Works of St. Thomas More,* ed. Edward Sturtz, S. J., and J. H. Hexter (New Haven: Yale University Press, 1965); hereafter this edition will be cited as CW 4; Thomas More, *Utopia: Latin Text and English Translation,* ed. George M. Logan, Robert M. Adams, and Clarence Miller (Cambridge: Cambridge University Press, 1995).

[2] The *Short-Title Catalogue* numbers are STC 18094 (1551), 18095 and 18095.5 (1556), STC 18096 (1597), STC 18097 (1624), and 18098 (1639); see A. W. Pollard and G. R. Redgrave, *A Short-Title Catalogue of Books Printed in England, Scotland, and Ireland and of English Books Printed Abroad, 1475–1640,* 2nd ed., ed. W. A. Jackson, F. S. Ferguson, and Katherine F. Pantzer, 3 vols. (London: Bibliographical Society, 1986–91), vol. 2, p. 161. After the Restoration, there were two further editions of the English translation, Wing STC 2691 (1684) and Wing STC 2692 (1685); see Donald Wing, *Short-Title Catalogue of Books Printed in England, Scotland, Ireland, Wales, and British America and of English Books Printed in Other Countries, 1641–1700,* 3 vols., 2nd ed., ed. Janice M. Hansel, Phebe A. Kirkham, Jeri S. Smith, et al. (New York: Modern Language Association of America, 1982), vol. 2, p. 577.

The 1551 edition of Robynson's translation was a bare-bones effort, lacking many of the features that distinguished the elegantly produced Latin versions from the presses of Louvain, Paris, Basel, and Florence, including the marginal notes, the maps of the island of Utopia, and the numerous other supplementary items supplied by More's friends and fellow humanists in support of his book. In 1556, Robynson and Abraham Vele, his publisher, went some way to remedy these shortcomings. Along with correcting errors that had crept into the 1551 version, they sought to make the book look more like its Latin cousins, adding marginal notes, most of them derived from those that Desiderius Erasmus and Peter Giles had originally created when they first put the book through Dirk Martens's press in Louvain, and presenting a selection from the original supplementary material.

The corrected second edition of this translation, with its marginal notes, forms the basis of the present version. I offer it here with modernized spelling and punctuation and with notes explaining some of the unfamiliar jokes and glossing archaic words and phrases. Insofar as possible, I have tried to suggest something of the appearance of the humanist text as it was sent into the literary marketplace by Robynson and Vele in 1556. But final decisions about format are made by Bedford/St. Martin's so as to conform to the design of the Bedford Series in History and Culture. I also offer Robynson's 1551 dedicatory letter to William Cecil, who was one of the principal secretaries of Edward VI's Privy Council when the first edition of the translation appeared. As discussed in the introduction, this dedicatory letter gives considerable insight into Robynson's purposes in first producing the translation and is usefully compared to the prefatory remarks to readers that begin the 1556 edition. Finally, to illustrate some of the material differences between the early Latin versions of *Utopia* and Vele's 1556 edition in English, I have provided reproductions of a few selected pages from the latter to compare to several special items drawn from John Froben's 1518 Basel edition in Latin, for which Vele could neither find nor create a substitute.

Until the twentieth century, Robynson's careful rendering, with its distinctive sixteenth-century phrases and idioms, has been the main means by which most readers of English have encountered the book's controversial social ideas and penetrating wit. Insofar as the work has influenced subsequent thinkers and commentators, its ideas have largely been couched in Robynson's phrasings. As argued in the introduction, they are what makes it possible for future ages to think that *Utopia* is best understood as *utopian,* a work intended to provide a never-to-be-realized or realizable model for social and economic policy rather than as a humanist satire on the relationship between the requirements of Christian virtue and the conduct of public affairs. Robynson's translation also gives us an example of how More's book was read and understood in the changing circumstances of sixteenth-century England. His translation, therefore, offers an excellent double entry into *Utopia*, allowing us to read this famous book not only as a commentary on the social and political life of sixteenth-century England, but also as an artifact of, and contributor to, this same history.

Utopia is an amazingly rich and sometimes puzzling work, one that touches on the widest range of historical and cultural subjects. Thomas More, a successful practicing lawyer and soon to be royal counselor to Henry VIII, was a man thoroughly engaged in the affairs of his times. He was also a committed humanist intellectual and devout Christian thinker, possessed of great learning and a wide range of scholarly friends on the continent as well as at home. The book he wrote drew significantly from the knowledge he gained from all the circles in which he moved.

The introduction to this present edition offers an account of the cultural and institutional framework within which it was written and read. It is historical in a broad sense, focused not just on recovering as much as possible the circumstances within which More and Robynson lived and worked, but in coming to terms with the major developments then unfolding in English and European society. The introduction begins with a discussion of More's book, the Latin work of 1516, understood as a learned text by one of the leading Christian humanists of the day. A second section considers the socioeconomic, ecclesiastical, and political context within which More lived and on which his book commented, attending particularly to the processes of historical change experienced by the English and affecting England's major institutions at the beginning of the sixteenth century. Finally, the concluding section focuses on a few of the major historical developments that reshaped England between 1516 and the 1550s and examines some of the distinctive features of Robynson's translation, seeing the way his approach to the book transformed it from a subtle humanist discussion of the relationship between ethics and politics into a work of socioeconomic advice and commentary.

The publication of More's *Utopia* was very much the product of joint efforts by colleagues and supporters among the community of literary patrons, learned scholars, innovative publishers, and skilled printers of his day. Much the same can be said about Robynson's translation. It too depended on the encouragement he received from friends and the creative efforts of those responsible for bringing his work to print. No less can be said about this present edition.

The dedication is to two friends who, in their different ways, brought me not just to the study of Thomas More and his *Utopia,* but to a deeper appreciation of the good fellowship of the scholarly life. Soon after we met, almost twenty years ago, Richard Marius entrusted me with reading and criticizing the manuscript of his magnificent biography of Thomas More, an experience that taught me as much about what it takes to make good writing for modern audiences as about the complicated nature of More's personality, character, and intellect and the ambiguous legacy of his career. Richard has now returned me the compliment of reading and commenting on the introduction to this present edition, offering his characteristically generous and helpful advice, for which I am exceptionally grateful. Richard also first introduced me to Jack Hexter, whose contributions to our understanding of the intellectual and cultural landscape of early modern England and Europe, in which More and his successors flourished, were matched only by his capacity for loyal friendship and his faith in the vigorous exchange of ideas.

At Reed College, my home institution, *Utopia* has an honored place in the curriculum of Humanities 210, a full-year, team-taught course focused on the study of the European humanities from the fourteenth to eighteenth centuries. My view of the book and its historical significance has been shaped by teaching in this course, and before that in Reed's Humanities 110, the first-year course devoted to ancient Greek, Roman, and early Christian civilization. I am especially grateful to the staff and students in those two courses for their patience as I explained my own views and for the instruction they have given me in return. I particularly want to thank the colleagues in Humanities 210 with whom I have been teaching *Utopia* in recent years: Mark Bedau, Ray Kierstead, Robert Knapp, Bill Ray, and Lisa Steinman. The introduction to this present edition also has benefited in important ways from the careful reading and commentary of David Cressy and Constance Jordan as well as two anonymous readers for Bedford/St. Martin's; each has helped make this edition better than it could possibly have been through my efforts alone.

I am also very grateful to Natalie Zemon Davis, editor of the series in which this book appears, not only for the invitation she gave me to do it, but equally for her encouragement and support on this project as on so many others. Similarly I must thank the editorial and production departments at Bedford/St. Martin's for the help they have provided, especially Louise Townsend, who gave it the benefit of her sound judgment through every stage from the earliest drafts to its final version. Much of the work and a good deal of the writing was done at the Folger Shakespeare Library; without the Library's magnificent collections and the assistance of its marvelous staff it would have been impossible to complete the work. I am especially grateful to Werner Gundersheimer, director of the Folger; Richard Kuhta, the Folger Librarian; Georgianna Ziegler, the Folger's reference librarian; and Betsy Walsh and her excellent colleagues in the Reading Room: Harold Batie, LuEllen DeHaven, Rosalind Larry, Camille Seerattan, and Sue Sehulster.

Finally, and most importantly, I must give my deepest thanks to my wife, Eleanor, who not only is responsible for transcribing and modernizing the text of Robynson's *Utopia,* working from a sometimes barely readable microfilm copy of the original 1556 edition, but who also assisted with her excellent editorial judgment and advice in ways too numerous to detail. Her faith and support has been vital to the completion of this project.

David Harris Sacks

Contents

APPENDICES

THE BEDFORD SERIES IN HISTORY AND CULTURE

Utopia

by Sir Thomas More

TRANSLATED BY RALPH ROBYNSON, 1556

Figure 1. Map of the Isle of Utopia, by Ambrosius Holbein, from John Froben's Latin edition of *Utopia,* printed in Basel in March 1518.
By permission of the Folger Shakespeare Library.

PART ONE

Introduction:
More's *Utopia* in
Historical Perspective

Thomas More's *Utopia* reports imagined conversations in Antwerp between the fictional Raphael Hythloday and a character called, like the author himself, "Thomas More."[1] The conversations are represented as having taken place during the summer of 1515, while the real More was in Antwerp in part to visit with Peter Giles, chief clerk of Antwerp's court of justice and a well-regarded and well-connected humanist scholar in his own right. According to the fiction, "More" first encountered Hythloday with Giles one morning after attending Mass at Antwerp's Church of Notre Dame. From Giles he learns that Hythloday, said to be Portuguese by birth, had sailed with Amerigo Vespucci on the latter's last three voyages to American waters. Intrigued to hear about these adventures in newfound lands, More invites Giles and Hythloday to the garden of his rented house. There Hythloday concentrates on providing a detailed description of the isle of Utopia, but he comes to this subject only in the course of considering and rejecting the proposition that philosophically minded men should become royal counselors — the subject that occupies most of The First Book.

After breaking for the midday meal, The Second Book takes up the task of description, beginning with the island's geography and something of its foundation and history. To demonstrate that a successful system of community property could indeed work, Hythloday describes the island's cities, and especially Amaurote, its capital; its form of government and the names and functions of its officials; the occupations of the Utopians; their customs and habits, including their dress, diet, and pastimes; the character of their economy; their learning, their system of education for men and women, and their moral outlook and principles; their management of their households and their family life; their laws and their institutions of law enforcement; their ideas and practices concerning war; and, finally, their religions.

The distinctiveness of this Utopian way of life centers on the absence of private property on the island, which makes possible its other unusual features: the production, distribution, and consumption of the necessities; habits and manners of social relations; the law, governmental institutions; the military; religious outlooks and practices; and a host of other matters. The Utopian life is marked by striking differences from prevailing European norms in relations between men and women. The family unit is conventional enough, with husbands and wives living together with their children in monogamous households. Women are subordinated to their husbands, just as children are to their parents. Nevertheless, men and women enjoy considerably more equality than was generally true in sixteenth-century Europe. Marriage is based on the principle of choice exercised by both parties. To ensure that the married couple will be appropriately matched, the Utopian custom requires that the future bride and groom be presented naked to each other before their wedding day. These same customs allow divorce to be initiated by either party, whether for adultery or other intolerable offenses. Women, like men, practice crafts or trades as well as work in the fields, although "as the weaker sort" they are assigned the lighter tasks, such as working wool or linen (136).[2] Like men, too, they are encouraged to seek learning, and many spend their free time reading and attending the scholarly public lectures given each morning before daybreak. Women are also eligible for service in the Utopian priesthood, although in practice only elderly widows ever attain these posts. Finally, women as well as men engage in regular military training, and wives are encouraged to join their husbands in military service and fight alongside them in war.

This last feature signifies with special clarity the commitment each Utopian, regardless of gender or personal circumstance, is expected to make to uphold and defend the Utopians' communal way of life. It also raises important questions about More's purpose as an author, since it pictures a society so remote from late medieval and early modern European practice that it would be hard to contemplate implementing it in his own day, if that indeed was his purpose.

When Hythloday has completed his description, "More," the character, grants that there are many things in the Utopian commonwealth "which in our cities I may rather wish for than hope after," but he remains unconvinced that the Utopian plan for social life could work in current European society (201–02). As readers, we are left to puzzle out for ourselves whether "More" or Hythloday is right.

In many ways, this subtle and cunning work of fiction needs no introduction. In dealing with human relations and the family, with wealth and poverty, with government and social order, and with faith and reason, it invites us into its fictional world to make up our own minds about a host of familiar issues about how best to live our lives. However, it is also the product of a milieu quite remote from ours in its institutions and practices, and in consequence it was written for an audience that brought to it different educational backgrounds, experiences, expectations, and assumptions than are common among us today. To further complicate the picture, More's world itself was rapidly changing in the early and mid-sixteenth century in a fashion that for later readers robbed some of More's most fondly held views and beliefs of their tacit acceptance or seeming self-evidence. This introduction attempts to offer some guidance on this history, concentrating first on the cultural and social environment in which More's Latin text first appeared and then on the setting in which Ralph Robynson's English translation was published.

TEXTS

We shall start with the text of *Utopia* as it relates to other texts. More was a learned scholar and already an accomplished writer when he published his book. He drew his literary inspiration and his philosophical ideas from a wide range of sources, and in doing so, he contributed in his own way to the development of the literary and philosophical traditions on which he was commenting. To understand what he was doing when he wrote *Utopia,* we need to attend first to its literary models and to the philosophical paradigms on which it depended.[3]

Literary Conventions

SEEING FORWARD

In a number of respects, *Utopia* might seem familiar territory. For example, it displays many of the features of a modern novel, especially in the way it represents itself as a description of an actual conversation between known people about a real place. Beginning with the dedicatory letter to Peter Giles, who is described as having been present at the conversations, the text uses a host of literary devices to create the illusion that it is recounting a history, not just telling a made-up tale. As already indicated, Giles himself was a real enough person; he made himself complicit in the book's fiction not just by contributing a letter of his own to the publication, but by speaking there of having been present during the supposed discussions (202–05). There are also a number of references to recent historical events, among them the 1497 revolt against Henry VII's high taxes (98) and the French invasions of Italy (114–15).

More also sought to increase his book's sense of verisimilitude by emulating accounts of actual travels to distant places by intrepid navigators and adventurers; accounts of this sort became popular in the aftermath of Christopher Columbus's voyages. As we have seen, Raphael Hythloday, *Utopia's* main protagonist, is represented as having sailed on the last three of the four voyages of Amerigo Vespucci, the famous Florentine who is remembered in the name America. Indeed, More explicitly drew on some of the factual materials contained in the two books that Vespucci wrote in 1504 about those voyages, as well as on Peter Martyr's *On the New World,* the first part of which was published in 1511. In his letters, Vespucci provided his fellow Europeans with evidence of peoples apparently living without any private possessions, but holding all things in common.[4] This fact helps make Hythloday's description appear as something more than a purely philosophical speculation.

This striving for what literary critics sometimes call a "reality effect" is itself a distinguishing feature of the fictional mode that *Utopia* introduced into early modern and modern literary culture. It establishes the work in the literary landscape between the purely imaginary tale, intended primarily for pleasure or entertainment, and the philosophical treatise, concerned to edify or convince, allowing it to partake of something from each. This sort of book almost instantly found a niche for itself in the publishing marketplace and was frequently imitated in the early modern period.[5] In the eighteenth century alone, some 215 descriptions of imaginary voyages were published in Europe, including Jonathan Swift's *Gulliver's Travels* (1726). The genre has persisted since then. Many of More's storytelling tricks are now commonly employed in contemporary fantasy literature, science fiction, and computer games.[6]

The word *utopia,* first coined by More for his book, also has a comfortable, modern feeling. It is now a very common term in English, most often carrying the meaning of a vain fantasy, a hopelessly unrealistic reform program, or an entirely impracticable set of social institutions. It was not long into its history that the word acquired this reputation for fictive foolishness. By the early 1530s, François Rabelais had satirically connected his *Gargantua and Pantagruel* with More's book by making Pantagruel a Utopian on his mother's side.[7] As early as 1570, John Foxe, the Protestant martyrologist, identified Purgatory and Utopia as two equally nonexistent places, treating their rigorous regimes of social discipline — the one being judged as the model for the other — as simultaneously false and fictitious.[8] More himself provided plenty of license for doubt about utopian possibilities in *Utopia* itself, perhaps nowhere more so than in the skeptical remarks he puts in the mouth of his namesake in the text.

Utopia is remarkably worldly and hardheaded in its grasp of the way societies work. The account of sixteenth-century socioeconomic life and of the conduct of contemporary politics in The First Book reveals a penetrating capacity for social criticism and pragmatic analysis. The treatment of the Utopian polity in The Second Book, despite its imaginary quality, shows a firm understanding of the institutions and mechanisms necessary to sustain an effectively functioning social order. More gives remarkable attention to the material conditions and commonplace details of everyday existence, and in a number of ways, Utopia shows a striking similarity to modern forms of social engineering. *Utopia* may be a visionary work, but the journey it portrays to a newfound land is some distance from being a medieval romance, and the imaginary island society it describes is very far from being a dreamy fantasy.

LOOKING BACKWARD

Although More's book undoubtedly helped create a familiar genre of fiction, in other respects it perhaps seems less like a modern work. For example, it conforms only in part to our model of individual literary authorship. The main body of the text, The First Book and The Second Book as we have them, is solely More's creative work. Even in this respect, however, the book differs somewhat from modern practice, since much of More's material is derived directly, without mention, from other sources, ancient and modern. More made no effort to conceal his borrowings, and his earliest readers — those familiar with Greek and Latin — would have spotted most of his sources without great difficulty. Indeed, a considerable measure of a reader's pleasure came from these moments of recognition, from seeing the inventive ways the author used familiar adages or images or stories in new contexts.

However, the *Utopia* that appeared in Louvain, and then in Paris, and then again in Basel was not the product of single authorship even in this expanded sense. It was, rather, very much a group project — the work of a number of European humanists who not only contributed prefaces, letters, illustrations, and other materials to frame it, but who supervised its press runs for More, who by then was back in England. The

1516 Louvain edition was left in the hands of Peter Giles and Desiderius Erasmus, the Dutch scholar and More's good friend. Responsibility for later editions fell to other friends.[9]

More's friends and supporters joined in the literary enterprise itself. Erasmus and Giles, for example, supplied the Latin editions with extensive marginal glosses, many of them offering biting remarks comparing Utopian virtues to the shortcomings of their present-day society. There is also a body of poetry, all of which appeared originally in the 1516 edition; More himself probably wrote only the six-line poem in Latin attributed to the Poet Laureate of Utopia. Particularly striking is the quatrain written in the Utopian language and alphabet, which appears along with a "translation" into Latin. It is very likely the work of Giles, not More. Two other brief Latin poems were supplied by Gerard Geldenhauer of Nijmegen and Cornelis de Schrijver, well-known humanist poets from the Low Countries. In addition, there is a great deal of commentary, some of it extended, by different hands, including important contributions by Guillaume Budé, the famous French humanist and legal scholar, and by Jerome Busleyden, a powerful patron of learning and a prominent official in the court of Charles, then the Prince of Castille and soon to be Charles V, the Holy Roman Emperor. Accompanying the work there is a map of the island. The one appearing in the 1517 and subsequent editions is the work of Ambrosius Holbein, brother of the famous artist Hans Holbein the younger, who himself supplied the border of the title page and several other printer's devices for the volume. Only a small portion of this material was retained by Ralph Robynson for his English translation.[10]

Humanist works, especially those published in the Erasmus circle, often appeared with such supporting documentation by many hands. One effect was to create a market for the book, giving it the endorsement of well-known and highly regarded writers, a pattern familiar enough on the dust jackets of today's best-sellers. In the print culture of early sixteenth-century Europe, this practice also allowed a group of like-minded scholar-authors to spread the individual fame of their friends and allies while building support for their common projects of intellectual enlightenment and social reform. Hence another function of the framing material was to set the text into a context of interpretation. Beyond these functions, the letters and other accompanying materials, by playing into More's fictions, contribute in some measure to the "reality effects" produced by the work.

These features of More's book make it appear in its externals rather different from most modern works, but there are substantive differences as well. As an account of a foreign journey to a previously unknown land, *Utopia* owes something of a debt to ancient and medieval tales of fantastic voyages. One model is certainly Lucian's *Menippus Goes to Hell,* written in Greek in the second century of the present era. About the year 1504, More and Erasmus translated Lucian's work from Greek into Latin. Reminding readers of the all-too-evident leveling effects of death, which reduces all human flesh to a common state of decay, this tale mocks the famous (including philosophers and ancient heroes) and the powerful (including kings and tyrants), focusing especially on the pretensions of the rich — "those whose wealth or political power had given them such an inflated idea of themselves," regularly engage in "lying, cheating, money grubbing, and charging exorbitant rates of interest," display their "utter contempt for the poor," and forget "that they and their possessions were strictly perishable."[11] A number of these topics receive extended treatment in *Utopia* as well. Another literary model is almost as surely Lucian's *The True History,* which imagines a voyage to strange lands lying beyond the Pillars of Hercules — that is, the present-day Gibraltar. Equally to the point, Lucian's "merry conceits and jests" are specifically said to have been adored by the Utopians (166).[12]

Obviously, the studied realism of *Utopia,* imitating Vespucci, contrasts markedly with the overtly mythic quality of Lucian and other examples of fantastic writing from the ancient and early modern period, perhaps nowhere more so than in More's repeated insistence that what he is describing truly happened. Lucian, in beginning his *True History,* took exactly the opposite position. In that story, Lucian tells his readers that "he shall be a . . . honest liar, for I am telling you frankly, here and now, that I have no intention whatever of telling the truth. Let this voluntary confession forestall any future criticism: I am writing about things entirely outside my own experience or anyone else's, things that have no reality whatever and never could have. So mind you do not believe a word I say." Lucian justifies his approach in comparison to the lying of other writers who offer their fictitious tales in the belief "that anyone could tell such lies and expect to get away with it."[13]

Viewed in this light, More's insistence on the truth of his narrative is itself an invitation to treat his claims with skepticism, calling into question the fundamental difference of his text from such fantasies as Lucian's. Nevertheless, the comparison between self-evidently fictional travelers' memoirs like Lucian's and professedly "true" histories like Vespucci's, implicit in *Utopia,* helps explain the curious literary effects produced by More's book — its tendency to undermine itself just as it is most insistent on its historical accuracy.[14] The clever irony subverts the realism that More in other respects was at such pains to display.

Although More had an impressive capacity to grasp and describe the mechanisms that keep society working, this skill was not something he could or would have wished to isolate from his deeper philosophical and religious commitments. His viewpoint was one that invited skeptical doubt about the ultimate importance of the very same worldly and material purposes that in other respects make *Utopia* seem so modern. More's own sense of realism was always tempered by a strong spirit of Christian devotion, which registered the persistence of sin in the world and expressly honored the power of godly grace in overcoming it and which consequently placed the ultimate fount of truth outside the realm of human reason and secular attainments. If "truth" is eternal and divine, as More, a deep student of Plato and Saint Augustine, believed, perhaps the best that can be expected from its representation on earth is only its dim reflection, whether we are experiencing actual events or reading about imagined ones.

Philosophical Convictions

ANCIENT REASONING

Despite what More's text shares in literary form with Lucian's satires and modern fiction, it is more closely associated with yet another genre, first invented by the ancients, which was still prominent in More's time but is not very evident today. More explicitly identified his book as a study of "the best state of a commonwealth," placing it in a long tradition of debate regarding the strengths and shortcomings of various ideal and real polities.[15] The first extended examples of the form are found in the writings of Plato and Aristotle, and there are later examples among Roman students of Greek intellectual traditions, such as Cicero and Seneca. Scholastic theorists like Marsiglio of Padua, following Aristotle, made it a subject in their writings during the Middle Ages, and humanist scholars and thinkers, Erasmus among them, following the classical Latin authors, particularly Cicero, kept it alive in the Renaissance.

In some obvious ways, More's greatest debt surely is to Plato, not only to *The Republic,* but also to *The Laws* and to the elegant portrayal of the lost island of Atlantis in the brief surviving fragment of his *Critias.* These are among the earliest philosophical works in which the characteristics of a best form of commonwealth are described and analyzed. In *The Republic,* Socrates constructs what is intended as the perfect model of a just city. A principal feature of it is the community of property among its class of Guardians or Philosopher-Kings. According to Socrates, this is a regime that can only come into being if philosophers become kings, or kings philosophers, something not logically impossible but not very likely, as Socrates himself implies.[16] The premise in *The Laws* is somewhat different: An unnamed "Athenian Stranger," often taken to be Plato himself, discusses plans for a colony reputedly to be founded on the isle of Crete. The book works up a code of constitutional, civil, and criminal laws and of administrative, religious, and social arrangements for what is understood to be a *second-best* regime. In contrast to *The Republic,* the fiction in *The Laws* is that its scheme for creating a new society is intended for implementation. Hence Plato allows for private property because its absence would be impractical, but he seeks in myriad ways to restrain the corrosive effects it has on personal morality and social harmony.[17]

Because community of property is the central feature of *Utopia,* its identification with *The Republic* is obvious; More himself is at pains to draw his readers' attention to it. Hythloday explicitly says that what "Plato feigneth in his weal public"— the Latin word here is *Respublica*— "the Utopians do in theirs" (122). The brief poem attributed to Anemolius, the Utopian poet laureate, also says that Utopia is "like to Plato's city":

> For what Plato's pen hath platted briefly
> In naked words, as in a glass,
> The same have I performed fully,
> With laws, with men, and treasure fitly (206).

On the whole, early readers of *Utopia* were especially struck by its connection to *The Republic,* especially in its advocacy of a form of communism. As Jerome Busleyden put it in the letter he contributed for early Latin editions of More's book, this feature was the very "pattern and perfect model of morality . . . so that every object and every action, whether public or private, regards not the greed of the many or the caprice of the few, but, however small it is, is totally directed to the maintenance of one uniform justice, equality, and communion." The consequence "of this absolute singleness of purpose is the complete elimination of everything that causes, promotes, and fosters intrigue, luxury, jealousy, and injustice. Into these evils mortals are themselves driven, even though reluctant, by the private ownership of property, or the burning thirst for gain, or that most pitiable of passions, ambition, to their immense and unparalleled loss."[18]

Nevertheless, *Utopia*'s reliance on a system of laws to establish a just and moral community, not simply on the reasoned judgment of philosopher-kings, shows that its debt to Plato's *The Laws* also is very great. There are a number of other striking similarities with this text, for example, in the relatively large social roles described for women and in the frank discussions of the sexual nature of marriage. It is in the area of government, however, that the parallels are perhaps the most important. The Utopian regime of magistrates, assemblies, and elections, though not exactly the same as the system that Plato prescribes for his second-best constitution, bears a significant resemblance to it — particularly in the effort made to ensure that officials will serve the communities they represent. Both regimes appear designed to situate their constitutions midway between monarchy and democracy, which the "Athenian Stranger" in *The Laws* says all "constitutional systems always should." [19] Neither regime envisions a single ruler over the whole polity or a complete reliance on popular sovereignty.[20]

In *The Laws,* Plato is quite clear about what distinguishes the "first-best society" from the "second-best." The former is one in which the old adage that "friends' property is common property" applies to the whole of society. In it, there is a perfect unity of purpose. In this view, there could be "no truer or better" society than one where "all means have been taken to eliminate everything we mean by the word *ownership* from life." [21] Under such a regime, there would be no need for laws, because the society would be governed by philosophical truth over which "no law or ordinance"— no mere political regime —"has the right of sovereignty." Nevertheless, Plato saw that, "as things are," the necessary philosophical "insight is nowhere to be met with, except in faint vestiges," and there is no available philosopher-king "able and willing to put the good into practice when he has perceived it." For this reason, the "Athenian Stranger" says, "we have to choose the second best, ordinance and law," a regime that regulates the magistrates along with the ordinary citizens, lest either pursue private advantage over the public good. "Mankind," he goes on, "must either give themselves a law and regulate their lives by it, or live no better than wild beasts." [22] Law, in short, is necessary to overcome the shortcomings of human nature.

What More created on his imagined island is an amalgam of the two kinds of regime that Plato had described. He extended the principle of community of property, adopted from *The Republic* where it was practiced only among the Guardians, to all of the island's inhabitants, but he eliminated the Philosopher-Kings and in their place followed the dictates of *The Laws* by substituting a system of councils and assemblies operating under the regulation of laws. The island of Utopia, therefore, is like the Athenian Stranger's imagined colony, a "law state"[23] and not an ideal community exclusively under the rule of philosophy, yielding to the undiluted love of wisdom and sure guidance of perfect knowledge. Put in other terms, it is a "first-best" society in its policies with a "second-best" constitution and system of laws.

The possible contradictions arising from More's use of Plato are made especially relevant because in considering the best state of a commonwealth, *Utopia* owes almost as great a debt to antithetical Aristotelian political and ethical ideas. In particular, More derived the arguments in favor of private property that he gives to his namesake at the end of The First Book and again at the end of The Second Book from Aristotle's own powerful and well-known criticisms of Plato's "communism." Aristotle believed that a political community by its very nature "is to be a plurality," a combination of people with differing qualities and skills, whose proper functioning depended on the principle of reciprocity.[24] Its self-sufficiency is achieved through proportional exchange, according to the value of each person's contribution, "and not on the basis of equality." Inevitably, therefore, a just society would display proportional differences in wealth between its richer and poorer members.[25]

In contrast to Plato, Aristotle saw the possession of private property as the very foundation of public and personal morality. If all was in common, he argued, no one would have particular responsibility for anything. The result would be poverty because each individual would expect the others to take care of the common good. "Everyone thinks chiefly of his own, hardly at all of the common interest; and only when he is himself concerned as an individual," Aristotle argued.[26] On the other hand, "when everyone has a distinct interest, men will not complain of one another, and they make more progress, because everyone will be attending to his own business." Aristotle also allowed that "by reason of goodness, and in respect of use, 'Friends,' as the proverb says, 'will have all things in common.'"[27] However, he put a very different interpretation on this adage than Plato did. When human beings are firmly in possession of what is their own, he argued, they have the incentive to share it with fellow human beings. For Aristotle, the possession of private property allows people to show their capacity for goodwill by choosing to be generous, and moral virtue is attributable only to actions about which there is a choice. On this argument, Plato's kind of "communism" would deprive people of the chance to be truly virtuous.[28]

Another source of great significance to More was Ciceronian civic humanism, as first articulated in Cicero's political and moral writings, such as *Of Duties,* and later rehearsed by numerous imitators and commentators, including Erasmus. Cicero also believed in the efficacy of private property, offering many of the same arguments in its defense as Aristotle. However, the Ciceronian approach to the question cast this discussion in a new context, debating whether social and political activity or philosophical contemplation was the best way of life. This discussion is also one that Hythloday and "More" engage in during their dialogue in The First Book.

As we have already noted, Hythloday forcefully insists that as things presently are, it would be pointless and foolhardy for a virtuous and philosophical person to serve the state. The character "More," answering in distinctly pragmatic terms, argues that it would be wrong nonetheless to abandon the commonwealth. "School philosophy," he tells Hythloday, can hardly be expected to receive a favorable hearing among such an audience, on such an occasion, and in such a setting. However, a more appropriate philosophy has a greater prospect of utility, one that is "more civil," that "knoweth . . . her own stage, and behaving herself in the play that she hath in hand, playing her part accordingly with comeliness, uttering nothing out of due order and fashion." "In a commonwealth" and "in consultations of kings and princes," "More" says,

> what part soever you have taken upon you, play that as well as you can and make the best of it. . . . If evil opinions and naughty persuasion cannot be utterly and quite plucked out of their hearts, if you cannot even as you would remedy vices which use and custom hath confirmed, yet for this cause you must not leave and forsake the commonwealth.

Instead, "you must with a crafty wile and subtle train study and endeavor yourself, as much as in you lieth, to handle the matter wittily and handsomely for the purpose, and that which you cannot turn to good so to order it that it be not very bad, for it is not possible for all things to be well unless all men were good, which I think will not be yet these good many years" (122).

How should we take this passage? The image of life as a stage play derives ultimately from a familiar analogy in Epictetus's *Enchieridion*— one that would have been well known to virtually all of the first readers of *Utopia:*

> Remember that you are an actor in a play, the character of which is determined by the Playwright: if He wishes the play to be short, it is short; if long, it is long; if He wishes you to play the part of a beggar, remember to act even this rôle adroitly; and so if your rôle be that of a

cripple, an official, or a layman. For this is your business to play the rôle assigned to you; but the selection of that rôle is Another's.[29]

In this passage, the play takes on the character of providential history and the playwright that of a god, and the roles he assigns become the equivalent of divinely ordained callings. Seen in this light, "More's" insistence that Hythloday act out his part in "the play that is in hand" (121) represents a serious moral challenge to the latter's philosophical high-mindedness.[30]

In many respects, Hythloday's and "More's" dispute reiterates the ancient debate between philosophy and rhetoric. Among the Greeks, Plato had put the interests of philosophical wisdom represented by Socrates, in whose voice Plato himself often spoke, against those of rhetorical science exemplified by the Sophists, teachers of verbal craft, which Plato viewed as aiming only at advantage and victory, not knowledge and truth.[31] Aristotle, however, had insisted on the importance of rhetoric for the flourishing of social and political life and had written a major treatise on the subject. In *The Politics,* he treats the capacity to speak and thereby "to set forth the expedient and inexpedient, and . . . likewise the just and unjust," as the trait that especially distinguishes human beings from all other animals.[32] Cicero also held a favorable view of rhetoric. In a series of well-known works — most notably *De Oratore*— he supported its merits against its philosophical enemies by urging a reunion of rhetoric with philosophy to harness the powers of persuasion with knowledge of the truth.[33] As with their differences over private property, therefore, Hythloday in this takes the side of Socrates and Plato, and "More" defends the Aristotelian and Ciceronian view.[34]

The debate also plays on another ancient theme, namely the relationship of philosophy to the active life of politics. In *The Republic,* Plato, again employing the voice of Socrates, argued that philosophers — people possessed of true wisdom — "who have also come to understand the madness of the multitude sufficiently and have seen that there is nothing . . . sound or right in any present politics" could not "escape destruction" in public life. Such a person "would be as a man who has fallen among wild beasts, unwilling to share in their misdeeds and unable to hold out singly against the savagery of all." "Before he could in any way benefit his friends or the state," he would "come to an untimely end without doing any good to himself or others." Hence Socrates recommends that the philosopher, living outside the perfect city, should remain "quiet," mind "his own affairs," and be "content" to "keep himself free from iniquity and unholy deeds through this life and take his departure with fair hope, serene and well content when the end comes."[35] Hythloday's arguments paraphrase this passage and conform closely to the paradigm (123–24).[36]

Hythloday, in defending his refusal of government service, argues that his choice allows him to "live at liberty after mine own mind and pleasure" (95). In the original Latin, the line reads, *Atque nunc sic uiuo ut uolo*—"As it is, I live now as I please."[37] It is a claim to philosophical freedom of the sort commonly made among Renaissance humanists pursuing a life of learning.[38] However, this wording harkens back to what Aristotle identified as "the false idea of freedom" that arises "in democracies of the more extreme type." In such places, he says, men think "that freedom means doing what one likes" and "every one lives as he pleases, or in the words of Euripedes, 'according to his fancy.'" This concept of liberty, Aristotle argues, is "contradictory to the true interests of the state" whose existence promotes "the good life."[39] Hythloday's phrasing also closely parallels the language used by Cicero as he considered whether a virtuous person should participate in government. Those who decline, Cicero argued, "have the same aims as kings — to suffer no want, to be subject to no authority, to enjoy their liberty, that is, in its essense, to live just as they please."[40]

"More's" criticism of Hythloday's refusal of governmental office is framed in similar Ciceronian terms as a defense of the active life. "Nature by the power of reason associates man with man in the common bonds of speech and life," Cicero argues, and "prompts men to meet in companies, to form public assemblies, and take part in them themselves." It also "stimulates . . . courage" to defend what is dear to them.[41] "We are not born for ourselves alone," he insists, "but our country claims a share of our being, and our friends a share." Hence "we ought to follow Nature as our guide, to contribute to the general good by an interchange of acts of kindness, by giving and receiving, and thus by our skill, our industry, and our talents to cement human society more closely together, man to man."[42]

In keeping with this view, the single-minded search for truth, admirable though it is, cannot be allowed to compete with most people's obligations to the commonwealth or to perform public responsibilities. Cicero recognized that a few "men of extraordinary genius" might be "excused for not taking part in public affairs,"[43] but for those with lesser skills "to be drawn by study away from active life is contrary to moral duty. For the whole glory of virtue is in activity."[44] Hence individuals "whom Nature has endowed with the capacity for administering public affairs should put aside all hesitation, enter into the race for public office, and take a hand in directing the government; for in no other way can a government be administered or greatness of spirit be made manifest."[45] In arguing in this way, Cicero proposes that Plato's view of philosophers is "inadequate." "Busied with the pursuit of truth" and despising and counting "as naught that which most men eagerly seek," they may do "no positive wrong to anyone" and thereby "secure one sort of justice." However, like the self-seeking individual engaged only in his own private business, they also "fall into the opposite injustice; for hampered by their pursuit of learning they leave to their fate those whom they ought to defend."[46]

It was a convention of moral theory, especially among Renaissance humanists, that true worthiness rested only in virtuous actions, freely chosen and performed. The mere holding of titles or lands or stocks of money could not grant it. Both Hythloday and "More" take these views as their own, but "More" does so in a way that raises a difficult problem for Hythloday's critique of private property. Hythloday is clear that private property brings out the worst in people by promoting their selfishness and by equating their worthiness with their possessions or their inherited positions, not with their actions. In response "More" asks, in effect, how is it possible to be virtuous without property and the freedom to act that came with it? Nevertheless, Hythloday's description of Utopia, grounded on evidence from Vespucci's voyages, suggests that there at least the goal had been achieved, whereas in England, where private property prevailed, poverty and crime seemingly flourished at the expense of virtue.

The name *Utopia,* encountered immediately on the title page, raises its own puzzle. It is a compound Greek word meaning literally "no place" or "nowhere," but the joke is not straightforward. In the brief poem "of Utopia" attributed to Anemolius (206), the name is made to pun on the Greek word *eutopia,* which means "happy" or "fortunate place." Moreover, in keeping with the book's overall spirit of jest, Anemolius's own name, also derived from Greek, means "windy" or "boastful." Are we to think, therefore, that only an imaginary "no place"—a Platonic "form"—can be a truly happy one? Or is even its fictional capacity to achieve full happiness to be doubted? What might be the best way to resolve this conundrum?

CHRISTIAN REVELATION

The island of Utopia exemplifies in a variety of aspects the virtues of the legendary Golden Age often written about by Greek and Roman poets.[47] Nevertheless, readers are also reminded that Christ himself favored the

Io.Clemens.   Hythlodæus.   Tho.Morus.   Pet.Aegid.

Figure 2. Headpiece, by Ambrosius Holbein, depicting Raphael Hythloday, Thomas More, and Peter Giles conversing in the garden of More's house in Antwerp, attended by More's servant, John Clement; from John Froben's Latin edition of *Utopia,* printed in March 1580.
By permission of The Folger Shakespeare Library.

Utopian ideal and had instituted a form of community of property among his first disciples that was still practiced in More's own day "amongst the rightest Christian companies," namely the monasteries (187). Is the Utopian regime therefore suited only to those, like the monks and friars of More's day, who would follow precisely in the footsteps of the earliest Christians, or were all Christians to strive to implement it in society as a whole?

Precisely because *Utopia* is framed as a dialogue and abounds with ironies and enigmas, jokes, and riddles, it is by no means certain how we should interpret its central debates. Our difficulty is made all the greater by ambiguities in the way More presents his two main protagonists. Hythloday's name derives from Greek and means, roughly, "cunning in nonsense"; "More," *Morus* in Latin, puns on a Latin word for "folly," *moria,* a connection that More's friend Erasmus had already advertised to the sixteenth-century reading public in *The Praise of Folly;* the Latin title of the latter is *Moriae Encomium.*[48] The effect is to construct a dialogue between alter egos: nonsense drawing on Greek roots facing folly with Latin ones.

This result is only compounded by the given, or "Christian" names, of these characters. They depend on biblical sources. Raphael was one of the four archangels in the Hebrew tradition, but he appears in an especially prominent role in the Book of Tobias, a text in the Roman Catholic canon of the Old Testament.[49] Among humanists, he was taken to symbolize the heavenly physician, someone who heals the soul.[50] The Book of Tobias involves the tribulations and triumphs of Tobit, a pious and charitable Jew in exile who is impoverished for his good works and blinded by disease but who in the end is restored to sight and good fortune through God's providence.

In the tale, Raphael, disguised as a kinsman, acts as a guide to Tobias, Tobit's son, taking him to a distant city and safely returning him with the family's wealth to his blind father, who through Raphael's agency is then restored to sight. Raphael sums up the meaning of the story in this way:

> A king's secret ought to be kept, but the works of God should be publicly acknowledged. Acknowledge them, therefore, and pay him honour. Do good, and no evil will befall you. Better prayer with sincerity, and almsgiving with righteousness, than wealth with wickedness. Better give alms than hoard up gold. Almsgiving preserves from death and wipes out every sin. Givers of alms will enjoy long life; but sinners and wrongdoers are their own enemies.[51]

The contrast between what is appropriate in celebrating the works of God and in performing the duties of a king's counselor is of special relevance in light of the views on royal service articulated by Hythloday in The First Book. Also of note is the role played by the archangel as a guide and healer in returning the son to the father and in bringing sight to the blind.

Is there also an allegorical meaning for "Thomas" in "More's" name, parallel with "Raphael"? In the New Testament, Thomas is one of the Twelve Apostles — the famous "doubting Thomas," who questions Christ's resurrection until it is proved to him directly with the evidence of his own eyes. When the resurrected Christ appears to him, he brings to his eyes the light of knowledge: the conviction of true belief. As Jesus says on the occasion, "Have you believed because you have seen me? Blessed are those who have not seen and yet believe."[52] Thomas's story is a model for confirmed belief in Christianity recorded for readers, as the Gospel puts it, in order "that you may believe that Jesus is the Christ, the Son of God, and that believing you may have life in his name."[53] Thomas, therefore, represents a New Testament inversion of Raphael, someone who confirms in a backhanded way what Tobit's story shows regarding knowledge of God. Thomas's doubt leads directly to divine knowledge. In this reading, Hythloday is associated with a divine or spiritual sort of healing, but also with an Old Testament story whose characters have no direct knowledge of Christ and can only anticipate his message. In contrast, "More" is connected with a kind of empirical or worldly skepticism, but one that eventually yields to firm knowledge of Christ's role in human salvation.

The ancients, of course, lacked Christian revelation and the benefits of the Christian sacraments, and so too do the Utopians, at least until the coming of Hythloday and his companions. They believed in divine providence and the immortality of the soul, but these ideas are attributed solely to the dictates of reason. In the course of The Second Book, however, we also learn that when informed about Christ and Christian practices, the Utopians were quite taken by them, although not all Utopians were converted. We are left with the sense that Utopia is primarily a pagan land, open to the possibility of a Christian life, whose occupants live according to rules and conceptions they had achieved without the benefit of the Bible or Christian training. Seen in this context, the Utopians, following the virtuous principles of the ancients, represent a challenge to More's own corrupted times: they might be seen to have come closer to achieving the ideals of Christianity than have ordinary Christians.

However, to a believing Christian, as More himself was, there could be no doubt that traditional Utopian religious life is not only incomplete, lacking as it does the knowledge that can come only from heaven-sent grace, but also is fundamentally in error in certain essentials. For example, the Utopians weigh pleasure so highly, we learn, that they believe it not only wise but godly and virtuous for those suffering "continual pain and anguish" from disease to commit suicide or to be put out of their misery by others (168–69). Among Christians, however, suicide was judged among the gravest of sins, and the practice of euthanasia would have been considered as nothing other than a form of murder — itself a grave sin.[54]

Utopia is largely concerned with how to weigh Europe's classical heritage in light of the demands of Christian belief and practice. This theme is also central to Saint Augustine's *City of God,* about which More had given a series of public lectures in London about the year 1501; the lectures themselves do not survive. Saint Augustine, in treating the City of God "both as it exists in this world of time, a stranger among the ungodly, living by faith, and as it stands in the security of its everlasting seat," stressed that its "final victory" must be awaited "in steadfast pa-

tience, until 'justice returns to judgement.'" For the present, we live under "the city of this world, a city which aims at dominion, which holds nations in enslavement, but is itself dominated by that very lust of domination." In this world, the greatest effort is "needed to convince the proud of the power and excellence of humility, an excellence which makes it soar above all the summits of this world, which sway in their temporal instability, overtopping them all with an eminence not arrogated by human pride, but granted by divine grace." Nevertheless, God "has revealed in the Scripture of his people this statement of the divine Law, 'God resists the proud, but he gives grace to the humble.' This is God's prerogative; but man's arrogant spirit in its swelling pride has claimed it as its own."[55]

In the absence of revelation, the Utopians could not achieve a perfect way of life according to these standards of Christianity. Was it nonetheless possible for them, using reason alone, to have arrived at "the best state of the commonwealth"? Perhaps reason could find ways to minimize the effects of sin in the world by channeling human pride away from its destructive paths. Hythloday certainly urged that the problem of crime would be alleviated, though not entirely eliminated, by removing the social incentives for it created by private property. Yet he also recognized the role of pride in clouding human judgment and resisting the establishment of the "best commonwealth" on this earth. If it were not for pride, he admitted, human self-interest "or else the authority of our Savior Christ (which for His great wisdom could not but know what were best, and for His inestimable goodness could not but counsel to that which He knew to be best) would have brought all the world long ago into the laws" of Utopia. "Pride," he says, "that one only beast, the princess and mother of all mischief," measures her achievements only in triumphing over others. "This hellhound creepeth into men's hearts . . . and is so deeply rooted in men's breasts that she cannot be plucked out" (200–01). If pride is so firmly in control of human beings, we may well ask, What is the best life we can live in this world?[56]

POLITICS

Utopia shares much with England or with England and Wales combined. Its breadth at its widest point, said to be two hundred miles, is roughly the same as that of England itself, according to the standard sources available in More's day. Its fifty-four "cities" equal the total number of English and Welsh counties plus London, and its capital city, Amaurote, situated on the river Anyder, corresponds closely to London on the

Thames. However, Amaurote, another word derived from Greek, refers to being obscured by darkness, suggesting that the city is no more than a phantom, while Anyder, comes from the Greek meaning "without water." In many respects More presents Utopia as the opposite of the world in which he and his English readers actually lived.

However, England and Wales do not themselves constitute an island. Rather, they represent those parts of one that were directly under the rule of England's King Henry VIII at the time More was writing. Scotland, to the north, was still politically independent. So the identification of More's nowhere land with the kingdom of which he himself was a subject is not purely topographical. It is also, and more significantly, political; it follows from the fact that England and Utopia, although in many respects mirror images of one another, each form a politically distinct community organized under its own regime of governance and law.

In this light, several important differences between the two polities should be noticed. As we have already observed, Utopia had no single ruler governing the whole island. The elected princes and counselors oversaw the affairs only of the individual cities. When matters of wider application arose, they were decided by a general council, not by an overlord or king. Utopus gave the island its constitution and first laws but had no successors; in any case, in More's Latin he is never referred to as "king," although Robynson does so in his translation.[57] England, of course, did have a single ruler, its monarch, who governed with the assistance of appointed officials and noble counselors and who made laws and raised taxes with the consent of his subjects — peers of the realm and church officials as well as commoners.

From this follows a second critical difference. In Utopia, the political hierarchy was grounded on recognized merit. The syphogrants and tranibores are elected annually, and the princes, or "first leaders," chosen from among those who are thought "most meet and expedient," serve for life unless "put down for suspicion of tyranny" (134–35).[58] In England, however, the hierarchy is based on birth and wealth. Kings and noblemen inherit their positions, while those bearing other offices, at least among the laity, are almost invariably important property holders. "More" alludes to these characteristics — "nobility, magnificence, worship, honor, and majesty" — in commenting at the close on shortcomings of the Utopian regime according to "common opinion" (201).

"More's" reference to "common opinion" in this passage itself locates the differences between England and Utopia, and between "More" and Hythloday, in the realm of politics, subtly shifting the ground from the domain of philosophy and universal knowledge where Hythloday earlier had placed it. In doing so, "More" also moves the discussion from what

might constitute the "best form of a commonwealth" to how, in practical terms, it might be brought into being. If Hythloday had accomplished nothing else in his description of the Utopian regime, he seems at least to have demonstrated to his questioner that the customary defense of private property needed to be rethought. In response, "More," in effect conceding the inadequacy of his previous arguments, concludes that though many aspects of the Utopian way of life would be desirable, there is little hope that they could be instituted in the face of prevailing views in defense of established interests. Does politics offer a potential solution to this dilemma? [59]

Utopia insistently places this subject at the forefront of its readers' attention. Rethinking the structure of the work as a whole, The First Book can be interpreted as addressing why the political practices of present-day monarchical councils and courts have failed to promote human happiness or generate virtuous actions. The Second Book can be seen as describing what sort of regime might produce political activities grounded in public good rather than the pursuit of personal pride and narrow self-interest. Finally, "More's" stress on the weight of "common opinion" in holding back the adoption of suitable reforms raises the question what sort of politics should prevail in the present day, especially in the face of the persistence of sin and the continuing power of pride in human life.

If the achievement of utopia is impossible in the world as it is at present, is there nonetheless a way to limit the consequences of sin for society and to ameliorate current social conditions? "More's" words and actions at the close of the narrative suggest a possible answer. In the final paragraph of The Second Book, he reveals that in listening to Hythloday's description he held back his criticisms of the Utopian way of life, especially its reliance on community of property, offering instead a polite "praising . . . of their institutions" and of Hythloday's description of them, while postponing to "another time" further examination of "the same matters" (201). Here "More," shaping his words to the occasion, follows the very same dictates of "civil philosophy" that he had earlier urged Hythloday himself to adopt. His actions allow the company to part on good terms, ready at the next occasion to take up their discussion where they had left off. They represent an implicit endorsement of the efficacy of rhetoric in making possible continued human sociability.[60] They also reveal that there is more to be said on the issues dividing "More" and Hythloday — that the discussion has not ended.

This sense that the debate needs to go on marks a vital difference between the island of Utopia and the world in which Hythloday and "More" conduct their dialogue. On the island of Utopia, there is plenty of room for discussions of various sorts. For example, the Utopians dispute the same ethical questions as Europeans do — questions "of the good qualities of the soul, of the body, and of fortune and whether the name of goodness may be applied to all these or only to the endowments and gifts of the soul," with the chief question being "in what thing, be it one or more, the felicity of man consisteth" (155). These subjects, derived from the ancient debates between the Stoics and the Epicureans, primarily concern the conduct of private life, and the Epicurean answer they receive from the majority of Utopians directly associates them with a philosophical sect that had famously withdrawn into strict privacy to pursue their hedonistic way of life in ancient Athens. It appears, therefore, that insofar as the Utopians debated among themselves about philosophical goals, they did so outside the political realm and without any consideration of the social means necessary for their achievement.

Nevertheless, the Utopians also relied to a considerable degree on debate in the conduct of their public affairs. The policies of their cities and "any controversies among the commoners" were settled in each place by the princes and their councils only after being "reasoned of and debated three days in the council." However, it was also deemed "death to have any consultation for the commonwealth out of the council or the place of the common election." In private political discourse, it is feared that the prince and his counselors might "conspire together to oppress the people by tyranny and to change the state of the weal public." To guard against this danger, "matters of great weight and importance" were brought to the local election houses by the annually elected leaders of the neighborhood who "open the matter to their families. And afterward, when they have consulted among themselves, they show their devise to the council" (135).

Among the Utopians, political discussion took place to establish good laws, not to deliberate about the larger ends for which those laws were put in place. However much their legislative procedures allowed for the public airing of major issues, they appear to make discussions like those between Hythloday and "More" virtually impossible. Nowhere on the island of Utopia does there seem to be room for a debate in the privacy of a quiet garden about the "best state of the commonwealth." One might argue, of course, that there was no need for such a debate in Utopia because, in Hythloday's view at least, the Utopians had already achieved this best state.

Debate itself has its virtues, however, such as exposing the verbal ambiguities, implicit contradictions, and practical limitations in the positions of the disputants. It represents one way of ensuring that what we "cannot turn to good" we might at least "order" so "that it be not very bad" (122). Debate has yet another virtue, particularly according to the theories of writers on rhetoric and "civil philosophy," such as Cicero. Effective debaters are able to move their audiences, not merely inform them, making them into a community by transforming principles or policies from intellectual abstractions into practical, political goals. Their persuasive skills can challenge prevailing views, conventional judgments, and "common opinion" by stressing their inconsistencies with the ultimate goals and best interests of the listeners. They have the capacity thereby not just to make philosophical truths attractive, but to bring them to fruition. "More" refers precisely to the essential and valuable skill of persuasion when he urges Hythloday to use "civil philosophy" rather than "school philosophy" in speaking at the council table.

To have a genuine debate, there must be common ground, not only in the questions addressed, but also in the means used to answer them. Thomas More may or may not have thought that through the establishment of community of property his imaginary Utopians had shown a way for human beings to achieve the best state of the commonwealth, a society where true virtue would thrive. However, in constructing his dialogue in *Utopia,* he held out hope that social and political benefits resulted from continued rational discussion of fundamental public questions in the commonwealth as it actually was.

The social capacity to exchange views on a common basis changes a mere association of people into a commonwealth — a community with ongoing interests and enterprises and a need for mutual support among its members, the sort of place about which it is possible to ask whether it has attained the best state. Here it might be said that there is more uniting than dividing Hythloday and "More." Both share common ends regarding the purposes of social life, and both rely on the uses of knowledge and wisdom, rather than on the exercise of power or brute force, as the preferred method for achieving these goals.

So too did the real More and his friend Erasmus, even though there is some reason to conclude that they were not in complete agreement on the themes explored in *Utopia.* One reason for so thinking is that it was only in *Utopia*'s third edition that Erasmus's own letter of comment appeared — a letter transmitting the book to John Froben in Basel for publication there. The letter reveals a certain skepticism: "Hitherto I have ever been exceedingly pleased with all of my friend More's writing," Erasmus says, "but, on account of our very close friendship, I somewhat distrusted my own verdict. Now, however, I see that all the learned unanimously subscribe to my judgment, and admire the man's divine genius even more than I. . . . I therefore openly applaud my opinion seriously, and shall in the future not hesitate from saying openly what I feel." The letter then goes on to point out how as a married man, a lawyer, and a public servant, More was "distracted" by domestic and state affairs and to wonder (implicitly) what he might have accomplished if he "were now totally devoted to the service of the Muses." It is hard to locate a word of direct praise at all.[61]

In his *Praise of Folly,* Erasmus had stressed that "the biggest fools of all"—the men and women infused with the divine folly exemplified in Saint Paul—were to be found among those who have been "wholly possessed by zeal for Christian piety. They squander their possessions, ignore insults, submit to being cheated, make no distinction between friends and enemies, shun pleasure, sustain themselves on fasting, vigils, tears, toil and humiliations, scorn life and desire only death."[62] He had grounded his hopes for the achievement of this divine grace on the capacities of eloquence and education to draw the very best qualities in the human soul toward God. In the voice of his Goddess "Folly," he, like Hythloday in *Utopia,* repeatedly ridiculed those who looked to worldly understanding and the activities of the secular state to achieve those ends. "Fortune," says the Goddess, "favours the injudicious and the venturesome, people who like to say 'the die is cast'," referring, of course to Caesar's reputed remark in crossing the Rubicon to begin a civil war. "But wisdom makes men weak and apprehensive, and consequently you'll generally find the wise associated with poverty, hunger, and the reek of smoke, living neglected, inglorious and disliked." Worldly "fools," like Caesar himself, "on the other hand, are rolling in money, and are put in charge of affairs of state; they flourish, in short, in every way. For if a man finds his happiness in pleasing princes and spending his time amongst those gilded and bejewelled godlike creatures, he'll learn that wisdom is no use at all to him, and is indeed descried above all by people like this."[63]

The view developed in *Utopia* exposed this Erasmian position to serious doubt. In light of the role of pride and greed among the fallen human beings living in worldly political communities, More seems to be saying to his friend Erasmus what "More," the character in the dialogue, had argued to Hythloday, namely that the means he proposed for achieving his virtuous and worthy aims are impracticable. Unless Christian humanists were prepared to use their learning and skills in advancing the good in the state, sin would go unchecked and rule everywhere. As Plato had insisted in the *Republic,* philosophers were obliged to return to

Figure 3. Desiderius Erasmus in 1517, by Quentin Massys.

the murkiness of the Cave after they had achieved their knowledge of the Good. For

> the law is not concerned with the special happiness of any class in the state, but is trying to produce this condition in the city as a whole, harmonizing and adapting the citizens to one another by persuasion and compulsion, requiring them to impart to one another any benefit which they are severally able to bestow upon the community, and that it itself creates such men in the state, not that it may allow each to take what course pleases him, but with a view to using them for the binding together of the commonwealth.[64]

Despite the arguments put forward by Hythloday, philosophers could not be allowed to "linger" on the heights "and refuse to go down among ... bondsmen and share their labors and honors" if the benefits of learning would accrue to the general good of the community.[65]

CONTEXTS

Thus far, we have been looking primarily at texts, examining a few aspects of *Utopia* itself and considering some of the literary and philosophical models and inspirations that helped shape it. In a sense, we have also been thinking about contexts, situating what More said within the web of language and ideas on which he depended and that he endorses or questions. However, More wrote not only to address literary traditions and philosophical currents, but also to engage with the social world of his own time and to participate in its political life. In 1516, he was already a public figure of some note, soon to become an even more important one. In addition to the debts *Utopia* owes or the relationships it enjoys to other books, there are also important contexts provided by the socioeconomic structures, legal and governmental institutions, and political events within which its author was immersed, on which he was commenting, and about which he hoped to have some say. We now need to situate More's book within this much more loosely-knit framework of sources and influences, foundations, and targets. We shall start with biography.

Personal Involvements

For all of *Utopia*'s literary cleverness and philosophical subtlety, it is also an intensely personal work, marked throughout by references to Thomas More's own life history. In The First Book, for example, when Hythloday reports the conversation he once had at the table of Cardinal

John Morton, Archbishop of Canterbury and Lord Chancellor of England, he was describing the very household in which More had served for two years as a page when he was a young boy.[66] More also made actual occurrences in his own life part of the fiction of his book, most notably his story of being in Antwerp during a lull in trade negotiations between England and the Low Countries. More had been appointed by Henry VIII to a five-person trade commission to Bruges, headed by Cuthbert Tunstall.[67]

The book is personal in a deeper sense, as well. First, it reflects More's own rearing and education. Born on February 7, 1478, or possibly a year earlier, he was the son of John More, a prominent London lawyer and jurist who eventually became one of the justices in the King's Bench, the most important of the common law courts. From the start, his father had wanted him also to be a lawyer, and although at times he was tempted by different possibilities, in the end he remained true to his father's wishes. As a young boy, Thomas was educated in Latin at Saint Anthony's school in London before spending two years in Archbishop Morton's household. In 1492, with Morton's patronage, he went up to Oxford to study Latin and Greek, sharpening his wits and his tongue for the law, and in the process acquiring a deep and abiding commitment to learning, especially the new humanist learning then spreading through the university. As was common at the time among those training for legal careers, he did not stay for a degree, but after two years came down to London to begin his formal legal training, ultimately at Lincoln's Inn, where he continued until he reached the rank of utter barrister in 1499 with the full right to appear at the bar in the main law courts of the realm.[68]

During these years, More became increasingly associated with the leading figures in the humanist movement, men engaged in trying to reform not only letters and learning, but also the church and social and political policy. At Oxford, he had studied Greek with William Grocyn and had become acquainted as well with Thomas Linacre, another important English humanist who had recently returned from Italy. Through these and similar connections, he was introduced to John Colet, who eventually became More's mentor and confessor. Colet had also studied in Italy, and in the late 1490s he had used his humanist training in framing lectures on the epistles of Saint Paul to large and learned audiences at Oxford.[69] Also in this period, More met Erasmus for the first time while the latter was making the first of his several visits to England.

If humanism had a leader in northern Europe, it was Erasmus.[70] He was connected everywhere with reform-minded statesmen as well as fellow scholars. It is perhaps symptomatic of his importance that More's

earliest meeting with him, in 1499, was in the household of Lord Mountjoy, a young Tudor nobleman and pupil of Erasmus's. During this visit,
the two men went to nearby Eltham Palace to meet the young prince
Henry, not yet heir to the throne but soon to be. As we have already
noted, Erasmus and More became quite close and within a few years col-
laborated in translating several of Lucian's satires from Greek into Latin,
a work first published at Paris in 1506.[71]

At the meeting with Prince Henry in 1499, More presented the boy
with a poem, an almost certain sign that he was seeking to store up goodwill and the prospect of favor from this royal figure. However, during the
same year, while More was still under twenty, he also became attracted
to the possibilities of a life in the church. He took up residence near the
Charterhouse in London so he could partake regularly of the spiritual
routines and regimens of the Carthusian community there. He also
adopted the wearing of a hair shirt next to his skin and other personal
austerities, practices that he never wholly abandoned during his life.
While continuing his legal career, he considered becoming a Franciscan
friar, taking up the ministry of preaching and public charity for which
the brotherhood was famous. It was during this period that he lectured
in London's church of Saint Lawrence Jewry on Saint Augustine's *The
City of God.*

After about four years, however, More made the decisive commitment to marriage and with it to the life of a lawyer and man of public affairs. However, he never entirely abandoned his deep religious commitments or his devotion to learning. By 1511, when his first wife died, he
had a burgeoning family of four children. To aid in bearing his household burdens, he quickly remarried, this time to a well-off merchant's
widow, seven years his senior, with a daughter of her own. In this respect, he never looked back to the call he had earlier felt to a clerical life.
In 1504, the year of his first marriage, he sat as an elected member of
Henry VII's last parliament, although for what constituency is not certain.[72] By 1510, More was a bencher in Lincoln's Inn, one of the senior
members responsible for its governance and for the education of its
students. He was then a noted lawyer who appeared frequently in important cases, especially those concerning commercial matters, and
who earned a handsome income from his practice, amounting, it is said,
to £400 per year.

In 1510, More also began serving as London's undersheriff, which
made him one of the City's chief legal advisers as well as judge in the
city's Sheriff's Court, which had local jurisdiction in a variety of civil and
commercial cases.[73] These judicial responsibilities gave More an acute
insight into London as a social and economic entity and, not coinciden-

tally, also as a highly litigious place — a community full of disputes over getting and spending and the failure to honor debts and meet other obligations. By the time he was in his early twenties, More also had begun to make himself known at court and in political circles.

In 1514, More's reputation as a master lawyer was enhanced when he skillfully and successfully defended papal interests before the Lord Chancellor and the rest of the judges in a case involving the king's claim to the forfeiture of one of the pope's great ships, then docked at Southampton.[74] His successful performance caught the eye of the king and some of his leading counselors, particularly Thomas Wolsey, the king's almoner at the time, whose ecclesiastical and political career was moving rapidly. More assisted regularly in the Chancery as an examiner and arbitrator, and in 1514 he was appointed a commissioner of sewers for the Thames district between Greenwich and Lambeth. Given these turns in More's career, it should be no surprise that when London's merchants fell into commercial disputes with the Netherlands, he seemed a good choice to all parties for service in the embassy sent to settle the matter.[75]

All of this is important not only for understanding the shape of More's career — its oscillation between religious and worldly callings — but the shape of his *Utopia,* as well. In January 1516, not long after he returned to England from his six-month sojourn in the Low Countries, More received an offer from Henry VIII and Wolsey to enter the king's service and of a pension from the royal coffers. In some respects, this offer represented a distinct recognition of, as well as a handsome reward for, what More had already done on the king's behalf. It was also the sort of benefit that an ambitious person, anxious for further advancement, would cherish. In certain ways, it was exactly the favor for which More arguably had been angling for some time.

Nevertheless, it confronted him with a hard choice. As a lawyer with an independent practice, he was able to keep up something of the life of letters, despite the time his practice took. It would not be as easy if he accepted the position as a royal counselor. Along with total loyalty to the king, government service also required a commitment of the counselor's talents fully to his royal master's interests and needs. It would no longer be possible for More to write freely on any subject that he might choose or to communicate ideas without considering the political effects they might have at court or abroad. The focus of his literary and intellectual life necessarily would shift from the academic philosophy Hythloday upheld in The First Book to the more "civil philosophy" "More" advocated in response. Was More — the lawyer and writer, the person — ready for this change?[76]

It appears that More used the writing of *Utopia,* in part, as a way to think through this question for himself and to expose its intricacies to his fellow humanists. Although he had finished much of the book by the time he left the Netherlands, he was held up for many months thereafter in completing what he had led Peter Giles and others to believe would only be final touches. The finished book did not actually appear in print in Louvain until December 1516, more than a year later.[77] In the interval, he appears to have rethought his aims in the book. Initially, it was simply to be an account of the Utopian commonwealth, and it was this writing that he had nearly finished before his departure from the Low Countries at the end of October 1515. In other words, in its original design, *Utopia* was to be a mock traveler's account almost entirely devoted to describing Utopian society. Thereafter, while in London, he added a large new section — the debate about counsel between Hythloday and "More" in The First Book and short portions at the end of The Second Book to round out this new material so that it fit into what had already been completed.[78]

What it became with the new material was something much richer, a work that critically linked a putative model for social reform with an examination of what it might take to accomplish it. The debate that More depicts between Hythloday and his namesake lays open the two sides of these intimately linked central issues. In doing so, it raises important philosophical and practical questions. If humanists wanted reform in state and society, did they grasp what accomplishing it might entail? Were they prepared to make the necessary adjustments in their lives and their intellectual habits to bring their beliefs to fruition? Were their fondest beliefs entirely coherent? Was it possible genuinely to pursue virtue in the public arena without also suppressing the trappings of honor and reward with which it was commonly recognized? More, the author, seems especially concerned to demonstrate — to himself as well as his friends — the exacting demands that public life imposed on men of learning and the limitations and contradictions inherent in the standard arguments made in answering questions about them. Taking his discussion seriously, it is not possible to think that a decision to accept royal office would be without costs.

However, it was not easy to say "no" to a king. Within months, More had accepted a royal pension of £100 a year, and it was not long before he was further involved in public affairs. In August 1517, he was nominated to serve on another foreign embassy, this time with the French at Calais. At the same time, he formally entered royal service, becoming a member of the King's Council. The following year, he was appointed

Master of Requests, an important office answering commoners' petitions, which required him to be in regular attendance on the king. By the summer of 1519, he was sufficiently ensconced at court to resign the office of undersheriff in London.

Historical Circumstances[79]

Not long after completing *Utopia,* More seems to have concluded that the powerful critique of government service he had articulated in the persona of Raphael Hythloday need not be correct in every case. What was it about the condition of England at that helped him to answer his book's most personally pressing question by accepting office under his king?

THE MORAL ECONOMY

There is perhaps no better place to start than with the embassy that brought More to the Netherlands in 1515. Its main purpose was to settle commercial disputes between English and Flemish traders that arose primarily from a commercial treaty, very favorable to English interests, agreed to in 1506 between Henry VII and Philip of Burgundy but never put in force.[80] English commercial interests in this era were significantly concentrated in the Low Countries, and increasingly in Antwerp in Flanders, the home of Peter Giles, a flourishing entrepôt for fine things. To a very considerable degree, England's overseas commerce with the Netherlands, as with nearly every other overseas market, was centered in London itself, which had already emerged as a great market for continental imports as well a major center of cloth manufacture and an exporter of English wares.[81]

The embassy, therefore, was vitally connected to the welfare of London's commercial community; it is no wonder that the city's leaders wanted their own interests represented in the mission by More, who not only enjoyed their respect but also that of the king and his chief minister. The significance of this embassy extended well beyond London itself, however. London's main export to the Low Countries was woolen cloth, much of it woven by country weavers in small cottages in the distant rural districts near the great sheep farms that produced the wool. London's clothiers and merchants took charge of financing and managing this complexly organized industry and trade, while its craftsmen dominated the finishing trades in the cloth industry. These facts made London's commercial life a vital feature in the prosperity of England as a whole and gave Londoners a presence in important economic activities throughout the realm.

There was not much fundamentally new in these arrangements. London had for centuries been the greatest entrepôt for trade in England, the place where the riches of the known world were most concentrated. Nevertheless, there is little doubt that by 1500 trading arrangements had become increasingly complicated as more and more of England's overseas commerce came to depend on the export of cloth, not raw wool. Although most people still lived in rural places, and most depended primarily on their own production or on highly localized markets for their essential needs, manufacture for and trade in national and even international markets were becoming a more significant feature in the lives of many ordinary people.[82]

London's commercial importance depended in large measure on its role as the center of the developing English state in the early modern period. In or near it were concentrated the royal household, the leading government departments, and the law courts, peopled by well-off officials who not only provided the growing range of governmental and legal services necessary in running a market-oriented economy, but who also were ready to buy the wide array of wares that the city's merchants and retailers had to offer. Similar tastes were displayed in the city by leading merchant magnates and in the countryside by wealthy landlords and rich churchmen, whose patterns of consumption emulated the style of the royal court. In turn, the habits of these figures often were emulated, as Hythloday argued, not only by "gentlemen's servants, but also handicraftsmen, yea, and almost the ploughmen of the country" (104).

As these developments unfolded, London became a more populous as well as a more prosperous place, its growth almost entirely the result of immigration from the countryside. At the end of the fifteenth century, the city may have had 40,000 to 50,000 inhabitants. By 1520, the number was approximately 55,000 to 60,000; by 1550, it was 100,000 or perhaps 120,000; and by 1600, it stood at around 200,000. During this period, an increasing portion of England's population as a whole came to live in significant-sized towns. According to some estimates, the percentage may have nearly doubled between 1500 and 1600.[83]

As the towns grew, a greater and greater share of the production of the surrounding countryside went to feed their populations, starting in the vicinity of London. These rural hinterlands became sources of raw materials and country manufactures for the urban marketplaces, suppliers of new urban population, and markets in their own right for imports as well as urban manufactures.[84] Many of these developments were felt directly on the land. In The First Book of *Utopia,* Hythloday speaks pointedly of sheep "that were wont to be so meek and tame and so small eaters" who now have become "so great devourers and so wild that they eat up and swallow down the very men themselves," consuming "whole fields, houses, and cities" (101). He refers here to the process of "enclosure," by which landlords or their tenants converted land previously under the plow into pasture, clearing it if necessary of houses and trees, and then hedging or fencing it for the exclusive use of the flocks.[85]

A significant percentage of the land in England, especially in upland regions and other areas where stock raising traditionally was a prime activity, had long been enclosed in some form. However, in regions with broad open country, including some places near London or in the Midlands, open-field farming had usually been the practice in the earlier Middle Ages. Here, rather than individuals fencing or hedging their own properties, large fields, divided into strips belonging to particular families, were worked collectively by the villagers, who also enjoyed access to the village commons, where sheep and other animals could be grazed. In such open-field communities, the fruits of agricultural endeavor belonged to the particular families themselves, who normally paid rent to a landlord for the land they tilled, but the work was in large measure communal. It involved the sharing of tools and plow animals under a regime of customary practices and rules. Even in regard to these places, however, we need to avoid taking a romanticized view of a once "merrie England" turned only in later days to greed and corruption by the spread of market forces. There was always a strong tendency among individual farmers to build up and consolidate holdings in order to make them more efficient and profitable, and many landlords, never adverse to finding additional sources of income from their properties, sometimes leased the lands they retained in their own hands in large units to well-off tenants capable of paying market rents.

These tendencies had received increased impetus following the so-called Black Death in England in the mid-fourteenth century. This outbreak of bubonic plague reduced the size of the population by at least a third to a level it maintained for the next hundred years. In this new demographic environment, land became relatively more plentiful and labor relatively scarcer than before, even as the number of people that needed to be fed had sharply declined. Rural labor became hard to find, food prices fell, and urban incomes rose, attracting workers to the towns. Not surprisingly, numerous landlords in the old open-field regions — many of them great men in the state or the church — used their considerable power to shift land use from arable farming to grazing, enclosing village wastes and commons and even the open fields themselves for sheep and their increasingly valuable wool. Families with weak claims to their holdings might well find themselves ousted from their customary rights. Sometimes, whole villages disappeared. In all, however, only about 10 percent of the once open fields were enclosed in this wave of agrarian change, most of them before 1485.

However, these patterns were beginning to shift again during More's lifetime. By the middle of the fifteenth century, the English population seems to have started growing, although at first only very slowly. Rural rents increased, even as the conversion of arable land into pasture eased. Prices also began to rise, at the outset mainly in the vicinity of London, whose growth created increased demand for food and other supplies. New forces were at work on the land, directed to supporting mixed agriculture, which sometimes also demanded enclosure to permit arable farming and stock raising to exist side by side. There was also a need among the landlords to improve their rental incomes to maintain their households. These processes of agrarian improvements, carried out by landlords of all ranks, from the king to the county gentry, often put increased pressure on customary tenants, racking their rents, eroding their ancient rights in village wastes and commons, and, in a number of cases, displacing them outright in favor of families able to pay landlords at higher rates.

These long-term socioeconomic developments eventually resulted in the expansion of commercial farming and the growth of larger holdings in rural England at the expense of small tenancies primarily devoted to subsistence agriculture. The number of rural wage earners also increased, and a widening gap opened between richer farmers and the rest, producing social dislocations, discontent, and unrest in the countryside. Hythloday pointedly mentions an "insurrection that the western Englishmen made against their king" (97), referring to the Cornish Rising of 1497.[86] Less dramatic, but of more widespread significance, were periodic, small-scale riots in which angry tenants forcibly removed the hedges or fences put up by their landlords. As potential sources of rural unrest, enclosures became matters of concern to the government. They were specifically attacked in parliamentary statutes in 1489 and 1515, in a royal proclamation in 1514, and in royal commissions of investigation in 1517 to 1518. However, there was not much sustained success in checking the spread of enclosures.

There were also signs of disorder and discontent in urban places.[87] One persistent problem for officials was vagabondage and the petty crimes that accompanied it. What especially caused anxiety was not just the burden that "sturdy rogues," as they were called, put on civic and charitable institutions, especially in times of famine or epidemic disease when the wandering poor flooded into the towns, but the challenge they seemed to represent to the idea of an ordered and disciplined community.[88]

England, in More's day, was not yet a fully integrated market society. Many of the socioeconomic changes necessary to bring it into being were only just taking shape in the countryside and town in the later fifteenth and early sixteenth centuries; they would only crystallize into definite form over the next century and later. Although large-scale manufacturing and commercial activities, particularly in the all-important wool and cloth trades, had long been conducted according to market principles, other aspects of the economic order lacked the impersonal character of this sort of market exchange. They arose, instead, in local settings where economic transactions were subject to important personal, social, and moral considerations.

To put this point in general terms, More's England possessed what might be described as a two-tiered, or dual, economy.[89] One segment, still small but growing, depended on buying and selling for profit in large-scale regional, national, and international markets. The other operated outside those markets, relying on exploitation of resources in the forests, commons, and wastes; cooperation among neighbors or gift exchange; customary services owed to superiors; and engagement only in a very localized trade in a limited number of items among known traders and neighbors.

In such dual economies, both sorts of activities are often present in the same communities, sometimes even in the undertakings of the same families or individuals. In the medieval and early modern English cloth industry, for example, weaving was commonly carried out in upland villages by residents who spent part of their time at their looms but also raised animals and tilled the soil for their own use. Under these conditions, the expansion of market-oriented and profit-driven aspects of economic life sometimes occurred at the expense of ingrained traditional practices closely associated with the most deeply felt moral beliefs and community feelings. Even open-field villages, which depended on traditional social bonds in their conduct of agriculture, were not entirely free from similar pressures, as the spread of enclosures makes abundantly clear. Whole villages sometimes found themselves pulled by market forces away from their customary practices.

In the towns, the story was bound to be somewhat different because urban life centered on the exchange of goods and services in the marketplace. Nevertheless, medieval urban markets were highly regulated by town governments as well as local gilds. Economic exchange normally occurred among long-time acquaintances, under the scrutiny of neighbors and local officials, and depended to a large measure on ties of kinship, patronage, and friendship rather than purely on market principles. However, as regional, national, and international markets grew, this old regulatory system was put under considerable strain, subjecting the towns to cross pressures similar to those affecting agrarian communities. In other words, in both countryside and town the dual economy was continually being subverted in More's day in favor of market-oriented activities, without entirely eliminating traditional practices or values.

If economic exchange in More's time was not yet fully under the control of impersonal market forces, neither is his description of it purely "economic" in the modern sense of the term. For More, economic activity is not merely instrumental, but moral — a way to assure the general welfare of the community and its members, not just to provide for subsistence and survival. What troubled More above all was the way the possession of power and wealth enhanced the capacity of greed to damage the powerless and the poor. In Hythloday's analysis, the cause of economic wrong is variously said to be "inordinate and unsatiable covetousness," "the unreasonable covetousness of a few," "great wantonness, importunate superfluity, and excessive riot." These moral failings are fueled by the concentration of property "into a few rich men's hands," who need not "sell before they lust" and who "lust not before they may sell as dear as they lust." "Because there be so few sellers," prices "falleth not one mite" no matter what the supply, and "dearth" follows; workers are deprived of the dignity of their labor, and idleness, beggary, and crime spread through the land (102–04). For Hythloday, the recommended cure for this moral pestilence itself is moral as well as legal. "Cast out these pernicious abominations," he says.

> Make a law that they, which plucked down farms and towns of husbandry, shall re-edify them, or else yield and uprender the possession thereof to such as will go to the cost of building them anew. Suffer not these rich men to buy up all, to engross and forestall, and with their monopoly to keep the market alone as please them (104).

Monopoly is the watchword in this passage.[90] Later in the sixteenth century, the word was applied specifically to royal grants or patents allowing individuals the exclusive right to manufacture and trade particular items. As More employs it, it refers more generally to such practices as cornering the markets in certain commodities — particularly wool — to gain control over their sale or holding back goods from trade to drive up their price artificially, phenomena called in Robynson's translation "engrossing" and "forestalling," respectively. These trading techniques, while hardly unheard of in the present day, have an extra significance in a dual economy in which the needs and interests of local and more distant markets sometimes conflict. When they do, it is often tempting for traders to bypass dealings with their neighbors to gain the higher prices available in the more impersonal markets farther afield. The consequence could be a strong sense of injustice and betrayal felt by those members of the local community deprived of what they might consider necessities for their livelihoods.

In this formulation, monopoly represents the dark side of market-oriented economic activities in England's dual economy — those impersonal forces that threaten to overwhelm the structures of authority and deference, the practices of beneficial goodwill, and the principles of harmonious social interchange on which its nonmarket-oriented aspects were thought to depend. However, More was no naive sentimentalist wishing to set England into a primitive economic state capable of producing goods only for bare subsistence. On the island of Utopia, he imagined a fairly complex division of labor. The Utopians, men and women, all practiced farming, but also had some other useful occupation, such as "clothworking in wool or flax . . . or the smith's craft" (136). Although luxuries were suppressed, the emphasis was less on what was produced than on the spirit of service and cooperation in which production was conducted. No one was to "sit idle"; everyone was to "apply his own craft with earnest diligence" for the common good (136–37).

To redress the damage to the moral community that he saw around him, More stresses ethical actions more than economic outcomes. In effect, he calls for production and consumption to be grounded in the values of face-to-face communal life of the sort believed to prevail in small villages and self-governing towns. More's treatment of the economy, therefore, is neither historical nor analytical, but ethical; it is not primarily concerned with explaining, but with judging and correcting. In this view, the proper cure for economic distress is the maintenance of a moral economy, grounded in the established, eternal values of personal charity and human fellowship, which preserves the community in its wholeness and makes a flourishing life possible within it.

CHURCH LIFE

One of the things that especially troubled More about the corrupt conditions in his day was the involvement of the clergy in so many of them. Although Cardinal John Morton appears as the very model of the good churchman and royal counselor, he is the only prelate or priest mentioned in The First Book of *Utopia* who is not subject to criticism or open ridicule. The problem was that the Church was not just a spiritual institution, but a worldly enterprise, possessed of material interests as well as religious duties and peopled by individuals with personal ambitions as well as godly callings. It had the highest ideals, but inevitably it was subject to human failings.

Considered narrowly as an organization of individuals under religious vows, the Church was populous.[91] At the beginning of the sixteenth century, there were perhaps 20,000 or 25,000 secular clergy in England and Wales, serving as parish rectors, vicars, and curates or as chantry priests, and possibly a further 9,000 to 10,000 regular clergy and 2,000 nuns living in religious houses. The total population of England and Wales at the time was less than 2.5 million, giving a ratio of approximately one priest, monk, friar, or nun for every seventy-five people, a level maintained through a continuous process of recruitment. Although many new recruits were the younger sons or daughters of the landed elite, who enjoyed advantages in the competition for the best offices, there was always pressure to find talented prospects from lesser families, and a number of them were able to rise into high places. Thomas Wolsey, for example, was the son of an Ipswich butcher and innkeeper, albeit a well-off one.

The Church was also exceedingly wealthy in More's day, holding, mostly under the control of its religious houses and cathedral chapters and its abbots and bishops, perhaps a fifth to a quarter of all agricultural land in England as well as impressive church buildings and extensive urban properties. Many of its leaders, the ecclesiastical equivalents of the lay nobility and gentry, lived in considerable luxury, housed in great palaces or mansions, attended by numerous servants who provided them with the finest in food and drink. Typically, these leading clerics managed their estates with the aim of seeking the best advantage from them, partly to ensure their own lordly status, which marked the honor of the Church as well as of themselves, and partly to provide sufficient revenues for the performance of their godly and charitable purposes, including almsgiving to those in need and hospitality to neighbors and strangers. This meant that the Church was often in the forefront of introducing improvements, such as enclosure, into the management of its properties. For a long while, the greatest sheep farmers in England were the Carthusian and Cistercian monks performing their daily routines of labor and prayer in remote regions. Because the Church's revenues were distributed into a large number of hands, they are difficult to estimate, but taken together, they almost certainly exceeded by several fold the crown's annual income, which in 1500 amounted to about £113,000 per year.

As a large, property-holding organization, the Church depended for its governance on a complex, hierarchical, bureaucratic structure, international in scope, headed in England by the archbishops of Canterbury and York, each in charge of his own ecclesiastical province. As a law-governed institution, it also had its own courts and its own system of law, which not only functioned to maintain the authority of its officials within the hierarchy, to control its finances, and to govern the activities of the clergy, but also enforced uniformity in ceremony and doctrine and regulated the laity in some of the most vital of their material affairs, such as marriage and probate. In addition, it took the lead in education. Schools and universities were church institutions, staffed by men in holy orders and engaged in large measure in educating future church officials.

For centuries, the Church claimed moral and legal superiority for itself as the representative of the whole body or commonwealth of Christendom, centered on papal authority or the power of a general council. It was understood to be independent, its leaders owing obedience only to God, while the state fell under ecclesiastical judgment and command in the performance of its own important functions in law enforcement and the provision of security against attack. In contrast, theorists for the state argued for an outright form of political dualism, according to which both Church and state enjoyed divinely ordained autonomous powers in their own spheres but cooperated in their performance of godly purposes. These differences were subtle, but they could lead to deep conflicts when interests clashed and, in practice, relations between the two spheres were vastly more complicated than any theory allowed.

In England, it was well recognized that in their temporal lives, all subjects, clerical as well as lay, fell under the common law and kingly rule. Only in matters of faith and morality did the Church's courts have independent powers, and even here proceedings could be stopped by the king's writ while their propriety was under scrutiny. The election and appointment of bishops and abbots also depended heavily on royal power and influence. Because high-ranking churchmen were also great landlords, responsible for governmental and military services, and sat in the House of Lords during parliaments, the state as well as the Church had a significant interest in ensuring their loyalty and effectiveness. Before their elections could go forward, formal procedures required the king's authorization; afterward, the successful candidate could only enter into his office with the king's approval, with his ecclesiastical income subjected to royal supervision. It is equally true that the church provided the monarchy with many of its most important officials. In the decades before More achieved the lord chancellorship, this office typically fell to high-ranking churchmen, such as Cardinal Morton and Archbishop William Warham, who were successively chancellors in Henry VII's and Henry VIII's reigns; each held the see of Canterbury while serving the king in the Chancery. Cardinal Wolsey, who followed Warham in the chancellorship in 1515, held the see of York. Many of the other leading royal counselors, especially those charged with running the state's major administrative departments and with conducting its foreign policy, also held high church offices.

The king, therefore, had a strong interest and was in a strong position to nominate candidates for these offices and to control their activities once they were installed. In consequence, most senior churchmen in More's day owed their advancement to the patronage of the king, although he usually acted in consultation with the pope and other church officials. Considered collectively, bishops and abbots were the Church's men, performing its godly duties and protecting its earthly privileges; considered individually, they were servants of the king, since he more than anyone had the capacity to satisfy their fondest personal ambitions. In fact, advancement in church and state often proceeded in step, good service to the king being rewarded by progress through the ranks of the ecclesiastical hierarchy.

Not surprisingly, there were often tensions in this intrinsically difficult relationship between church and state. The independent role of the ecclesiastical courts was one source of trouble, especially in connection with their jurisdiction over the private businesses of the laity, such as defamation and breach of promise. The Church's ability to offer sanctuary to felons and to protect many of them from punishment for their crimes through "benefit of clergy" also produced vexation.

Many of these issues came to a head early in Henry VIII's reign, when a number of Church officials fell under scrutiny for the murder of Richard Hunne, a well-to-do merchant tailor and citizen of London who had become entangled in a series of legal disputes with the ecclesiastical authorities.[92] Accused by them of heresy and jailed, he was subsequently found dead by hanging while in Church custody. A London coroner's jury delivered a verdict of willful murder against Hunne's jailers, but they were protected from trial by the ecclesiastical authorities; in the end, the controversy was accommodated only through the intervention of the king. More, as an important London official at the time, was well aware of these events. He was present at the judgment against Hunne that condemned his books and his body to be burned. When More wrote about the matter later, he sided with the clergy in seeing Hunne as a heretic, a conclusion supported in part by More's judgment that he had indeed taken his own life.[93]

The Hunne affair signaled no general rejection of the Church or its doctrines, but it unfolded in something of a new cultural environment. Several features stand out. One concerns the charge of heresy leveled against Hunne. There had long been an element of heresy in England, especially in London, although the number of heretics was never large. Most of the heretics were Lollards, that is, followers of John Wycliffe (1324?–1384), who advocated a scriptural religion based on reading the Bible in the vernacular and who rejected a number of the key doctrines and practices of orthodox Catholicism, such as transubstantiation and the veneration of saints. During the fifteenth century, his lay followers were almost all poorer men and women, particularly those engaged in the cloth-making crafts. However, in the early sixteenth century, the movement, though remaining small, had begun to spread into wealthier segments of the population, particularly in London. This is one reason why the bishop of London was so concerned by the Hunne affair and why he and some of his colleagues elsewhere took such aggressive stances against the Lollard sect. If the social prominence of heretics increased, it was feared that the influence of their views would as well, especially among increasingly literate and independent-minded urban dwellers.[94]

A second new element concerns the character of lay piety.[95] Traditional Catholicism was very much a communal religion, centered on collective acts of public worship in the Mass and on the performance of group rituals, such as the great procession of the elevated Host on Corpus Christi and the festive celebration of saints' days. These features remained firmly in place in More's time, but among literate men and women, there was also an increasing emphasis on personal forms of devotion, individual acts of piety, and the inner life of the spirit. Private and family prayers and personal meditations became more important. So too did attendance at sermons and the reading of devotional literature, the latter made more readily available by the spread of printing. These impulses were furthered as well by increased attention to the confessional and the requirements of individual penance, which stressed the importance of conscience and personal responsibility for good works as well as sin. These developments set the practices of the Church in a context that especially stressed its role in individual salvation, without diminishing its responsibilities for moral leadership and the maintenance of social peace. The paradoxical effect was to enhance the awareness among some ordinary Christians of the Church's flaws as an institution and of the moral and intellectual limitations among some of its clergy.

Added to this deepening of the personal and inward aspects of religion were more formal and systematic efforts to achieve a closer relationship with the divine through direct, mystical, religious experiences and the disciplines of contemplation. Much of the resulting writing originated in the monasteries and was concerned with the spiritual lives of the monks. Considerable attention among the learned was also given to an intensely intellectual and philosophically dense neoplatonism, drawing particularly on the writings of Marsilio Ficino and Giovanni Pico della Mirandolla. However, popular threads of mysticism and lay piety similarly thrived in such widely circulated works as *The Cloud of Unknowing, The Book of Margery Kempe,* and *The Imitation of Christ;* the latter detailed the strict contemplative routines of the Brethren of the Common Life, a lay religious and charitable movement in the Netherlands. These texts spoke directly to the personal religious yearnings of a significant lay reading public.

In a number of respects, Thomas More's early life seems immersed in these spiritual developments. Although he was not following the letter of *The Imitation of Christ,* he seems to have been taken by a very similar spirit. In addition, through his friendships with Erasmus and John Colet, he had significant connections with neoplatonism and in 1510 had published an English translation of a Latin biography of Giovanni Pico della Mirandola, including as an addendum a verse paraphrase of Pico's *Twelve Rules of a Christian Life.*[96] More's heightened religious awareness and his belief in the Church as a potent source of goodness in the world made its failings all the harder to take. He was no outspoken anticlerical but nonetheless was a critic of the Church because he was a deeply devout, orthodox Catholic whose inner life was firmly shaped by his sense of membership in the spiritual body of Christendom.

Christian humanism in its Erasmian form represents yet a third new element in the early Tudor cultural environment.[97] Erasmus, himself educated among the Brethren of the Common Life in the Netherlands, stood at the head of a movement to employ the new scholarly and critical insights of humanism to the interpretation of religious texts. The movement's aim was not merely to produce more accurate and more accessible versions of these works, but to transform the institutions of the Church and society in accordance with the understanding of Christ's message that resulted from this new philological, literary, and historical learning. The emphasis was on the practice of Christian love in acts of piety, not on the formalities of theology or strict adherence to ceremony and certainly not on the legal rights and material interests of the institutional Church.

Erasmus's message provided the foundation for an important reform movement in England, particularly in the schools and universities and in the Church. Believing that ecclesiastical and clerical reform would logically result in the reform of society, his English supporters, led by John Colet, were especially concerned to withdraw the church from its worldly entanglements, to turn the clergy from their ignorance and sin, and to focus them instead on prayer, the study of Scripture, the preaching of God's word, and the performance of the sacraments. The inadequacies and wickedness of priests, monks, and friars, they believed, only opened the door to heresy. More shared this view.

One must guard against seeing these important features of religious and intellectual culture as the direct precursors of an inevitable Reformation. There was neither a crisis of corruption among the clergy at the beginning of Henry VIII's reign nor a crisis of antagonism to the Church. Anticlericalism had long been a feature of the Church's relations to the state and to society.[98] It flared from time to time in response to particular events — the Hunne case was hardly the first — without signaling contempt for the Church as a whole or the beginnings of a general conflagration. Often it was churchmen themselves who led the criticism of the Church and sought its spiritual and moral reform. Popular devotion to the Catholic Church also remained high, judging by the gifts the Church continued to receive in lay people's wills and by the spirit of piety with which its liturgy, its system of penance, and other practices were accepted. A sophisticated Italian visitor reported around 1500 that the English seemed especially pious — committed to worship, active in almsgiving, anxious to appear good Christians, concerned about religious ideas, and argumentative in their opinions.[99] If he had met More at the time, he almost certainly would have considered him an exemplary representative of these English characteristics: pious and skeptical at the same time — a good model for the character "Thomas More" whom we meet in *Utopia*.

THE MONARCHICAL STATE [100]

In the medieval English state, a substantial majority of governmental officials had been churchmen. Although clergy occupied many important senior positions in Henry VIII's government, the early Tudors relied more and more on laymen as leading counselors, and the ecclesiastical presence elsewhere in royal administration had waned. Laymen, especially those trained in the classics and the law, increasingly filled posts in the major governmental departments and in the royal household. More's selection for membership in the royal council and his subsequent rise to importance as an official should be seen as part of this trend in early Tudor government.

These changes in the social composition of the royal administration went hand in hand with the impetus to reform the state and build up its revenues, which Edward IV and Richard III, the Yorkist kings, put at the heart of their programs and which the early Tudors took up in a determined way. Alongside the assertion of the supremacy of royal justice over ecclesiastical immunities, there was a systematic program to advance monarchical prerogatives against the king's principal feudal tenants and the holders of franchises.[101] At the same time, pains were taken to resume control of all alienated royal estates, based on the theory that the crown's endowment in land, from which it derived the revenues necessary to perform its divinely ordained functions, was intrinsically inalienable and should pass intact from one reign to the next.

Although much attention was given to strengthening the independent power of the king, late medieval England was a consent-based monarchy. Sir John Fortescue, Chief Justice in the King's Bench during Henry VI's reign, identified it as a *dominium politicum et regale,* a regime in which executive authority belonged exclusively to the king and his officials, but where lawmaking and taxation required the formal acceptance of the people through their representatives in Parliament. There was as yet no full-scale theory of the "state" — no conception, that is, of an autonomous political entity enjoying rights, having interests, and undertaking actions distinct from the person and power of the monarch. However, there was a deepening sense that the king stood at the head of a corporate body politic, a commonwealth whose members had a collective identity and collective interests.[102]

With the advent of the new Tudor dynasty, fiscally weak and installed only after a civil war, these well-established political doctrines took on new significance. Henry VII was able to improve not only the power but the authority of the monarchy at home and abroad, by aggressively asserting the higher purposes of royal rule and the king's claims to superiority in the realm. His policies aimed to check the rebelliousness and undermine the independent military power of the great nobility, quiet the violence of their factional divisions, and build up royal revenues. This form of government was inherently personal and dynastic, dependent on the royal will not only in the formulation of policy, but also in its enforcement. It was not possible in practice for a subject to be obedient and loyal to the kingdom without also being obedient and loyal to the person of the king. Similarly, the interests of the nation could not readily be disentangled from the interests of the royal family that ruled it.

Under Henry VII, who took great pains with administrative details and day-to-day decisions, government centered on his household as well as his council. Henry VIII, however, was less inclined to immerse himself in the daily business of governance. No less committed than his father to promoting his own, his family's, and his country's interests and no less personal in his exercise of his royal office, he preferred to rule through the administrative skills of leading ministers, often settling the main responsibility on a single figure. The first of them was Wolsey, who had achieved this status by 1515.

The political situation that Wolsey faced was significantly shaped by what had happened during the fifteenth century to England's relations with continental Europe. From the time William the Conqueror crossed the Channel from Normandy in 1066 to the era of the Hundred Years' War, the English king had been almost as much involved, militarily as well as politically, in France as in the British isles. During this long period, England remained in control of substantial French possessions, especially Gascony and Aquitaine, and for considerable intervals during the Hundred Years' War itself, the English were in the dominant position vis-à-vis the French king. All this ended, however, when the military tide reversed after the death of Henry V in 1425. In 1453, England lost Bordeaux and its region, its last truly valuable and substantial French holdings. Thereafter, its only foothold on the continent was at Calais. In Queen Mary's reign, even this stronghold was lost, never to be recovered. England was now essentially an island nation in political as well as geographic terms. Its successes and failures in the world depended primarily on what it could accomplish in the British isles themselves.[103]

These developments had profound effects on English affairs.[104] It was deemed especially important to restore England's European trading links, which had been seriously disrupted not only in France, but also in the Low Countries, by England's defeat in the Hundred Years' War. A flourishing trade was necessary to keep up the domestic economy and the crown's customs revenues and to ensure high levels of employment in the cloth-making industry and the maintenance of the king's power in the land. It is not surprising, therefore, that a good deal of English diplomacy in this period, including the embassy that took Thomas More to Bruges and Antwerp in 1515, had as a main purpose the improvement of commercial relations.

However, to protect the dynasty from Yorkist attacks originating abroad, it was also necessary to win acceptance for the Tudor regime on the continent. In Henry VII's reign, foreign policy was on the whole successfully directed toward that goal. It was equally essential to quiet any threats from Scotland, something that Henry VII accomplished mainly through diplomacy, but that his son achieved militarily at the battle of Flodden in 1513. Since in this period war remained a valuable source of prestige for a monarch and his nobles as well as a vehicle of state policy, voices opposing war normally went unheeded, as Hythloday pointedly argues in The First Book of *Utopia*.

England's defeat in the Hundred Years' War left it a considerably weaker power. Only deft political judgment, diplomatic cunning, and a degree of ruthlessness had any prospect of salvaging the situation. It was these qualities that Henry VIII saw in Wolsey. The latter recognized that success for England could not be achieved by frontal attack, but instead required the careful and concealed manipulation of events on the continent in England's long-term interests. The policy was intrinsically aggressive, but given the strict limitations of English resources and arms, which Wolsey recognized, stress was put on keeping the peace, with the aim of winning what was desired through maneuver and concessions from the French, rather than violence and opposition. Wolsey followed this strategy after ending the Anglo-French war by arranging the marriage in 1514 of Henry's younger sister Mary to Louis XII. During the next several years, he maneuvered to achieve a treaty of universal peace, intended to cover all of Europe, at the heart of which would be a permanent Anglo-French alliance. In fact, such a document, short-lived though it turned out to be, was signed at London by England and France in 1518.

These were the international conditions confronting England as More considered his offer from Henry and Wolsey to join the royal council. Whether the coming of peace would have positive results for social good depended ultimately on the virtue and goodwill of the king and his advisers. What would it take to ensure that government pursued the common good and not just the ruler's own advantage and the personal ambitions of his counselors? Hythloday's answer in *Utopia* turned on the elimination of private property. Given the unlikelihood of this proposal being accepted, what, if anything, might be done instead?

More was not politically naive, as he makes abundantly clear through the voice of Hythloday. Along with his friends Erasmus and Colet, however, he abhorred war and all the miseries it brought with it. Here was the prospect that an era of peace might be at hand. Peace, desirable in its own right, would also bring a number of other desirable goals somewhat closer. By redirecting the energies of the government, it might promote justice and help the poor at home. By relieving the political pressures on the papacy in Italy, it might also allow the church to attend to much needed renovation. If he thought that Henry and Wolsey, the leading minister, might be ready to follow "good counsel," he could hardly refuse. What might have made him think so?

By the time of his accession, Henry VIII himself had earned a brilliant reputation for scholarship as well as virtue. In a letter written to Erasmus at the time of Henry's accession, Lord Mountjoy said that "heaven smiles, earth rejoices; all is milk and honey and nectar. Tight-fistedness is well and truly banished. Generosity scatters wealth with unstinting hand. Our king's heart is not set upon gold or jewels or mines of ore, but upon virtue, reputation, and eternal renown."[105] Erasmus was himself impressed by Henry's learning as well as his grace and at one time even said that the Tudor court was the only one in Europe he would consider joining.[106] The king knew Latin and several modern languages, was adept in mathematics, astronomy, and theology, and was genuinely gifted in music. At the outset of his reign, Henry signaled an intention to bring justice and reform to his government by imprisoning and eventually executing Sir Richard Empson and Edmund Dudley, his father's most aggressive and hated officials. It was therefore possible to believe that the new king might truly be committed to a course of peace abroad and social improvement at home once he began to follow Wolsey's lead.

In these early years of Henry's reign, Wolsey himself also had a reputation as a reformer — someone willing to listen to philosophers.[107] He had been a student at Oxford and a fellow of Magdelene College there in the 1480s and 1490s as the humanist movement began to take hold.

Figure 4. Hans Holbein the Younger's ink and watercolor study of Henry VIII with Henry VII for his now-destroyed Whitehall mural of 1537. By courtesy of the National Portrait Gallery, London.

Although he seems to have been more an adminstrator than a scholar, he took degrees in theology as well as arts, which demonstrates a commitment to learning. He was, at least briefly, master of Magdelene College's school for young boys, where he had pedagogical responsibilities as well. Even in his early days as a royal official, there were high hopes among the humanists that he would prove to be a supporter of their circle and their program, and as he rose in rank at the council table, these aspirations were to some degree fulfilled. The domestic policies he

Figure 5. Anonymous portrait of Cardinal Thomas Wolsey.
By courtesy of the National Portrait Gallery, London.

pursued had a reformist character, including efforts to restrain the inequities caused by enclosure, to ensure fair dealings in the marketplace, and to ameliorate the social problems arising from poverty and vagabondage. Moreover, many of his appointments went to humanist scholars, a number trained in Italy — men seeking to translate their liberal educations into worthy careers in public service. Notable among such figures were Richard Sampson, Richard Pace, and Cuthbert Tunstall, men who had studied in the great centers of humanist learning abroad (Sampson at Paris, Pace and Tunstall at Padua). Erasmus certainly regarded Wolsey as a supporter of humanism's broad mission, one of the main reasons why Henry VIII's court was deemed such a worthy place for the flourishing of letters.

Despite the fact that Henry's and Wolsey's support for learning and interest in reform were well known when More received their offer of membership in the royal council, he delayed in accepting. It is uncertain what during the ensuing year convinced him to join. It may only be that as a family man with a legal career to pursue, he found it impossible as a practical matter to reject the patronage of the king and his principal minister.[108] His first duty as a member of the royal council in 1517 was to serve in a commercial embassy to France. He was invited, therefore, not just to promote English domestic prosperity, with all the positive consequences this might have for London's welfare and the improvement of conditions for the poor, but also to join in the pursuit of peace with France. Perhaps the offer of this assignment helped him make up his mind to become the king's good servant.[109]

Thereafter, his career took off. In 1521, he became undertreasurer in the Exchequer, an important financial office, and was knighted. In 1523, he was elected, on Wolsey's urging, as speaker of the House of Commons for that year's parliamentary session. There he did his part to ensure the grant of taxes to the king. In 1525, he added the chancellorship of the Duchy of Cornwall, another important financial office, to his growing list of positions. More's membership on the royal council left him well placed to perform good service not only to his king, but also to the commonwealth. During these years, he acted as unofficial secretary to the king, answering correspondence and petitions; played the role of intermediary between him and Wolsey; served frequently on diplomatic missions; and assisted Henry VIII in publishing a defense of the seven sacraments against Luther (1521). In 1523, he also wrote his own response to Luther in Latin. A bit later, in 1528, Cuthbert Tunstall, by now bishop of London, commissioned him to write works in the vernacular attacking Luther and Lutheranism, the first of which appeared the following year.[110] For all of this, he was handsomely rewarded by the king with substantial grants of lands and pensions. When Wolsey fell from grace in 1529, having failed his master on the vital matter of the king's divorce, More himself became lord chancellor.

The lord chancellor was the most senior judicial figure in the realm, head of his own Court of Chancery, present as a judge to hear state trials in the king's council sitting in the Star Chamber, keeper of the king's conscience touching matters of justice and equity, and invariably consulted on all important legal matters. These roles inevitably made the chancellor a central figure in any reign. Frequently, as in the case of Wolsey, he was also the king's main minister, operating at the hub of all government policy, domestic and foreign, and therefore was well positioned not only to advance English interests abroad, but also to promote a vigorous reform in the realm, especially as regards the provision of justice to ordinary people in the law courts. For someone with More's aspirations to advance the common good, there could not have been a better post. Although he could hardly have expected to build a utopia on this foundation, he surely would be in a position to ensure that what he could not "turn to good," he could so "order it that it be not very bad" (122). However, as we shall see, events soon took a turn that made even this limited goal impossible to achieve.

DEVELOPMENTS

As far as we know, More never attempted to translate *Utopia* into English, even though he wrote and published in English as well as in Latin throughout his later career. Given the direction More's career took after he published his book, he may himself have become less preoccupied by its main themes, especially those addressed in The First Book. For whatever reason, *Utopia*— More's most famous piece of writing — turned out for him to have been the book of a particular period of his life, something to which he did not return once his career in high office was under way.

Nevertheless, *Utopia* did not lose its appeal to readers. As we noted earlier, there remained a good market for it in Latin in the sixteenth century. It was also not long before there arose a demand for it in the vernacular. However, its publication in English for the first time in 1551 placed it in a very different context from the one in which it had initially appeared. More, Erasmus, Wolsey, and Henry were all dead, and many of the great issues that had stirred them in the earlier sixteenth century had been transformed or made irrelevant by the events of the Reformation. Relations between the clergy and the laity were forever altered, and there was an increasing focus in English public affairs on the formation of a conception of nationhood, on the maintenance of a stable social order, and on the curing of a host of secular ills affecting the lives and livelihoods of the poor and the middling sort. Ralph Robynson's translation is, in many respects, part of this new environment. In this final section of the introduction, we will consider some of the main historical changes that separate Robynson's world from More's and point out a few of their consequences for the reception and interpretation of *Utopia*.

Transition

Thomas More himself died a martyr to his beliefs.[111] His appointment to the lord chancellorship placed him in a position to do much good for the commonwealth, but also put him in an office where he could not escape the same great matter that had brought down Wolsey. For years after

Wolsey's fall, the king's desire to shed his first wife and seek another in his quest for a legitimate male heir continued to dominate governmental policy, foreign affairs, and relations with the pope and the Church. More, whose views on the sanctity of marriage were entirely orthodox and unyielding,[112] had not been prepared to accept the chancellorship if it meant openly committing himself to a policy of "divorce." At first, he had declined Henry VIII's invitation; he agreed only when the king offered to have the issue of his marriage handled exclusively by those among his advisers whose consciences would not be troubled. More's presence and prestige, Henry hoped, would help bring some unity to his faction-ridden council, which was deeply divided on how to proceed toward the king's professed goal. It was a task beyond even More's great rhetorical skills, and he soon found himself assisting his king in pursuit of a policy for which he did not approve while simultaneously siding with the opposing faction in the council.[113]

More struggled with this inherently ambiguous and thoroughly intractable political situation for two and a half years in hopes of winning victory for Catherine of Aragon, Henry's queen, and of protecting the Church, where the authority lay to grant Henry his petition in the marriage case. At the same time, More pursued an aggressive policy against heresy, actively joining in the arrest, imprisonment, and interrogation of heretics, treating them as menaces to secular as well as spiritual life, whose death by burning he believed was fully justified. Because England enjoyed the benefits of the true Christian religion, he allowed no room in his official practices for the free religious discussion and toleration that we find in Utopia.[114] However, with "The Submission, the Clergy" in May 1532, by which England's bishops surrendered their independent legislative authority to the crown, More could stay in office no longer. The "very bad" had not been prevented. He resigned to go into private life, keeping his personal views on the king's marriages from the public, intending to live in retirement while the storms raged about him.

However, although he did not openly resist the king's marriage policy, he could not entirely withdraw from the controversies it touched on or helped stir.[115] As a committed Catholic, the spirit of service to orthodox Christian belief had never left him in his political career. Even when he was no longer a public official, he still remained a public figure. With publications in 1533 attacking the English Lutherans and defending his own actions in persecuting heretics, he was still someone engaged — with the greatest vituperation — in the central religious issues of his day.[116]

While More was thus occupied, the king's great matter further unfolded. In January 1533, Henry secretly married Anne Boleyn, already pregnant with the future Queen Elizabeth I. In April, the convocation of the Archdiocese of Canterbury, where the case of Henry's marriage to Catherine now rested, decided in Henry's favor that the two had never been legally wed according to divine law. The following March, Parliament approved the Act of Succession, which endorsed the convocation's action, recognized the king's new marriage, and made it treason to attack it. The statute ordered all English subjects to swear obedience to any heirs born to the king by his new queen. Within weeks, the oath of succession was submitted to More, who refused to swear the oath as a matter of conscience, although he was willing to acknowledge the succession as a matter of law. For this he was accused of violations of the Acts of Supremacy (1534) and Treason (1534) and was quickly imprisoned in the Tower of London. While there, he occupied himself with writing a number of works of religious solace and devotion, some in English and some in Latin.[117]

As his case proceeded, More never explicitly denied the king's statutory supremacy over the church nor insisted on absolute papal authority. Instead, he rested his arguments on his right to remain silent about the views he held in conscience. It was a legally deft as well as an intellectually radical stance. However, in the face of a strong royal interest in crushing all resistance to the king's claims to supremacy, backed by a developing theory of the power of parliamentary statute to determine all questions of law, it did not — it could not — prevail. In a little more than a year, More was convicted of treason after a brief trial, and on July 7, 1535, he was beheaded on Tower Hill. At his execution, More is said to have professed himself the king's good servant, but God's first. His lifelong effort to reconcile a worldly career to God's spiritual commandments had finally proved impossible to achieve, and he went to his death a martyr to his most profound convictions. Had Hythloday, his alter ego, been right after all? Was it impossible for a virtuous man to be a good royal counselor in Tudor England and for a good counselor to be a virtuous man?

Only after his conviction did More speak openly against the parliamentary statute that had authorized the supremacy, calling it "directly oppugnant to the laws of God and His Holy Church, the supreme government of which" belonged only to the "See of Rome" and "no temporal prince."[118] He remained steadfast in his belief that individual kingdoms or states were subordinate to the whole Christian commonwealth, which was made up not only of its living members on earth but its saints in heaven. England, "being but one member and a small part of the Church," he argued, "might not make a particular law dischargeable with the general law of Christ's universal Catholic Church, no more than the City of London, being but one poor member in respect of the whole Realm, might make a law against an act of Parliament to bind the whole Realm." Hence an act of "the council of one realm against the general council of Christendom" was "in law, amongst Christian men, insufficient to charge any Christian."[119]

More's arguments directly challenged the most profound changes to the legal standing of the Church in England that had been wrought by Henry VIII. The theory was succinctly stated in the Act in Restraint of Appeals (1533), which restricted the trial of all ecclesiastical cases before Church courts in England, cutting off papal jurisdiction, on the grounds that "England is an empire . . . governed by one supreme head and king having the dignity and royal estate of the imperial crown of the same, unto whom a body politic . . . be bounden and owe to bear next to God a natural and humble obedience."[120] The central terms are *empire* and *imperial crown*. They insist not only that England is divinely ordained to be an independent realm, owing obedience to no other earthly ruler, but that its king is the sovereign head not just of the state, but also of the Church.[121]

The Act in Restraint of Appeals, therefore, resolved the medieval debate over the jurisdictions of Church and state firmly in favor of the state. The Church was viewed essentially as a state institution to which had been delegated certain religious and administrative responsibilities, subject to the king's appointment powers and to legislative regulation by sovereign acts of the king-in-parliament in the form of statutes. This position was confirmed by the Act of Supremacy, which held the king and his successors to be "the only supreme head in earth of the Church of England called Anglicana Ecclesia . . . annexed and united to the imperial crown of this realm."[122]

The religious and ecclesiastical life of England was also affected by a second set of changes in Henry VIII's reign. Beginning under Wolsey as a movement for monastic reform, and continuing in the 1530s as a more systematic effort to dismantle entirely the religious orders in England, every house of monks, friars, and nuns in the realm was dissolved by 1540, and their vast properties were redistributed. Some went to endow educational institutions, others to found several new bishoprics, but the bulk passed initially into the hands of the king, from whence they were almost immediately sold for the crown's benefit to private individuals or lay corporations.[123] By the end of the sixteenth century, hardly any of these former monastic holdings were left in the crown's hands. The reign of Edward VI, Henry's heir, witnessed similar seizures of chantry properties — endowments for the singing of masses for the dead, often associated with altars or chapels devoted to the veneration of particular saints. Some of these lands were used to endow schools and charitable activities, but again most passed into private hands.

In one way, this massive redistribution of property followed directly from the royal supremacy, since the church's holdings were simply treated as resources to support the imperial crown in the performance of its wide range of functions. However, the dissolutions also had a deep cultural, intellectual, and spiritual significance. The main function of monasteries and chantries was intercession with Christ on behalf of the dead to plea for their salvation and ease their penance in Purgatory. An attack on the religious orders, therefore, did not just advance the political and material interests of the state, it also struck a blow to the substance of traditional Catholic belief and practice and threatened the church's ability to perform its traditional intercessory functions. What made this attack all the more telling was that once the Church's lands had come into a large number of private estates, the prospect of reconstituting the endowments and restoring the religious orders was considerably dimmed.

These developments were accompanied by the spread of Protestant beliefs and practices, although the pace of this reformation in conscience is extremely hard to assess. It certainly proceeded faster in London than elsewhere and with more early fervor in southeast England, near to London and the universities, in cities and the cloth-making districts, and among the prosperous and literate. As a religion of the Word, Protestantism's advance also depended directly on preaching and print, both of which were more readily available in the regions and among the social groupings just mentioned. However, they were subject to governmental regulation and the twists and turns of ecclesiastical politics.

Access to the Bible was probably the most crucial stimulant. Wycliffe's fourteenth-century English translation already existed, but it was not widely available, and although William Tyndale, the English Lutheran, had begun a new Protestant translation in the 1520s, he was able to complete and publish only the New Testament, the Pentateuch, and the Book of Jonah. In any case, because his work was unauthorized, these texts could only be sold illicitly. In the course of the 1530s, however, several authorized translations became available, and with the support of Thomas Cromwell, Henry VIII's principal minister at the time, and of Thomas Cranmer, the archbishop of Canterbury, laymen were being officially urged to read the Scripture as part of their regular religious devotion. Henry VIII's own views on theology and the sacraments were highly conservative, and by 1540 he had turned firmly against the Protestants, subjecting them to persecution and punishment for heresy. However, as long as the Bible still remained available, reading and discussion of it laid the foundation among numerous clergy and laymen for serious spiritual reevaluation.

Despite this persecution, the spread of Protestantism was not checked. Although it is not possible to be certain of percentages, there can be little doubt that by Henry VIII's death in 1547, significant numbers of the clergy, of the gentry, and of the middling sort in the towns had accepted Protestant doctrine. However, the course of change was slow and uneven. Perhaps 20 percent of Londoners were Protestants in 1547, and this figure was reached probably only in the other major towns of southern England and in the country districts near them. Elsewhere, and especially in the north of England, the figures were much lower. However, many Englishmen and women in this period, as in other times, were dutiful rather than passionate followers of religious convention, conforming their practices to the requirements of the law and the pull of events rather than the pricks of troubled consciences. In this climate, the numbers of active and committed Protestants mattered less, perhaps, than the fact that many were prosperous and prominent members of their communities, capable of leading others.

Edward VI's brief reign (1547–53) confirmed and advanced the trends that were set in motion under his father.[124] When he succeeded to the throne, he was a boy of nine, which made it necessary for him to rule through a regency council. The latter was headed by his maternal uncle, Edward Seymour, the duke of Somerset, and excluded the most religiously conservative of Henry VIII's advisers from its membership. Possibly, Somerset was already a Protestant himself when he became lord protector, but whether he was or not, he sought to secure the regime by promoting the Protestant cause. At the same time, Archbishop Thomas Cranmer prepared a new English prayer book to replace the Latin texts previously in use. Although this first *Book of Common Prayer* did not provide a fully Protestant liturgy, it adopted a formula for the sacrament of the Lord's Supper that permitted a distinctly Protestant interpretation. The dissolution of the chantries, which also came in 1549, was part of this pro-Protestant policy and was even more significant in altering the religious landscape. In consequence, Robynson's translation of *Utopia* first appeared in a country that was officially Protestant.

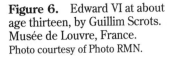

Figure 6. Edward VI at about age thirteen, by Guillim Scrots. Musée de Louvre, France.
Photo courtesy of Photo RMN.

Between 1516 and 1551, Reformation issues also became intertwined with the principal social and economic questions of the era — many of them the same ones More had addressed in *Utopia*. The pace of demographic growth had increased, and by 1551, England's population had expanded by a third or more from what it had been at the beginning of the century. By some measures, the problems arising from enclosure and from poverty had correspondingly worsened. Pressure was felt, especially in the vicinity of London, which itself had now begun to grow very rapidly. The metropolis was almost twice as large as it had been at the beginning of the century. Prices had also taken off, more than doubling in the same interval. To make matters worse, the 1540s witnessed a very costly war between England and France that was financed partly by the crown's rapid sales of recently seized monastic lands, partly by heavy domestic taxation, and partly by repeated devaluations of the currency. In the resulting inflation, cloth exports grew somewhat, but so too did the price of every domestic product. Real wages fell in both town and country. When bad harvests came, as they did between 1549 and 1552, and worse yet between 1555 and 1557, they transformed the already deficient living conditions of the laboring classes and the poor into grim destitution.

These economic strains were accompanied by increased evidence of social instability and rural unrest in England. Although London's population had exploded, many of the leading provincial towns remained in a stagnant or decayed condition, even as structural economic change was altering England's emerging urban network. The problem of vagrancy seems to have grown, relieved in the mid-1540s only by the demand for manpower in the royal armies to fight in France. However, when the soldiers returned to England at the end of Henry's reign, their presence only compounded the problems of poverty and unemployment. There were also more frequent and more serious enclosure riots, at least as reported in the court of the Star Chamber. Most of these riots, however, were very localized, were quite limited in their social aims, and had little to do with religion. In 1549, worsening economic conditions and grievances arising from enclosure contributed to a series of riots and revolts throughout England. During the summer and fall, more than half of the counties were affected in some way.[125]

Two of these outbreaks, the Western Rising in Devon and Cornwall and Kett's Rebellion in East Anglia, were particularly threatening to public order and required the calling out of county musters and the use of mercenaries.[126] In the west, the problem of enclosure and the prospect of a heavy tax on sheep raising combined with anxiety and misunderstanding about the new *Book of Common Prayer* to cause major bloodshed. The East Anglian rebellion was more concerned with enclosure, agrarian rents, and other economic matters and revealed a sharp strain of antagonism against the wealthy and powerful. But it also had a strong anticlerical tone, with many criticisms of the rapaciousness and laziness of the priesthood, and something of a Protestant flavor, especially in demands that ministers do more preaching and "that all bond men may be made free for God made all free with his precious blood shedding."[127]

These unsettled social, economic, and political conditions were the focus of a considerable body of criticism and commentary at the time, much of it from the pens of Protestant "commonwealthmen" who combined Protestant religious ideas on the inward nature of conversion with medieval Christian theories of social justice and community cooperation.[128] Encouraged by Protector Somerset, there was a concerted effort by the government to seek remedies for social wrongs, to ameliorate the material conditions of the laboring poor, and thereby to maintain the stability of the commonwealth's hierarchical social order. Bills proposing "commonwealth" remedies to restore tillage, keep up food supplies, and prevent price gouging were introduced in Edward VI's first parliament, albeit without becoming law. Somerset himself appointed a commission to survey enclosures, similar to the one instituted by Wolsey in 1517 to 1518; it had begun its inquiries, only to have its work overtaken by the risings and rebellions of 1549. Somerset's mishandling of these revolts, especially in the face of his ambitious social policies and his reputation for leniency toward the poor, led to his downfall. He was replaced by John Dudley, earl of Warwick and soon to be duke of Northumberland, who supported an advanced form of Protestantism accompanied by the rigorous imposition of godly discipline to ensure the maintenance of public order and the control of the poor.

Between the first appearance of *Utopia* in print and its first publication in English, England had made a decisive transition. What was new about the cultural environment was first the royal supremacy, whose deepening effects on the state, the Church, and the nation were already evident at the time of More's execution, and second the growing political and social importance of Protestant beliefs and practices in the centers of power in Edward VI's reign. What was familiar were the myriad social and economic problems arising from the increasing importance of market-oriented economic activity, the growing commercialization of agriculture, the dislocations caused by demographic change, and the spread of indigency. On social and economic issues, *Utopia* still had much of practical significance and moral power to say, but on government, politics, and religion it was very much a book of the previous age, before Henry VIII had begun to seek an end to his first marriage and before Protestant dissent had begun to spread in England. These facts not only encouraged *Utopia*'s publication in English, but also shaped how it was received and interpreted.

Translation

Abraham Vele, newly established in 1550 as a bookseller in London's St. Paul's Churchyard, first published Ralph Robynson's translation of *Utopia* in 1551 in an edition by Steven Mierdman, an Antwerp-born printer residing in London during Edward VI's reign. All three men were among the growing group of Protestants living and working in Reformation London. We know little about Robynson himself. He was a humanist-trained scholar, born in 1521 in Lincolnshire, where he was educated

in grammar schools along with William Cecil, one of Edward's two principal secretaries. Later, Robynson entered Corpus Christi College, Oxford, took a bachelor's degree, and became a fellow there. He eventually left Oxford to go to London, where he entered the livery of the Goldsmith's Company and began seeking the patronage of his old school friend. He tells us that he was persuaded to translate and publish More's book by George Tadlowe, "an honest citizen of London" (211). In fact, Tadlowe, a member of London's Company of Haberdashers, was a prominent city figure, a great supporter of humanist literature and anticlerical satire in the 1540s, and probably a moderate Protestant in his religious beliefs. As a member of the city's common council in the 1550s, he was staunchly loyal to Edward VI's regime under Protector Somerset.[129]

These facts associate Robynson with Somerset and his program — not as a propagandist already in governmental service, but as someone seeking favor in these circles. In the dedicatory letter he addressed to William Cecil, his school friend, he says that he undertook his translation out of a "bounden duty to God and to my country" and "for the advancement and commodity of the public wealth . . . seeing every sort and kind of people in their vocation and degree busily occupied about the commonwealth's affairs, and especially learned men daily putting forth in writing new inventions and devices to the furtherance of the same" (210). These thoughts connect him with the views on public service expressed by "Thomas More" in The First Book of *Utopia*.

In its printed form, the book Robynson produced is strikingly different from the Latin editions, and especially from Froben's fine 1518 volume. There is nothing to duplicate the imaginative map of the island of Utopia that appeared in 1516 or the even more detailed one that Ambrosius Holbein supplied in 1518.[130] The title page is crude, not at all like the elegant design that Hans Holbein the younger had produced for Froben. The best that Mierdman and Vele could manage were a few stock devices and ornamental letters, none of them comparable in quality to Froben's.[131] Held in the hand, Robynson's volume appears cheaply made

---

Top: **Figure 7.** The family of Henry VIII showing the Tudor succession. The painting dates from c. 1572 and is attributed to Lucas de Heere.
Photo courtesy of National Museums and Galleries of Wales.

Bottom: **Figure 8.** Thomas More, his father, his household and his descendants, painted in 1593 by Rowland Lockey and based on Hans Holbein the Younger's lost group portrait.
By courtesy of the National Portrait Gallery, London.

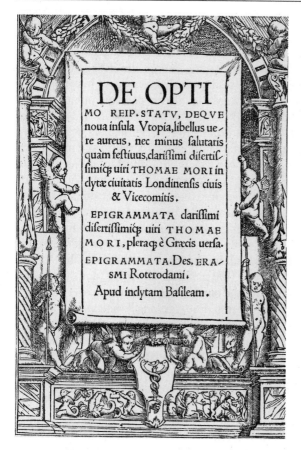

Figure 9. The title page of John Froben's Latin edition of *Utopia,* printed in Basel in March 1518. The rich border is by Hans Holbein the Younger.

By permission of The Folger Shakespeare Library.

compared to what the continental printers had produced. The expense Vele thus saved on fancy print undoubtedly helped keep down the book's price and made it available to a wider market, including the "middling sort" as well as the rich.

Robynson's edition also differed in other more substantive ways from the earlier Latin ones. In 1551, apart from Thomas More's letter to Peter Giles, none of the original group of supporting letters and commentaries appeared. In their place we have only Robynson's dedicatory letter to William Cecil (209–12). Almost none of the original front matter was included, not even the brief poem attributed to "Anemolius," which points out the punning relationship between the words *utopia* and *eutopia.*

Figure 10. The title page produced by Abraham Vele and Steven Mierdman for the first edition of Ralph Robynson's translation of *Utopia*. By permission of The Folger Shakespeare Library.

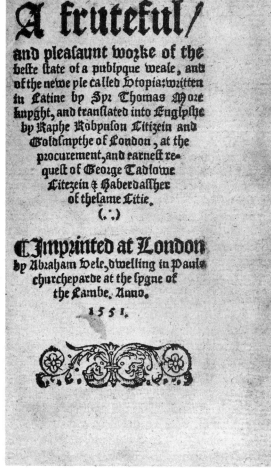

There were also no marginal notes. The volume was entirely made up of a translation of the main body of More's text. For the second, corrected edition of 1556, some additions were made, including marginal notes, a translation of "Anemolius's" verses, and the short poem in the Utopian tongue that Giles had supplied for the original Latin editions.[132] Most important, the dedicatory letter to Cecil was omitted: With the accession of Queen Mary to the throne and the consequent reversal of royal religious policy, Cecil was no longer in favor; in addition, some of Robynson's own remarks in that letter might have proved dangerous to him. Instead, Robynson supplied a brief epistle to the reader apologizing for the translation errors that had slipped into the 1551 version. In other words, this second edition, which forms the basis for our text, is still almost entirely a translation of The First Book and The Second Book, not of the printed work as published in 1516, 1517, or 1518.

The effects of these differences were to remove *Utopia* from its original moorings in Erasmian humanism. The missing endorsements, supporting letters, and marginal notes in the Latin version had set the book in a distinct philosophical and interpretive framework. These materials had especially helped shape readers' judgments about the relationship of ancient moral theory to Christianity and about More's intentions regarding community of property. They had placed More's book in an ongoing debate about the best form of a commonwealth, tracing its heritage back to classical Greece and Rome. All of this was now gone.

The translation also altered the book in some important ways for readers lacking classical training. Much of the fun and a good deal of the intellectual ambiguity of the original text arises from the clever verbal jokes and puns based in ancient languages that More used to establish the relationship between the island of Utopia and England, the former a "no place" that nonetheless might have discovered the best form of a commonwealth, and the latter a "someplace" that had many shortcomings but nevertheless enjoyed the blessings of Christianity. The force of this juxtaposition depends, in large measure, on seeing that "Utopia" means *no place,* that its principal topographical features have similarly antithetical names, that the name of the poet laureate who praises Utopia as "Plato's city" marks him as a windbag, that the name of the main narrator identifies him as a purveyor of nonsense, and so on. To readers with no knowledge of Greek, a good deal of this would have been lost. The inclusion in 1556 of a rather crude translation of "Anemolius's" poem may have done little to illuminate the point for those who did not already get its jokes, and there was nothing at all to help with Amaurote or Anyder, Hythloday or Anemolius himself.

It is not just a lack of the ancient languages that posed a problem. Readers untrained in Greek and Latin were also likely to have been without an education in the ancient philosophical texts. Most of them would have found it difficult to discern the links between Utopian religion and Epicureanism or to see *Utopia*'s relationship to the writings of Plato, Aristotle, and Cicero. Some help was offered in 1556 with passing references to Plato's *Republic* in Giles's letter to Busleyden as well as in "Anemolius's" poem. However, unless readers already knew *The Repub-*

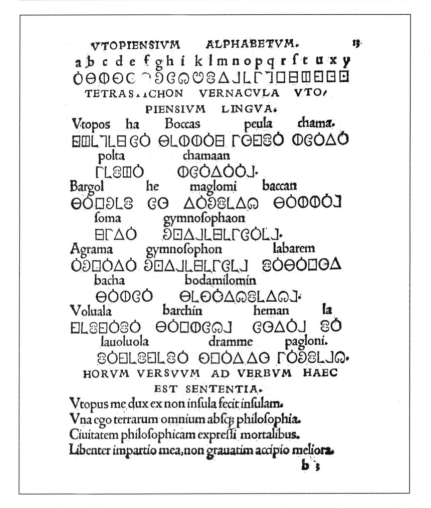

Figure 11. The Utopian alphabet and the poem in the Utopian language, with its Latin translation, from John Froben's Latin edition of *Utopia,* printed in Basel in March 1518. For contrast with the 1556 English edition, see Figure 13. By permission of the Folger Shakespeare Library.

lic, they were unlikely to make very much from these brief hints, and in 1551, of course, even these items were absent. Robynson's English version, therefore, not only somewhat diminished the philosophical richness of the book, but also made it available to a reading public less likely to read it in the way that the learned had when it first appeared — less

likely in particular to see its clever juxtapositioning of ancient philosophical doctrines and Christian beliefs and practices.

Although in most respects Robynson offers a very accurate rendering
of More's Latin text, albeit in the idioms, syntax, and rather prolix style
of mid-sixteenth-century English prose, there can be little doubt that
something important was lost in his translation. However, something
was also gained by moving the book into the new cultural and political
environment of Reformation England. Robynson acknowledged that
More was a famous and great intellect, someone well known "for the excellent qualities, wherewith the great goodness of God had plentifully
endowed him, and for the high place and room, whereunto his prince
had most graciously called him" (210), but he also recognized that
More's Catholic religious views might make his ideas unacceptable in
the present political climate. "It is much to be lamented," Robynson says
to Cecil,

> and not only of us Englishmen, that a man of so incomparable wit,
> of so profound knowledge, of so absolute learning, and of so fine elo-
> quence was yet nevertheless so much blinded, rather with obstinacy
> than with ignorance, that he could not or rather would not see the
> shining light of God's holy truth in certain principal points of Christian
> religion, but did rather choose to persevere and continue in his willful
> and stubborn obstinacy even to the very death (210–11).

Nevertheless, Robynson also insisted that More, being "a man of late
time, yea, almost of these our days," had focused on conditions that were
still present in England and that *Utopia* remained a "fruitful and profitable" book. Robynson was prepared therefore to let More's religious errors "pass," to concentrate instead on "the good and wholesome lessons
which be there in great plenty and abundance" (210–11).

More, of course, had devoted considerable attention in *Utopia* to the
relationship between religious and philosophical truth, focusing especially on whether it is possible to have the best form of commonwealth
without the guidance of Christian revelation. Even though he was able to
praise many Utopian practices despite the Utopians' ignorance of Christianity, he was not equally willing to disregard willful obstinacy in the
face of incontrovertible truth. On the island of Utopia, there may have
been a general freedom "for every man to favor and follow what religion
he would" (188), but those who rejected fundamental religious truth
were excluded "from all offices and . . . common administrations in the
weal public" and were neither counted "in the number of men" nor permitted to dispute their views publicly. In addition, believers whose stubborn wrongheadedness on religious matters led to political dissension

or sedition were punished by exile (188–89). As lord chancellor More was not only a fervent prosecutor of heretics, but also assiduous in regulating the book trade to prevent the dissemination of their ideas. It is unlikely, therefore, that he would have agreed with Robynson in sharply separating the philosophical truths and the practical lessons of a book from its religious errors.

In his dedicatory letter, Robynson also praises the Latin version of *Utopia* for "the sweet eloquence of the writer and also in the witty invention and fine convenience or disposition of the matter." Nevertheless, Robynson professed himself to fear that through the "rudeness and ignorance" of his "simple translation . . . all the grace and pleasure of the eloquence, wherewith the matter in Latin is finely set forth may seem to be utterly excluded and lost, and therefore the fruitfulness of the matter itself much peradventure diminished and appaired" (211). He was disinclined to publish his translation, he says, until Tadlowe persuaded him otherwise. Here Robynson raises the issue of the relationship between truth and its presentation, a subject central to the Erasmians, who had firmly argued on behalf of eloquence as creating the necessary path to wisdom. In effect, Robynson represents himself as initially siding with the rhetoricians, only to yield in the end to Tadlowe's arguments regarding the social utility of the ideas conveyed in the book despite "the barbarous rudeness" of the translation.

Just as Robynson was able to disengage the secular and practical virtues of *Utopia* from the religious errors of its author, he was also able to disengage its intellectual content from its rhetorical presentation. He places his emphasis on the book's "good and wholesome lessons," not its transcendent truths, and on substance, not form. These are rhetorical moves in their own right, of course, working to disassociate Robynson from More's Catholicism and to disarm potential critics. Their effect is also to take the book from its original context in pre-Reformation humanist debate and resituate it in the world of the commonwealthmen with their focus on particular social ills and specific governmental remedies for them.

The publication history of Robynson's translation lends credence to this interpretation. It appeared for the first time in 1551 in the aftermath of one of the worst outbreaks of social unrest England had experienced since Jack Cade's Rebellion a century before. The year itself had been one of high food prices, the result of a bad harvest. Food prices and harvest conditions were even worse in 1556, when Vele published the second, revised edition of the Robynson translation.[133] The next publication came in 1597, the year after a serious revolt in Oxfordshire against enclosures. The years 1596 and 1597 also witnessed terrible harvests, extremely high food prices, and widespread destitution throughout England. In fact, they represent the low point for real wages in the early modern period. A further edition of Robynson's translation appeared in 1624, in yet another period of economic distress, this time the consequence of a deep trade depression and widespread unemployment in the cloth-making industry.[134] This publication pattern strongly suggests that *Utopia* in translation had come to be viewed, at least by publishers, primarily as a work speaking to the social, and especially the agrarian, problems of the age.

With Robynson's translation, *Utopia* was transformed from a book primarily challenging the intellectual conventions and answering the philosophical questions of a learned international audience, to one offering commentary on current social, economic, and political ills focused mainly on England and directed to a mixed readership, led by figures like William Cecil and George Tadlowe who possessed power in their own spheres to promote social good. It was now a work more of social amelioration than of philosophical inquiry and political satire. It is perhaps for this reason that Robynson persists in treating Utopus, the conqueror of Utopia and the maker of its laws, as a king. If *Utopia* was to be a truly practical book leading toward the elimination of present-day social evils and toward the improvement of conditions for the poor, it was not possible to rely solely on bringing the hearts and minds of the people to clear insight. Any specific reform would require the concerted action of the political classes under the initiative and with the approval of the prince.

What was found in translation, therefore, was a book not so much about the best state of the commonwealth as about good government and the practical requirements of reform. With this change the word *utopia* could take on its modern meaning as a hopelessly impracticable fantasy, something that might intellectually challenge present shortcomings and produce a modicum of good through its criticisms, but that otherwise we "may rather wish for than hope after" (202).

NOTES

[1] In this Introduction, quotation marks are used to designate "Thomas More," the character in *Utopia,* and to distinguish him from Thomas More, the historical figure who was its author.

[2] The numbers in parentheses following quotations refer to the page in the text of *Utopia* on which the quotation can be found.

[3] In addition to the extensive introductory essays by J. H. Hexter and Edward Surtz in

CW 4, pp. xv–cxciv, More's *Utopia* has been the subject of numerous commentaries. See the bibliography, section III A.

[4] Amerigo Vespucci, *Mundus Novus: Letter to Lorenzo Pietro di Medici,* trans. G. T. Northrup (Princeton: Princeton University Press, 1916); Amerigo Vespucci, *The First Four Voyages of Amerigo Vespucci Reproduced in Facsimile and Translated from the Rare Original Edition* (Florence, 1505–6; London: Bernard Quartitch, 1893); Peter Martyr d'Anghiera, *The Decades of the New Worlde or West India,* trans. Richard Eden (London, 1555; STC 645); Peter Martyr d'Anghiera, *De orbe novo,* trans. F. M. MacNutt (New York: G. P. Putnam's Sons, 1912).

[5] See, e.g., Tommaso Campanella, *La Città del Sole: Dialogo Poetico/The City of the Sun: A Poetical Dialogue,* ed. and trans. Daniel J. Donno (Berkeley and Los Angeles: University of California Press, 1981), which first appeared in 1623; Francis Bacon's unfinished *New Atlantis,* dating from 1626, of which there are numerous modern editions: see Francis Bacon, *New Atlantis,* in Brian Vickers, ed., *Francis Bacon* (Oxford: Oxford University Press, 1996), pp. 456–88; or Joseph Hall's "dystopia" *Mundus Alter et Idem* [Another world and yet the same], first published in Latin in 1605 and in English in 1609 in a translation by John Healey: see Joseph Hall, *The Discovery of a New World (Mundus Alter et Idem),* ed. Huntington Brown (Cambridge, Mass.: Harvard University Press, 1937).

[6] See, e.g., Samuel Butler's *Erewhon* (1872), Edward Bellamy's *Looking Backward* (1887), William Morris's *News from Lord of the Flies Nowhere* (1890), Aldous Huxley's *Brave New World* (1932), B. F. Skinner's *Walden Two* (1948), and William Golding's *Lord of the Flies* (1954). Many of the same features also appear in television programs and motion pictures devoted to science fiction themes, such as *Star Trek.*

[7] According to Pantagruel's fictional genealogy, he was the son of Badebeo, who herself was the daughter of the king of the Amaurots in Utopia. His father, of course, was Gargantua; François Rabelais, *Gargantua and Pantagruel,* trans. J. M. Cohen (Harmondsworth: Penguin, 1955), p. 174.

[8] John Foxe, *The Acts and Monuments of John Foxe,* ed. George Townsend, 8 vols. (New York: AMS Press, 1965), vol. 4, p. 665; see also pp. 643, 675.

[9] The 1517 Paris edition was supervised by Thomas Lupset, a young English humanist living there at the time, and work on the two 1518 Basel editions, printed by John Froben, the great Swiss master of the printer's art, was overseen by Beatus Rhenanaus, a noted German humanist. For the early publication history of *Utopia,* see CW 4, *intro.,* pp. clxxxiii–cxcii.

[10] The additions to the main body of More's early sixteenth-century Latin texts are best consulted in CW 4, pp. 2–37, 249–45; cf. the text of Robynson's translation in this book.

[11] Lucian, *Satirical Sketches,* trans. Paul Turner first Midland Book ed. (Bloomington: Indiana University Press, 1990), pp. 98, 104, 109–10. For the Latin, see Lucian, *"Menippus siue Necromantia,"* in Thomas More, *Translations of Lucian,* in *The Yale Edition of the Complete Works of St. Thomas More,* vol. 3, pt. 1, ed. Craig R. Thompson (New Haven: Yale University Press, 1974), pp. 25–43.

[12] Lucian, *Satirical Sketches,* pp. 248–94. There were other early precedents as well, including among ancient works Homer's *Odyssey,* Pliny's *Natural History,* and the traveler's tales attributed to Iambulus by Diodorus Siculus; and among medieval ones *Mandeville's Travels,* a narrative filled with marvels reputedly discovered by one Sir John Mandeville, a fictitious English knight, on his supposed travels to the East.

[13] Lucian, *Satirical Sketches,* p. 250.

[14] More cunningly suggested as much in a second letter to Giles published with the 1517 Paris edition of the text; Thomas More to Peter Giles, in CW 4, pp. 251–52.

[15] The original title of More's book is *De optimo reipublicae statu deque nove insula Utopia,* which means *Concerning the Best State of a Commonwealth and the New Island of Utopia.* Ralph Robynson's English title of 1551 is *A fruteful and pleasaunt worke of the beste state of a publyque weale, and of the newe yle called Vtopia.*

[16] *Republic* 5.473c; Plato, *Republic,* trans. Paul Shorey, in *The Collected Dialogues of Plato, Including the Letters,* ed. Edith Hamilton and Huntington Cairns (New York: Pantheon, 1961), p. 712.

[17]The discussion of the model city begins at *Laws,* 3.702b, Plato, *Laws,* trans. A. E. Taylor, in *Collected Dialogues,* p. 1295.

[18]Jerome Busleyden to Thomas More, CW 4, pp. 32–37.

[19]*Laws,* 6.756e, in *Collected Dialogues,* p. 1336; see also 3.693e in *Collected Dialogues,* p. 1228.

[20]In Plato's imagined colony a Nocturnal Council of wise gentlemen-farmers exercises philosophical oversight, but there is also an elected executive council, a group of elected Guardians of the Law charged with enforcement, and an assembly made up of all the male citizens; *Laws,* 6.756b–66b, 8.850b, 12.951a–68a, in *Collected Dialogues,* pp. 1336–44, 1414, 1496–1512. On the island of Utopia, elected "princes"—note the plural—rule over only their particular cities, with the counsel of elected officials gathered in a kind of senate or parliament. There is no single prince for the island as a whole; all collective business must be done by a general council.

[21]*Laws,* 5.739b–d, in *Collected Dialogues,* p. 1324.

[22]*Laws,* 9.874e–875d, in *Collected Dialogues* pp. 1433–34.

[23]This term is adopted from Trevor J. Saunders, "Plato's Later Political Thought," in Richard Kraut, ed., *The Cambridge Companion to Plato* (Cambridge: Cambridge University Press, 1992), p. 477.

[24]*Politics,* II.2.1261a; Aristotle, *Politics,* trans. B. Jowett, in Aristotle, *The Complete Works of Aristotle: The Revised Oxford Translation,* 2 vols., ed. Jonathan Barnes (Princeton: Princeton University Press, 1984), vol. 2, p. 2001.

[25]*Nicomachean Ethics,* V.5; the quoted passage is at 1132b32–33, in Aristotle, *Nicomachean Ethics,* trans. W. D. Ross, rev. J. O. Urmson, in *Complete Works,* vol. 2, pp. 1787–89, with the quote at p. 1788.

[26]*Politics,* II.3.1161b35, in *Complete Works,* vol. 2, p. 2002.

[27]*Politics,* II.3.1163a26–30, in *Complete Works,* vol. 2, p. 2004.

[28]*Politics,* II.5.1263a25–b14, in *Complete Works,* vol. 2, pp. 2004–5; see also T. H. Adkin, "Aristotle's Defense of Private Property," in David Keyt and Fred D. Miller, eds., *A Companion to Aristotle's Politics* (Oxford: Blackwell, 1991), pp. 200–25; and R. F. Stalley, "Aristotle's Criticism of Plato's *Republic,*" in Keyt and Miller, eds., *Companion,* pp. 182–99.

[29]*Enchieridion,* 17, in Epictetus, *The Discourses as Reported by Arrian, the Manual, and Fragments,* trans. W. A. Oldfather, 2 vols. (Cambridge, Mass.: Harvard University Press, 1929), pp. 496–97.

[30]Many of the first readers of *Utopia* would have recognized that this passage alludes to a very similar discussion in Erasmus's own *Praise of Folly,* first published in 1511. There the Goddess Folly asks, "Now what else is the whole of life but a sort of play? Actors come on wearing different masks and all play their parts until the producer orders them off the stage, and he can often tell the same man to appear in different costume, so that now he plays a king in purple and now a humble slave in rags. It's all a sort of pretence, but it's the only way to act out this farce"; Desiderius Erasmus, *Praise of Folly and Letter to Maarten van Dorp,* 1515, trans. Betty Radice, ed. A. H. T. Levi (Harmondsworth: Penguin, 1971), p. 104.

[31]The point is raised obliquely in the exchange between Thrasymachus and Socrates in Book I of *The Republic,* 1.336b–54b, in *Collected Dialogues,* pp. 586–605; and more directly by Socrates in his debate with Gorgias, in the dialogue bearing the latter's name: Plato, *Gorgias,* trans. W. D. Woodhead, in *Collected Dialogues,* pp. 229–307.

[32]*Politics* I.1253a7–18, in *Complete Works,* vol. 2, p. 1988; Aristotle, *Rhetoric,* trans. W. Rhys Roberts, in *Complete Works,* vol. 2, pp. 2152–2269; see Amélie Oksenberg Rorty, ed., *Essays on Aristotle's Rhetoric* (Berkeley and Los Angeles: University of California Press, 1996), especially the essays by Robert Wardy, M. F. Burnyeat, Troels Engberg-Pederson, T. H. Irwin, Stephen Halliwell, and C. D. C. Reeve, pp. 56–205.

[33]Cicero, *De Oratore,* 2 vols., trans. E. W. Sutton, ed. H. Rackham (Cambridge, Mass.: Harvard University Press, 1988). Cicero wrote extensively on rhetoric; see especially *Ad C. Herrenium. De Ratione Dicendi [Rhetorica ad Herennium],* ed. and trans. Harry Caplan (Cambridge, Mass.: Harvard University Press, 1954); Cicero, *Rhetorici Libri Duo qui Vo-*

cantur de Inventione/Two Books on Rhetoric Commonly Called on Invention, in Cicero, *De Inventione. De Optimo Genere Oratorum. Topica,* ed. and trans. H. M. Hubbell (Cambridge, Mass.: Harvard University Press, 1949), pp. 1–345.

[34] See Brian Vickers, *In Defense of Rhetoric* (Oxford: Clarendon Press, 1988), pp. 1–213; for early modern uses of rhetoric, see Quentin Skinner, *Reason and Rhetoric in the Philosophy of Thomas Hobbes* (Cambridge: Cambridge University Press, 1996), pp. 19–211.

[35] *Republic,* 5.496c–e, in *Collected Dialogues,* p. 732.

[36] Aristotle raised a similar issue in his *Nicomachean Ethics* in considering whether the highest excellence for human beings was "contemplation" or the active life of participation in a *polis*—a political community; *Nicomachean Ethics,* 10.7.1177a11–10.8.1178b31, in *Complete Works,* vol. 2, pp. 1860–1864.

[37] CW 4, pp. 56–57.

[38] For instances, see CW 4, pp. 309–10.

[39] *Politics,* 5.9.1310a26–34, in *Complete Works,* vol. 2, p. 2080; see also 1.2.1252b28–35, 6.2.1317b10–17, 7.3.1325a16–25b32, pp. 1988, 2091, 2103.

[40] *De Officiis,* I.xx.69; Cicero, *De Officiis,* ed. and trans. Walter Miller (Cambridge, Mass.: Harvard University Press, 1975), pp. 70–71; Cicero, *On Duties,* ed. and trans. M. T. Griffin and E. M. Adkins (Cambridge: Cambridge University Press, 1991), p. 28.

[41] *De Officiis,* I.iv.12, Cicero, pp. 12–15.; Cicero, *On Duties,* p. 6.

[42] *De Officiis,* I.vii.22, pp. 22–25; Cicero, *On Duties,* pp. 9–10. Cicero allowed that there were those who, "occupied solely with their own affairs," claimed that they thereby did no one "any injury." Against this view he held that "while they steer clear of one kind of injustice, they fall into another: they are traitors to social life, for they contribute to it none of their interest, none of their effort, none of their means"; *De Officiis,* I.ix.29, pp. 28–31; Cicero, *On Duties,* p. 12.

[43] *De Officiis,* I.xxi.71, pp. 72–73; Cicero, *On Duties,* pp. 28–29.

[44] *De Officiis,* I.vi.19, pp. 20–21; Cicero, *On Duties,* p. 9.

[45] *De Officiis,* I.xxi.72, pp. 72–75; Cicero, *On Duties,* p. 29.

[46] *De Officiis,* I.ix.28, pp. 28–29; Cicero, *On Duties,* p. 12.

[47] For example, Budé identified it with the "Fortunate Isles, perhaps close to the Elysian Fields"; CW 4, p. 13.

[48] See Erasmus, *Praise of Folly,* pp. 56, n.2, 67; Erasmus went to some pains in making this pun, since the standard Latin word for "fool" is *stultitia.* The word Erasmus chose derived from the Greek, *moros,* and entered into Latin only very late, significantly at the time of Saint Augustine.

[49] *Liber Tobiae/Book of Tobias,* in *Biblia Sacra juxta Vugatam Clementinam* (Rome: Societatis S. Joannis Evang., 1947), pp. 469–79. In Protestant Bibles, the narrative appears as the Book of Tobit in the *Apochrypha; Book of Tobit,* in *The Oxford Annotated Bible with the Apocrypha: Revised Standard Version,* ed. Herbert G. May and Bruce M. Metzger (New York: Oxford University Press, 1965), *Apocrypha of the Old Testament,* ed. Meltzer, pp. 63–75.

[50] *Tobit,* 5:14–15, in *Oxford Annotated Bible, Apochrypha,* p. 68; CW 4, pp. 301–2.

[51] *Tobit,* 12:7–10, *Oxford Annotated Bible, Apochrypha,* p. 73.

[52] *John,* 20:24–29, *Oxford Annotated Bible,* pp. 1314–15.

[53] *John,* 20:31, *Oxford Annotated Bible,* p. 1315.

[54] On these points, see Skinner, "Sir Thomas More's *Utopia,*" in Pagden, ed., *The Languages of Political Theory,* pp. 150–51.

[55] Saint Augustine, *City of God,* trans. Henry Bettenson, with an introduction by John O'Meara (Harmondworth: Penguin, 1984), p. 5.

[56] Compare this passage to the following from Peter Martyr's description of the island peoples first encountered by Columbus:

> The inhabitants of these Islands have been ever so used to live at liberty, in play and pastime, that they can hardly away [bear] with the yoke of servitude which they attempt to shake of by all means they may.... A few things content them, having no

delight in such superfluities, for which in other places men take infinite pains and commit many unlawful acts, and yet are never satisfied, whereas many have too much, and none enough. But among these simple souls, a few clothes serve the naked: weights and measures are not needful [needed] to such as cannot skill of craft and deceit [do not cheat] and have not the use of pestiferous money, the seed of innumerable mischiefs. So that if we shall not be ashamed to confess the truth, they seem to live in that golden world of the which old writers speak so much: wherein men lived simply and innocently without enforcement of laws, without quarrelling judges and libels, content only to satisfy nature, without further vexation for knowledge of things to come[;] yet these naked people also are tormented with ambition for the desire they have to enlarge their dominions: by reason whereof they keep [engage in] war & destroy one another: from the which plague I suppose the golden world was not free. For even then also, *Cede, non cedam,* that is 'give place, & I will not give place,' had entered among men.

In other words, while these people arguably had escaped the sin of greed, at least for the present, they had not escaped sin itself, for they manifested the sin of pride and the will to dominate others. Martyr is clear that only "if they had received our religion, would [he] think their life moste happy of all men," despite their enjoying what he calls "their ancient liberty." Even in their near perfect social order, the lust for power, and all that follows from it, remained in force among them. Martyr d'Anghiera, *Decades,* p. 8 (spelling modernized).

[57]See the text (128, 133, 188, 205). When Utopus is mentioned in More's Latin text, he is identified only by his name, without any title. Giles, in "translating" into Latin the poem in the Utopian language he supplied for the text, says *Utopus me dux,* i.e., "Utopus my leader"; *dux* in Latin identifies a supreme military commander; it is the root for the noble title *duke,* not for *king (rex),* the term More regularly uses when he wishes to identify the kings of places other than Utopia; CW 4, pp. 18, 112, 120, 219, 220. On this point, see Thomas More, *Utopia,* ed. Richard Marius (London: J. M. Dent and Sons, 1991), pp. xi–xii.

[58]In More's Latin, the "first leader" of each of the fifty-four cities is identified as *principes,* the root of the title *prince.* See CW 4, pp. 122, 132, 192, 194. Robynson uses the term *prince* (134, 135, 139, 172, 173). In the context of Utopian institutions, however, the term *principes* might more appropriately be translated as "governor," as Surtz does in CW 4, pp. 123, 133, 193, 195. See More, *Utopia,* ed. Marius, pp. xi–xii.

[59]For more on these points, see Skinner, "Sir Thomas More's *Utopia,*" pp. 152–57.

[60]Curiously, Hythloday had made a somewhat similar rhetorical move in responding to "More's" arguments about "civil philosophy." In reframing "More's" remark, Hythloday not only employs rhetorical maneuver, but does so in a way that shifts the ground from what might be universally true for all philosophers to what is true for him — itself a concession to the power of "civil philosophy" (122).

[61]CW 4, pp. 2–3; see also Thomas More, *Utopia,* ed. and trans. George M. Logan and Robert M. Adams (Cambridge: Cambridge University Press, 1989), pp. 114–15.

[62]Erasmus, *Praise of Folly,* p. 201.

[63]Ibid., p. 184.

[64]*Republic,* 7.519d–521c. Quote at *Republic,* 7.519e–520a, in *Collected Dialogues,* pp. 752–53.

[65]*Republic,* 7.519d, in *Collected Dialogues,* p. 752.

[66]CW 4, p. 314. More wrote about Morton in very similar terms in *The History of King Richard III,* in *Complete Works,* vol. 2, pp. 90–92.

[67]The embassy is discussed in most works dealing with More's career or with *Utopia.* For details, see Edward Surtz, "St. Thomas More and His Utopian Embassy of 1515," *Catholic Historical Review,* 39 (1953), pp. 272–97. In 1515, Tunstall was a rising star in the church and state, soon to become master of the rolls in the Chancery and, a bit later, keeper of the privy seal and bishop of London. For more on him, see Charles Sturge, *Cuth-*

bert Tunstall: Churchman, Scholar, Statesman, and Administrator (London: Longmans, Green, 1938).

[68] For biographies of More, see the bibliography, section IV A.

[69] On Colet, see Joseph Hirst Lupton, *A Life of John Colet, D.D., Dean of St. Paul's and Founder of St. Paul's School* (London: G. Bell and Sons, 1909); John B. Gleason, *John Colet* (Berkeley: University of California Press, 1989); and J. B. Trapp, *Erasmus, Colet, and More: The Early Humanists and Their Books* (London: British Library, 1991).

[70] Erasmus's life and work have been the subject of numerous studies; see the bibliography, section IV B.

[71] See More, *Translations of Lucian,* in *Complete Works,* vol. 3, pt. 1.

[72] Perhaps it was Gatton, in the county of Surrey, for which John Colt, his father-in-law, had sat in 1492. S. T. Bindoff, ed., *The House of Commons, 1509–1558,* 3 vols. (London: History of Parliament Trust, 1982), vol. 2, p. 620.

[73] The title pages of the original Latin editions of *Utopia* incorrectly state that he was "sheriff." See CW 4, p. 1. In fact, as regards the work of the Sheriff's Court, he was the annually elected sheriff's permanent deputy. See J. A. Guy, *The Public Career of Sir Thomas More* (New Haven and London: Yale University Press, 1980), pp. 5–6 and the works cited there.

[74] See William Roper, *The Life of Sir Thomas More,* in Richard S. Sylvester and Davis P. Harding, eds., *Two Early Tudor Lives* (New Haven: Yale University Press, 1962), p. 201.

[75] See Guy, *Public Career,* pp. 6–8; and G. R. Elton, "Thomas More, Councillor," in G. R. Elton, *Studies in Tudor and Stuart Politics and Government,* 4 vols. (Cambridge: Cambridge University Press, 1974–92), vol. 1, pp. 129–33.

[76] The argument in this and the next several paragraphs depends on Hexter's treatment in *More's Utopia: The Biography of an Idea,* pp. 15–30; and J. H. Hexter, "Utopia and Its Historical Milieu," introductory essay in CW 4, esp. pp. xv–xxii, xxx–xxxviii.

[77] More says himself, in the letter he wrote to Giles when he sent him the manuscript, that he had expected to complete it "within a month and a half" of his return to England, since he "was already disburdened of all the labor and study belonging to the invention of this work" (83).

[78] More opened a seam in his text to insert the new material early in The First Book, not long after "More" is introduced to Hythloday (94). "More" tells us he is going to "rehearse" what he had heard "of the manners, customs, laws, and ordinances of the Utopians," but we have to wait until The Second Book, and a break for the midday meal, before we get there.

[79] For an overview of the history of this era, the best guide is John Guy, *Tudor England* (Oxford: Oxford University Press, 1988). See also the bibliography, section V.

[80] CW 4, p. 295.

[81] See F. J. Fisher, "Commercial Trends and Policy in Sixteenth-Century England," in F. J. Fisher, *London and the English Economy, 1500–1700,* ed. P. J. Corfield and N. B. Harte (London and Ronceverte: Hambleton Press, 1990), pp. 81–104; and G. D. Ramsay, "The Antwerp Mart," in G. D. Ramsay, *English Overseas Trade during the Centuries of Emergence: Studies in Some Modern Origins of the English-Speaking World* (London: Macmillan, 1957), pp. 1–33. For more on this issue, see the works in the bibliography, section VI.

[82] See C. G. A. Clay, *Economic Expansion and Social Change: England, 1500–1700,* 2 vols. (Cambridge: Cambridge University Press, 1984).

[83] See Roger Finlay and Beatrice Shearer, "Population Growth and Suburban Expansion," in *London, 1500–1700,* pp. 37–59; E. A. Wrigley, "Urban Growth and Agricultural Change: England and the Continent in the Early Modern Period," in E. A. Wrigley, *People, Cities and Wealth: The Transformation of Traditional Society* (Oxford: Blackwell, 1987), pp. 158–67; E. A. Wrigley, "A Simple Model of London's Importance in Changing English Society and Economy, 1650–1750," in Wrigley, *People, Cities and Wealth,* pp. 133–56, and Jan de Vries, *European Urbanization, 1500–1800* (Cambridge, Mass.: Harvard University Press, 1984), appendix 1, pp. 269–87.

[84] F. J. Fisher, "The Development of the London Food Market, 1540–1640," "The Development of London as a Centre of Conspicuous Consumption in the Sixteenth and Seventeenth Centuries," "The Growth of London," and "London and an 'Engine of Economic Growth,'" in Fisher, *London and the Growth of the English Economy,* pp. 61–80; 105–18, 173–84, and 185–98, respectively; and Michael Reed, "London and Its Hinterland, 1600–1800: The View from the Provinces," in *Capital Cities and their Hinterlands in Early Modern Europe,* ed. Peter Clark and Bernard Lepetit (Aldershot: Scolar Press, 1996), pp. 51–83.

[85] For more on this point and the issues discussed in the next four paragraphs, see Joan Thirsk, ed., *The Agrarian History of England and Wales, Vol. 4: 1500–1640* (Cambridge: Cambridge University Press, 1967); and Eric Kerridge, *Agrarian Problems in the Sixteenth Century and After* (London: George Allen and Unwin, 1969). See also other works cited in the bibliography, section VI.

[86] In the Cornish Rising of 1497, 15,000 people rebelled against the royal taxes that had been levied for war against Scotland; more than a thousand were slain in the battle at Blackheath in Kent that was fought to suppress them. The classic discussion is in Francis Bacon, *The History of the Reign of King Henry VII and Selected Works,* ed. Brian Vickers (Cambridge: Cambridge University Press, 1998), pp. 135–44; Bacon's history was first published in 1622. See also Ian Arthurson, "The Rising of 1497: A Revolt of the Peasantry?," in Joel Rosenthal and Colin Richmond, eds., *People, Politics, and Community in the Later Middle Ages* (New York: St. Martin's Press, 1987), pp. 1–18. There had been a similar tax rebellion in Yorkshire in 1489 and further trouble in collecting taxes in 1513–15. See Anthony Fletcher and Diarmaid MacCulloch, *Tudor Rebellions,* 4th ed. (London: Longman, 1997), pp. 13–21.

[87] For an overview of the history of early modern English towns, see Peter Clark and Paul Slack, *English Towns in Transition, 1500–1700* (London: Oxford University, 1976); and John Patten, *English Towns, 1500–1700* (Hamden, Conn.: Archon, 1978). See also the works cited in the bibliography, section VI.

[88] J. C. K. Cornwall, *Wealth and Society in Early Sixteenth-Century England* (London: Routledge and Kegan Paul, 1988), pp. 198–230; and Paul Slack, *Poverty and Policy in Tudor and Stuart England* (London: Longman, 1988). For more, see the bibliography, section VI.

[89] For the discussion that follows, see David Harris Sacks, "The Paradox of Taxation: Fiscal Crises, Parliament, and Liberty in England, 1450–1640," in Philip T. Hoffman and Kathryn Norberg, eds., *Fiscal Crises, Liberty, and Representative Government, 1450–1789* (Stanford: Stanford University Press, 1994), pp. 27–28.

[90] For the discussion that follows, see David Harris Sacks, "The Greed of Judas: Avarice, Monopoly, and the Moral Economy, c. 1350–1600," *Journal of Medieval and Early Modern Studies* 28, no. 2 (Spring 1998): 267–311.

[91] For the following discussion, see R. N. Swanson, *Church and Society in Late Medieval England* (Oxford: Basil Blackwell, 1989); and the works cited in the bibliography, section VII.

[92] On the Hunne case, the classic account is in Foxe, *Acts and Monuments,* ed. Townsend, vol. 4, pp. 183–205. For modern commentaries, see Arthur Ogle, *The Tragedy of Lollards' Tower: The Case of Richard Hunne with Its Aftermath in the Reformation Parliament, 1529–1532* (Oxford: Pen-in-Hand, 1949); Dickens, *English Reformation,* pp. 112–15; J. A. F. Thomson, *The Later Lollards, 1414–1520* (Oxford: Oxford University Press, 1965), pp. 162–70; Peter Gwyn, *The King's Cardinal: The Rise and Fall of Thomas Wolsey* (London: Barrie and Jenkins, 1990), pp. 34–41; J. Duncan M. Derrett, "The Affairs of Richard Hunne and Friar Standish," in Thomas More, *The Apology,* in *The Yale Edition of the Complete Works of St. Thomas More,* vol. 9, ed. J. B. Trapp (New Haven: Yale University Press, 1979), appendix B, pp. 213–46; Richard M. Wunderli, "Pre-Reformation London Summoners and the Case of Richard Hunne," *Journal of Ecclesiastical History* 33, no. 3 (1982): 209–24; S. J. Smart, "John Foxe and 'The Story of Richard Hun, Martyr,'" *Journal of Ecclesiastical History* 37, no. 1 (1986): 1–14; Susan Brigden, *London and the Refor-*

mation (Oxford: Clarendon Press, 1989), pp. 98–103; and Haigh, *English Reformations,* pp. 77–87.

[93] See Thomas More, *A Dialogue Concerning Heresies,* in *The Yale Edition of the Complete Works of St. Thomas More,* vol. 6, ed. Thomas M. C. Lawler, Germain Marc'hardour, and Richard C. Marius (New Haven: Yale University Press, 1981), pt. 1, pp. 317–30; and Thomas More, *Supplication of the Souls,* ed. Germain Marc'hardour, in *The Yale Edition of the Complete Works of St. Thomas More,* vol. 7, ed. Frank Manley, Germain Marc'hardour, Richard Marius, and Clarence Miller (New Haven: Yale University Press, 1990), pp. 116–17, 132–36.

[94] On Wycliffe, the Lollards, and Lollardy, see A. G. Dickens, *The English Reformation,* 2nd ed. (London: B. T. Batsford, 1989), pp. 46–60; Thomson, *Later Lollards,* esp. pp. 5–19, 139–72, 220–53; and the works cited in the bibliography, section VII. Londoners accused of heresy included members of the family of a lord mayor of London, several goldsmiths, a member of the Merchants of the Staple, and Hunne himself, a merchant tailor.

[95] See Eamon Duffy, *The Stripping of the Altars: Traditional Religion in England, c. 1400–c.1580* (New Haven: Yale University Press, 1992), pp. 1–376; Dickens, *English Reformation,* pp. 38–43; J. J. Scarisbrick, *The Reformation and the English People* (Oxford: Basil Blackwell, 1984), pp. 1–39; and Christopher Haigh, *English Reformations: Religion, Politics, and Society under the Tudors* (Oxford: Clarendon Press, 1993), pp. 25–55.

[96] Thomas More, *Life of Pico,* in *The Yale Edition of the Complete Works of St. Thomas More,* vol. 1, ed. Anthony S. G. Edwards, Katherine Gardiner Rodgers, and Clarence H. Miller (New Haven: Yale University Press, 1997), pp. 47–122.

[97] See James McConica, *English Humanists and Reformation Politics under Henry VIII and Edward VI* (Oxford: Clarendon Press, 1965); Roberto Weiss, *Humanism in England during the Fifteenth Century,* 2nd ed. (Oxford: Basil Blackwell, 1957), pp. 39–70; and Gordon Zeeveld, *The Foundations of Tudor Policy* (Cambridge, Mass.: Harvard University Press, 1948).

[98] See Christopher Haigh, "Anticlericalism and the English Reformation," in Christopher Haigh, ed., *The English Reformation Revised* (Cambridge: Cambridge University Press, 1987), pp. 56–74.

[99] *A Relation, or Rather a True Account, of the Island of England . . . about the Year 1500,* ed. C. A. Sneyd (London: Camden Society, no. 37, 1847), p. 23; see also pp. 34, 35, 40–41.

[100] For overviews, see Guy, *Tudor England;* Penry Williams, *The Tudor Regime* (Oxford: Clarendon Press, 1979); and the works cited in the bibliography, section V.

[101] I. D. Thornley, "The Destruction of Sanctuary," in R. W. Seton-Watson, ed., *Tudor Studies Presented by the Board of Studies in History in the University of London to Albert Frederick Pollard* (London: Longmans, Green, 1924), pp. 182–207; Harold Garrett-Goodyear, "The Tudor Revival of Quo Warranto and Local Contributions to State Building," in M. S. Arnold, T. A. Green, and S. D. White, eds. *Of the Laws and Customs of England: Essays in Honor of S. E. Thorne* (Chapel Hill: University of North Carolina Press, 1981), pp. 225–29; Robert Constable, *Prerogativa Regis: Tertia Lectura Roberti Constable de Lyncolnis Inne anno. 11 H. 7,* ed. Samuel E. Thorne (New Haven: Yale University Press, 1949), pp. v–li; Joel Hurstfield, "The Revival of Feudalism in Early Tudor England," *History,* new ser., 37 (1952), pp. 131–45; and H. E. Bell, *An Introduction to the History and Records of the Court of Wards and Liveries* (Cambridge: Cambridge University Press, 1953), pp. 1–15. See also J. M. W. Bean, *The Decline of English Feudalism, 1215–1540* (Manchester: Manchester University Press, 1968), esp. pp. 235–56; and Joel Hurstfield, *The Queen's Wards: Wardship and Marriage under Elizabeth I* (London: Longmans, Green, 1957), pp. xiii–xxi, 3–17.

[102] Sir John Fortescue, *On the Laws and Governance of England,* ed. Shelly Lockwood (Cambridge: Cambridge University Press, 1997); and Quentin Skinner, *The Foundations of Modern Political Thought,* 2 vols. (Cambridge: Cambridge University Press, 1978), vol. 2, 353. See also Quentin Skinner, "The State," in Terence Ball, James Farr, and Russell L.

Hanson, eds., *Political Innovation and Conceptual Change* (Cambridge: Cambridge University Press, 1989), pp. 90–131; Sacks, "Paradox of Taxation," in Hoffman and Norberg, eds., *Fiscal Crises,* pp. 31–33; and David Harris Sacks, "Political Culture," in David Scott Kastan, ed., *Blackwell's Companion to Shakespeare* (Oxford: Blackwell, 1999), pp. 117–36.

[103] See Fernand Braudel, *Civilization and Capitalism, 15th–18th Century,* 3 vols., trans. Siân Reynolds (New York: Harper and Row, 1984), vol. 3: *The Perspective of the World,* pp. 352–56; see also Hugh F. Kearney, *The British Isles: A History of Four Nations* (Cambridge: Cambridge University Press, 1989), pp. 89–127.

[104] For the following discussion, see Guy, *Tudor England,* 53–56, 74–77, 80–115 passim; Gwyn, *King's Cardinal,* pp. 58–103; and R. B. Wernham, *Before the Armada: The Emergence of the English Nation, 1485–1588* (New York: Harcourt, Brace and World, 1966), pp. 11–97.

[105] Mountjoy to Erasmus, Greenwich, 27 May 1509, in *The Correspondence of Erasmus, Letters 142 to 297, 1501 to 1514,* trans. R. A. B. Mynors and D. F. S. Thomson, in *Collected Works of Erasmus,* vol. 2 (Toronto: University of Toronto Press, 1975), Letter 215, pp. 147–48.

[106] Erasmus to Henry VIII, Louvain, 25 April 1518, in *The Correspondence of Erasmus, Letters 594 to 841, 1517 to 1518,* trans. R. A. B. Mynors and D. F. S. Thomson, in *Collected Works of Erasmus,* vol. 5 (Toronto: University of Toronto Press, 1979), Letter 834, pp. 410–11. See also Erasmus to Pace, Louvain, 22 April 1518, in *Collected Works,* vol. 5, Letter 821, pp. 392–93.

[107] See Gwyn, *King's Cardinal,* pp. 1–32.

[108] On these points, see Hexter, *More's Utopia,* pp. 131–55; Hexter, "*Utopia* and Its Historical Milieu," in CW 4, pp. xxxiii–xxxviii; Richard C. Marius, *Thomas More, A Biography* (New York: Alfred A. Knopf, 1984), pp. 189–93; Peter Ackroyd, *The Life of Thomas More* (London: Chatto and Windus, 1998), pp. 176–81; Guy, *Public Career,* pp. 6–12; Elton, "Thomas More, Councillor," in Elton, *Studies,* vol. 3, pp. 129–33; and J. J. Scarisbrick, "Thomas More: The King's Good Servant," *Thought: Fordham University Quarterly* 52, no. 3 (1977): 252–58.

[109] Guy, *Public Career,* pp. 7, 11–12.

[110] Ibid., pp. 12–33; Henry VIII, *Assertio Septem Sarcramentorum, aduersus Martinum Lutherum* (London, 1521; STC 13079); Thomas More, *Responsio ad Lutherum,* in *Complete Works of St. Thomas More,* vol. 4, pts. 1 and 2, trans. Sister Scholastica Manderville, ed. John Headley (New Haven: Yale University Press, 1969); More, *Dialogue Concerning Heresies,* in *Compete Works,* vol. 6; and Thomas More, *Supplication of Souls,* in *The Yale Edition of the Complete Works of St. Thomas More,* vol. 7, eds. Frank Manley, Germain Marc 'hadour, Richard Marius, and Clarence H. Miller (New Haven: Yale University Press, 1990), pp. 109–228.

[111] For the details of More's last years, see the works cited in the bibliography, section IV A.

[112] See the text (170–71).

[113] For More's political activities as lord chancellor, see Guy, *Public Career,* pp. 97–203; Marius, *Thomas More,* pp. 325–417; Ackroyd, *Life of Thomas More,* pp. 280–320; Elton, "Thomas More, Councillor," in Elton, *Studies,* pp. 146–54; and Scarisbrick, "Thomas More: The King's Good Servant," pp. 259–65. Technically, Henry was not pursuing a "divorce" but rather ecclesiastical recognition that he had never been legally married to Catherine of Aragon, who had been the wife of Arthur, Prince of Wales, Henry's deceased older brother. Henry's case rested first on passages in Leviticus that appeared to suggest that it was against divine law to marry a deceased brother's wife and second on the grounds that the papal dispensation granted to him on the occasion of his marriage was invalid. See Scarisbrick, *Henry VIII,* pp. 163–97; and Henry Ansgar Kelly, *The Matrimonial Trials of Henry VIII* (Stanford: Stanford University Press, 1976).

[114] See the text (187–89).

[115]See G. R. Elton, "Sir Thomas More and the Opposition to Henry VIII," in Elton, *Studies*, vol. 1, pp. 155–72; Marius, *Thomas More*, pp. 418–60; Ackroyd, *Life of Thomas More*, pp. 321–49.

[116]In 1524, for example, he wrote *Four Last Things*, a devotional work published only after his death; in *Complete Works*, vol. 1. Later, he produced a series of polemical anti-Protestant works in the vernacular, some while he was lord chancellor: *A Dialogue Concerning Heresies* (1529), in *Complete Works*, vol. 6; *Supplication of Souls* (1529) and *A Letter Impugning the Erroneous Writings of John Frith* (1532), both in *Complete Works*, vol. 7; and the first part of the *Confutation of Tyndale's Answer* (1532). The second part of the *Confutation of Tyndale's Answer* (1533) was published after his resignation; both are in *The Yale Edition of the Complete Works of St. Thomas More*, vol. 8, pts. 1, 2, and 3, ed. Louis A. Shuster, Richard C. Marius, James Lusardi, and Richard J. Schoeck (New Haven: Yale University Press, 1973). Also published after his resignation were *Apology of Sir Thomas More, Knight* (1533) in *Complete Works*, vol. 9; *The Debellation of Salem and Bizance* (1533), in *The Yale Edition of the Complete Works of St. Thomas More*, vol. 10, ed. John Guy, Ralph Keen, Clarence H. Miller, and Ruth McGugan (New Haven: Yale University Press, 1987); and *Answer to a Poisoned Book which a Nameless Heretic Hath Called the Supper of the Lord* (1533) in *The Yale Edition of the Complete Works of St. Thomas More*, vol. 11, ed. S. M. Foley and Clarence H. Miller (New Haven: Yale University Press, 1985).

[117]In English: *A Treatise on the Passion, Treatise on the Blessed Body and Instructions and Prayers* in *The Yale Edition of the Complete Works of St. Thomas More*, vol. 13, ed. Garry E. Haupt (New Haven: Yale University Press, 1976); and *A Dialogue of Comfort against Tribulation* in *The Yale Edition of the Complete Works of St. Thomas More*, vol. 12, ed. Louis L. Martz and Frank Manley (New Haven: Yale University Press, 1976). In Latin: *De Tristitia Christi* (*On the Sadness of Christ*) in *The Yale Edition of the Complete Works of St. Thomas More*, vol. 12, ed. and trans. Clarence H. Miller (New Haven: Yale University Press, 1976). All were first published in the 1550s during Queen Mary's reign.

[118]Roper, *Life of Sir Thomas More*, in *Two Early Tudor Lives*, p. 248.

[119]Ibid., pp. 248–50.

[120]Act in Restraint of Appeals, 24 Hen. VIII. c. 12 (1533), in G. R. Elton, ed., *The Tudor Constitution: Documents and Commentary*, 2nd ed. (Cambridge: Cambridge University Press, 1982), pp. 353–56; quote at p. 353.

[121]See Walter Ullmann, "'This Realm of England Is an Empire,'" *Journal of Ecclesiastical History* 30, no. 3 (1979); 175–203; R. Koebner, "'The Imperial Crown of This Realm': Henry VIII, Constantine the Great, and Polydore Vergil," *Bulletin of the Institute of Historical Research* 26 (1953): 29–52; G. R. Elton, *England under the Tudors*, 2nd ed. (London: Methuen, 1974), pp. 160–92; and Dale Hoak, "The Iconography of the Imperial Crown," in Dale Hoak, ed., *Tudor Political Culture* (Cambridge: Cambridge University Press, 1995), pp. 54–103. See also G. Nicholson, "The Act of Appeals and the English Reformation," in Claire Cross, David Loades, and J. J. Scarisbrick, eds., *Law and Government under the Tudors* (Cambridge: Cambridge University Press, 1988), pp. 19–30.

[122]Act of Supremacy, 26 Hen. VIII, c. 1 (1534), in Elton, ed., *Tudor Constitution*, pp. 364–65, quote at p. 364.

[123]See David Knowles, *The Religious Orders in England*, 3 vols. (Cambridge: Cambridge University Press, 1948–1961), vol. 3: *The Tudor Age*, pp. 195–417; G. W. O. Woodward, *The Dissolution of the Monasteries* (London: Blandford Press, 1966); and Joyce Youings, *The Dissolution of the Monasteries* (London: George Allen and Unwin, 1971).

[124]For developments in the reign of Edward VI, see Guy, *Tudor England*, pp. 212–49; Cross, *Church and People*, pp. 81–100; W. K. Jordan, *Edward VI: The Threshold of Power: The Protectorship of the Duke of Somerset* (London: Allen and Unwin, 1968); W. K. Jordan, *Edward VI: The Young King. The Dominance of the Duke of Northumberland* (London: Allen and Unwin, 1970); Jennifer Loach and Robert Tittler, eds., *The Mid-Tudor Polity, c. 1540–1560* (London: Macmillan, 1980); M. L. Bush, *The Government Policy of Protector Somerset*

(London: Edward Arnold, 1975); Whitney R. D. Jones, *The Mid-Tudor Crisis, 1539–1563* (London: Macmillan, 1973); Diarmaid MacCulloch, *Thomas Cranmer: A Life* (New Haven: Yale University Press, 1996); Dickens, *English Reformation*, pp. 222–86; Duffy, *Stripping of the Altars*, pp. 448–77; and Haigh, *English Reformations*, pp. 168–202.

[125] See Barrett L. Beer, *Rebellion and Riot: Popular Disorder in England during the Reign of Edward VI* (Kent, Ohio: Kent State University Press, 1982); and Andrew Charlesworth, ed., *An Atlas of Rural Protest in Britain, 1548–1900* (Philadelphia: University of Pennsylvania Press, 1983), pp. 29–31. See also Manning, *Village Revolts*, pp. 31–54.

[126] See Frances J. Rose-Troup, *The Western Rebellion of 1549: An Account of the Insurrections in Devonshire and Cornwall against Religious Innovations in the Reign of Edward VI* (London: Smith, Elder, 1913); S. T. Bindoff, *Ket's Rebellion, 1549*, reprinted in Joel Hurstfield, ed., *The Historical Association Book of the Tudors* (London: Sidgwick and Jackson, 1973), pp. 72–102; Julian Cornwall, *Revolt of the Peasantry, 1549* (London: Routledge & Kegan Paul, 1977); and Stephen Land, *Kett's Rebellion: The Norfolk Rising of 1549* (Totowa, N.J.: Rowman and Littlefield, 1977). See also Joyce Youings, "The Southwestern Rebellion of 1549," *Southern History* 1, no. 2 (1979): 99–122; and J. D. Alsop, "Latimer, the 'Commonwealth of Kent' and the 1549 Rebellions," *Historical Journal* 28, no. 3 (1985): 379–83.

[127] Brit. Lib., Harl. MS 304, f. 75; printed in Land, *Kett's Rebellion*, p. 64.

[128] See A. B. Ferguson, *The Articulate Citizen and the English Renaissance* (Durham: Duke University Press, 1965); Whitney R. D. Jones, *The Tudor Commonwealth, 1529–1559: A Study of the Impact of the Social and Economic Development of England upon Contemporary Concepts of the Nature and Duties of the Commonwealth* (London: Athlone Press, 1970); Zeeveld, *Foundations of Tudor Policy.* The commonwealthmen included writers such as Bishop Hugh Latimer, Thomas Starkey, Sir Thomas Smith, Henry Brinklow, Robert Crowley, Thomas Becon, and Thomas Lever.

[129] See Bridgen, *London and the Reformation*, pp. 344–45, 497.

[130] The artist of the 1516 rendering is unidentified and unknown.

[131] In addition, no attempt at all was made to produce the letters of the Utopian alphabet that were such a strikingly clever feature of the original Latin editions. In 1556, for the second edition of the translation, Vele apologized for their lack, saying that he had "not as yet the true characters of forms of the Utopian letters" but promised that they would appear in "the next impression" (207). In 1551, he seems to have made no attempt at all in this connection. Since he produced no subsequent edition, he never did get them into the English version. For the alphabet as it appeared in 1518, see Figure 11.

[132] By the time this second edition appeared, also published by Vele, Mierdman had returned to the continent and was printing at Emden; probably he left England in the face of its return to Roman Catholicism under Mary I. The second edition was printed for Vele by Richard Tottel, who was a Catholic. See Edward J. Baskerville, *A Chronological Bibliography of Propaganda and Polemic Published in English between 1553 and 1558 from the Death of Edward VI to the Death of Mary I* (Philadelphia: American Philosophical Society, 1979), pp. 7–8.

[133] Because *Utopia* was originally a Latin work, it was not included in the 1557 edition of the collected works of More, published under the editorship of William Rastell, even though one of the printers was Richard Tottel, who had printed the 1556 revised version of Robynson's translation for Abraham Vele; see *The Workes of Sir Thomas More Knyght, Sometyme Lorde Chauncellour of England, Wrytten by Him in the Englyshe Tonge*, 2 vols. (London, 1557; STC 18076).

[134] For evidence of social and economic stress in the 1550s, 1590s, and 1620s, see Joan Thirsk, ed., *The Agrarian History of England and Wales, Vol. IV: 1500–1640* (Cambridge: Cambridge University Press, 1967), statistical appendix, Tables I, VI, VII, pp. 818, 820–21, 848–50, 853–55; E. H. Phelps Brown and Sheila Hopkins, "Seven Centuries of the Prices of Consumables, Compared with Builder's Wage-Rates," in E. M. Carus-Wilson, ed., *Essays*

in Economic History, 3 vols. (London: Edward Arnold, 1962), vol. 2, pp. 194–95; E. A. Wrigley and Roger Schofield, *The Population History of England, 1541–1871: A Reconstruction* (London: Edward Arnold, 1981), App. 9, Table 9.2, pp. 642–43; and the works cited in the bibliography, section VI. The context for the 1639 edition (STC 18098) was not so much social unrest, but political dissension and disorder. Consequently, the discussion of counsel in The First Book was probably of greater weight than the discussion of society and the economy. It was dedicated by Bernard Alsop, one of the printers of the volume, to Cresacre More, Sir Thomas's great-grandson, who in 1631 had himself published a biography of his great-grandfather.

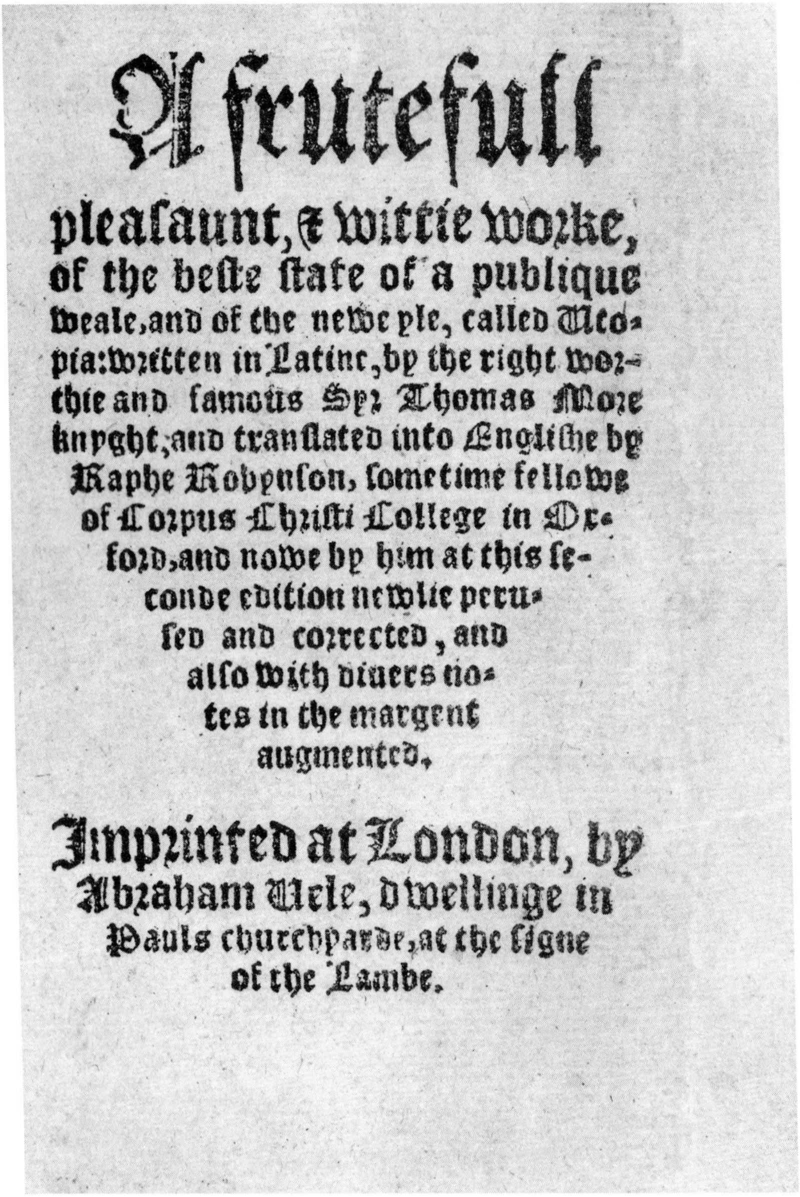

A frutefull

pleasaunt, & wittie worke,
of the beste state of a publique
weale, and of the newe yle, called Utopia: written in Latine, by the right wor-
thie and famous Syr Thomas More
knyght, and translated into Englishe by
Raphe Robynson, sometime fellowe
of Corpus Christi College in Ox-
forde, and nowe by him at this se-
conde edition newlie perused and corrected, and
also with diuers no-
tes in the margent
augmented.

Imprinted at London, by

Abraham Uele, dwellinge in
Pauls churchyarde, at the signe
of the Lambe.

Figure 12. Title page of the second, corrected edition of Ralph Robynson's translation of More's *Utopia,* printed in 1556.
By permission of the Folger Shakespeare Library.

PART TWO

Utopia

A fruitful,

pleasant, and witty work,

of the best state of a public

weal and of the new isle called Utopia,
written in Latin by the right worthy
and famous Sir Thomas More,
knight, and translated into English by
Ralph Robynson, sometime fellow
of Corpus Christi College in
Oxford, and now by him at this
second edition newly perused
and corrected, and
also with divers notes
in the margin
augmented.

Imprinted at London by
Abraham Vele, dwelling in
Paul's churchyard at the sign
of the Lamb.

THE TRANSLATOR TO THE GENTLE READER.

Thou shalt understand, gentle reader, that though this work of Utopia in English come now the second time forth in print, yet was it never my mind nor intent that it should ever have been imprinted at all, as who for no such purpose took upon me at the first the translation thereof, but did it only at the request of a friend for his own private use, upon hope that he would have kept it secret to himself alone.[1] Whom though I knew to be a man indeed, both very witty and also skillful, yet was I certain that, in the knowledge of the Latin tongue, he was not so well seen as to be able to judge of the fineness or coarseness of my translation. Wherefore, I went the more slightly through with it, propounding to myself therein, rather to please my said friend's judgment than mine own. To the meanness of whole learning I thought it my part to submit and attemper[2] my style. Lightly, therefore, I overran the whole work and in short time, with more haste than good speed, I brought it to an end. But as the Latin proverb saith; the hasty bitch bringeth forth blind whelps, for, when this my work was finished, the rudeness thereof showed it to be done in posthaste. Howbeit, rude and base though it were, yet fortune so ruled the matter that to imprinting it came, and that partly against my will. Howbeit, not being able in this behalf to resist the pithy persuasions of my friends, and perceiving, therefore, none other remedy but that forth it should, I comforted myself for the time only with this notable saying of Terence:

> *Ita vita est hominum, quasi quum ludas tesseris*
> *Si illud, quod est maxume opus, iactu non cadit:*
> *Illud, quod cecidit forte, id arte ut corrigas.*[3]

In which verses the poet likeneth or compareth the life of man to a dice playing or a game at the tables. Meaning therein, if that chance rise not, which is most for the players' advantage, that then the chance which fortune hath sent ought so cunningly to be played, as may be to the player

---

[1] This letter to the reader is Ralph Robynson's preface to the second (1556) edition of his translation. In the letter to William Cecil, which prefaced the 1551 edition, Robynson explained that the friend was George Tadlowe, a prominent London haberdasher and patron of humanist literature. See pp. 61, 211.

[2] "Attemper" = "regulate."

[3] Translation: "Human life is like a game with dice; if you don't get the throw you most want, you must show your skill in making the best throw which you can get." Terence, *Adelphi/The Brothers,* lines 739–41; *Terence,* 2 vols., ed. and trans. John Sargent (London: William Heinemann, 1931), vol. 2, pp. 295, 297. In modern editions, the Latin reads; *Ita vitast hominum quasi quom ludas tesseris: / si illus quod maxime opus est iactu non cadet, / illud quod cedidit forte, id arte ut corrigas; Terence,* vol. 2, pp. 294, 296.

least damage. By the which worthy similitude surely the witty poet giveth us to understand that though in any of our acts and doings (as it oft chanceth), we happen to fail and miss of our good pretensed purpose so that the success and our intent prove things far odd, yet so we ought with witty circumspection to handle the matter that no evil or incommodity, as far forth as may be, and as in us lieth, do thereof ensue. According to the which counsel, though I am, indeed, in comparison of an expert gamester and a cunning player but a very bungler, yet have I in this by chance that on my side unawares hath fallen, so (I suppose) behaved myself that, as doubtless it might have been of me much more cunningly handled had I forethought so much, or doubted any such request at the beginning of my play, so I am sure it had been much worse than it is if I had not in the end looked somewhat earnestly to my game. For though this work came not from me so fine, so perfect, and so exact that at first, as surely for my small learning it should have done, if I had then meant the publishing thereof in print. Yet I trust I have now in this second edition taken about it such pains that very few great faults and notable errors are in it to be found. Now, therefore, most gentle reader, the meanness of this simple translation and the faults that be therein (as I fear much there be some), I doubt not but thou wilt, in just consideration of the premises, gently and favorably wink at them. So doing you shall minister unto my good cause to think my labor and pains herein not altogether bestowed in vain.

Vale

THE EPISTLE

Thomas More to Peter Giles sendeth greeting.

I am almost ashamed, right well-beloved Peter Giles,[1] to send unto you this book of the Utopian commonwealth well nigh after a year's space, which I am sure you looked for within a month and a half. And no marvel. For you knew well enough that I was already disburdened of all the labor and study belonging to the invention of this work, and that I had no need at all to trouble my brains about the disposition or conveyance of

---

[1] Peter Giles (1486–1533), chief clerk of Antwerp's court of justice, was a prominent humanist in his own right.

the matter, and therefore had herein nothing else to do, but only to rehearse those things which you and I together heard Master Raphael tell
and declare. Wherefore, there was no cause why I should study to set
forth the matter with eloquence. Forasmuch as his talk could not be fine
and eloquent, being first not studied for, but sudden and unpremedi-
tate and then, as you know, of a man better seen in the Greek language
than in the Latin tongue. And my writing, the nigher[2]

it should approach to his homely, plain, and simple
speech, so much the nigher should it go to the truth,
which is the only mark whereunto I do and ought to di-

*Truth loveth simplicity
and plainness.*[3]

rect all my travail and study herein. I grant and confess, friend Peter, myself discharged of so much labor, having all these things ready done to
my hand, that almost there was nothing left for me to do, else either the
invention or the disposition of this matter might have required of a wit
neither base, neither at all unlearned, both some time and leisure and
also some study. But if it were requisite and necessary that the matter
should also have been written eloquently and not alone truly, of a surety
that thing could I have performed by no time nor study. But now, seeing
all these cares, stays, and lets were taken away, wherein else so much labor and study should have been employed, and that there remained no
other thing for me to do but only to write plainly the matter as I hath it
spoken, that, indeed, was a thing light and to be done.

Howbeit, to the dispatching of this so little business, my other cares
and troubles did leave almost less than no leisure. Whiles[4] I do daily
bestow my time about law matters: some to plead,
some to hear, some as an arbitrator with mine award to
determine, some as an umpire or a judge with mine

*The author's business
and lets.*[5]

sentence finally to discuss.[6] Whiles I go one way to see and visit my
friend; another way about mine own private affairs. Whiles I spend almost all the day abroad amongst others and the residue at home among

---

[2]"Nigher" = "nearer."

[3]This marginal note and the others, absent from the 1551 edition of Robynson's translation, parallel the marginal notes supplied by Desiderius Erasmus and Peter Giles for the
original Latin editions of *Utopia*. Abraham Vele, the book's publisher, provided this set of
marginal notes for the second edition to make the English translation appear closer in
form to the original Latin ones; he may himself have been their author. Some of the notes
paraphrase or translate the original Latin, but this one and many others do not.

[4]"Whiles" = "sometimes."

[5]"Lets" = "hindrances."

[6]More here is describing his activities as a lawyer, especially as the undersheriff of London, acting as judge in the city's Sheriff's Court, and as an arbiter and special examiner in
the Court of Chancery. See the introduction.

mine own, I leave to myself, I mean to my book, no time. For when I am come home, I must common[7] with my wife, chat with my children, and talk with my servants, all the which things I reckon and account among business, for as much as they must of necessity be done, and done must they needs be unless a man will be stranger in his own house. And in any wise, a man must so fashion and order his conditions and so appoint and dispose himself that he be merry, jocund, and pleasant among them whom either nature hath provided or chance hath made or he himself hath chosen to be the fellows and companions of his life. So that with too much gentle behavior and familiarity, he do not mar them and, by too much sufferance of his servants, make them his masters. Among these things now rehearsed stealeth away the day, the month, the year. When do I write then? And all this while have I spoken no word of sleep, neither yet of meat,[8] which among a great number doth waste no less time than doth sleep, wherein almost half the lifetime of man creepeth away.

Meat & sleep: great wasters of time.

I, therefore, do win and get only that time which I steal from sleep and meat. Which time, because it is very little, and yet somewhat it is, therefore, have I once at the last, though it be long first, finished *Utopia* and have sent it to you, friend Peter, to read and peruse to the intent that if anything have escaped me, you might put me in remembrance of it.

For though in this behalf I do not greatly mistrust myself (which would God I were somewhat in wit and learning, as I am not all of the worst and dullest memory), yet have I not so great trust and confidence in it that I think nothing could fall out of my mind. For John Clement, my boy,[9] who as you know was there present with us, whom I suffer to be away from no talk wherein may be any profit or goodness (for out of this young-bladed and new-shot-up corn, which hath already begun to spring up both in Latin and Greek learning, I look for plentiful increase at length of goodly ripe grain), he, I say, hath brought me into a great doubt. For, whereas Hythloday[10] (unless my memory fail me) said that the bridge

John Clement.

---

[7]"Common" = "commune," "discourse."

[8]"Meat" = "feeding," "eating."

[9]John Clement, a young humanist and one of the first pupils of John Colet's St. Paul's grammar school, founded circa 1509, had entered More's household as a servant by 1514 and accompanied More as his "boy," or servant, on the embassy to the Netherlands in 1515. Later, he became a learned physician and in 1544 was elected president of the College of Physicians. He died abroad in 1572.

[10]Hythloday in the original Latin is *Hythlodaeus,* a compound word derived from Greek meaning "cunning" or "expert in nonsense."

of Amaurote[11] which goeth over the river of Anyder[12] is 500 paces, that is to say half a mile in length, my John saith that 200 of those paces must be plucked away, for that the river containeth there not above 300 paces in breadth. I pray you heartily call the matter to your remembrance, for if you agree with him, I also will say as you say and confess myself deceived. But if you cannot remember the thing, then surely I will write as I have done and as mine own remembrance serveth me. For as I will take good heed that there be in my book nothing false, so if there be anything doubtful, I will rather tell a lie than make a lie, because I had rather be good than wily.

A diversity between making a lie and telling a lie.[13]

Howbeit, this matter may easily be remedied if you will take the pains to ask the question of Raphael himself by word of mouth if he be now with you, or else by your letters, which you must needs do for another doubt also that hath chanced, through whose fault I cannot tell, whether through mine or yours or Raphael's. For neither we remembered to inquire of him nor he to tell us in what part of the new world Utopia[14] is situate, the which thing I had rather have spent no small sum of money than that it should thus have escaped us, as well for that I am ashamed to be ignorant in what sea that island standeth, whereof I write so long a treatise, as also because there be with us certain men, and especially one virtuous and godly man, and a professor of divinity, who is exceeding desirous to go unto Utopia, not for a vain and curious desire to see news, but to the intent he may further and increase

In what part of the world Utopia standeth it is unknown.

It is thought of some that here is unfainedly meant the late famous vicar of Croydon in Surrey.[15]

our religion, which is there already luckily begun. And that he may the better accomplish and perform this his good intent, he is minded to procure that he may be sent thither by the high bishop. Yea, and that he himself may be made Bishop of Utopia, being nothing scrupulous herein, that he must obtain this bishopric with suit. For he counteth that a godly suit, which pro-

A godly suit.

---

[11] "Amaurote" in the original Latin is *Amauroticum,* derived from a Greek word meaning "made dark" or "made dim," hence a "dark place."

[12] "Anyder" in the original Latin is *Andrus,* derived from a Greek word meaning "waterless."

[13] In the original Latin editions, Erasmus and Giles here supplied a comment to "note the Theological distinction between an intentional and an objective falsehood." See CW 4, pp. 40–41.

[14] The name Utopia derives from the Greek *u-topos,* meaning literally "no place."

[15] The person intended by the author of the marginal note is Rowland Phillips, an Oxford-educated divine and a royal chaplain. Whether More himself meant this individual or was speaking generically is uncertain. See CW 4, p. 292.

ceedeth not of the desire of honor or lucre, but only of a godly zeal. Wherefore, I most earnestly desire you, friend Peter, to talk with Hythloday, if you can face to face, or else to write your letters to him, and so to work in this matter, that in this my book there may neither anything be found which is untrue, neither anything be lacking which is true. And I think, verily, it shall be well done that you show unto him the book itself, for if I have missed or failed in any point, or if any fault have escaped me, no man can so well correct and amend it as he can, and, yet, that can he not do unless he peruse and read over my book written. Moreover, by this means shall you perceive whether he be well willing and content that I should undertake to put this work in writing, for if he be minded to publish and put forth his own labors and travails himself, perchance he would be loathe, and so would I also, that in publishing the Utopian weal public [16] I should prevent him and take from him the flower and grace of the novelty of this his history.

Howbeit, to say the very truth, I am not yet fully determined with myself whether I will put forth my book or no, for the natures of men be so divers, the fantasies of some so wayward, their minds so unkind, their judgments so corrupt that they which lead a merry and a jocund life, following their own sensual pleasures and carnal lusts, may seem to be in a much better state

> The unkind judgments of men.

or case than they that vex and unquiet themselves with cares and study for the putting forth and publishing of something that may be either profit or pleasure to others, which others nevertheless will disdainfully, scornfully, and unkindly accept the same. The most part of all be unlearned, and a great number hath learning in contempt. The rude and barbarous alloweth nothing but that which is very barbarous indeed. If it be one that hath a little smack of learning, he rejecteth as homely gear and common ware whatsoever is not stuffed full of old moth-eaten terms and that be worn out of use. Some there be that have pleasure only in old rusty antiquities, and some only in their own doings. One is so sour, so crabbed, and so unpleasant that he can away with no mirth nor sport; another is so narrow between the shoulders that he can bear no jests nor taunts. Some silly poor souls be so afraid that at every snappish word their nose shall be bitten off that they stand in no less dread of every quick and sharp word than he that is bitten of a mad dog feareth water. Some be so mutable and wavering that every hour they be in a new mind, saying one thing sitting and another thing standing. Another sort sitteth upon their ale benches, and there among their cups they give judgment

---

[16] "Weal public" = "commonweal," "commonwealth."

of the wits of writers, and with great authority they condemn even as pleaseth them, every writer according to his writing, in most spiteful manner mocking, louting, and flouting them, being themselves in the mean season safe and, as saith the proverb, out of all danger of gunshot. For why they be so smug and smooth that they have not so much as one hair of an honest man whereby one may take hold of them. There be, moreover, some so unkind and ungentle that though they take great pleasure and delectation in the work, yet for all that they cannot find in their hearts to love the author thereof, nor to afford him a good word, be-ing much like the uncourteous, unthankful, and churl-ish guests which, when they have with good and dainty   A fit similitude. meats well-filled their bellies, depart home, giving no thanks to the feast maker. Go your ways now and make a costly feast at your own charges for guests so dainty-mouthed, so divers in taste, and, besides that, of so unkind and unthankful natures. But nevertheless (friend Peter) do, I pray you, with Hythloday as I willed you before, and as for this matter I shall be at my liberty afterwards to take new advise-ment. Howbeit, seeing I have taken great pains and labor in writing this matter, if it may stand with his mind and pleasure, I will, as touching the edition or publishing of the book, follow the counsel and advice of my friends, and especially yours. Thus, fare you well right heartily beloved friend Peter, with your gentle wife, and love me as you have ever done for I love you better than ever I did.

THE FIRST BOOK

of the communication of Raphael Hythloday
concerning the best state of a commonwealth.

The most victorious and triumphant king of England, Henry the Eight of that name, in all royal virtues a prince most peerless, had of late in controversy with Charles, the right high and mighty king of Castile, weighty matters and of great importance. For the debatement and final determination whereof, the king's majesty sent me ambassador into Flanders joined in commission with Cuthbert Tun-stall,[1] a man doubtless out of comparison and whom the king's majesty of late, to the great rejoicing of all men,   Cuthbert Tunstall.

[1]In the original Latin, Charles, son of Philip, Duke of Burgundy, and of Joanna, the third child of Ferdinand and Isabella of Spain, is designated correctly as "Prince of Castile," not king. Born in February 1500 and ultimately elected Holy Roman Emperor in 1519, Charles had succeeded officially to his father's titles and possessions in the Netherlands

did prefer to the office of Master of the Rolls.[2] But of this man's praises I will say nothing, not because I do fear that small credence shall be given to the testimony that cometh out of a friend's mouth, but because his virtue and learning be greater and of more excellency than that I am able to praise them, and also in all places so famous and so perfectly well known that they need not, nor ought not, of me to be praised unless I would seem to show and set forth the brightness of the sun with a candle, as the proverb saith.

There met us at Bruges (for thus it was before agreed) they whom their prince had for that matter appointed commissioners, excellent men all. The chief and the head of them was the Margrave (as they call him) of Bruges,[3] a right honorable man, but the wisest and the best spoken of them was George Temsice, provost of Cassel,[4] a man not only by learning but also by nature of singular eloquence and in the laws profoundly learned. But in reasoning and debating of matters, what by his natural wit and what by daily exercise, surely he had few fellows. After that we had once or twice met, and upon certain points or articles could not fully and thoroughly agree, they for a certain space took their leave of us and departed to Brussels, there to know their prince's pleasure.

I in the meantime (for so my business lay) went straight thence to Antwerp. Whiles I was there abiding, often times among other, but which to me was more welcome than any other, did visit me one Peter Giles, citizen of Antwerp, a man there Peter Giles. in his country of honest reputation and also preferred to high promotions, worthy truly of the highest, for it is hard to say whether the young man be in learning or in honesty more excellent. For he is both of wonderful virtuous conditions and also singularly well learned, and towards all sorts of people exceeding gentle, but towards his friends so kindhearted, so loving, so faithful, so trusty, and of

---

and Burgundy on the latter's death in 1506. At the time of More's embassy to Bruges in 1515, Charles's maternal grandfather, Ferdinand, King of Castile, was still alive; the latter died in January 1516, and his grandson was formally recognized as ruler, conjointly with his mother, only in 1518. See Karl Brandi, *The Emperor Charles V,* trans. C. V. Wedgewood (London: Jonathan Cape, 1949), pp. 39–45, 71–72; CW 4, p. 296.

[2]The royal commission, naming More along with Tunstall and three others as commissioners, dates from May 7, 1515. Tunstall (1474–1559), a humanist-educated official, became Master of the Rolls on the Chancery and Vice-Chancellor of England under Wolsey in May 1516. See pp. 27, 72n67.

[3]In the original Latin, the title is given as *praefectus,* meaning "governor" or, in this urban context, "mayor."

[4]Georges de Themsecke (d. 1536) was a doctor of laws and a prominent official in Flanders.

so earnest affection that it were very hard in any place to find a man that with him in all points of friendship may be compared. No man can be more lowly or courteous; no man useth less simulation or dissimulation; in no man is more prudent simplicity. Besides this, he is in his talk and communication so merry and pleasant, yea, and that without harm that, through his gentle entertainment and his sweet and delectable communication, in me was greatly abated and diminished the fervent desire that I had to see my native country, my wife, and my children, whom then I did much long and covet to see, because at that time I had been more than four months from them.

Upon a certain day when I had heard the divine service in Our Lady's Church,[5] which is the fairest, the most gorgeous and curious church of building in all the city, and also most frequented of people, and, the service being done, was ready to go home to my lodging, I chanced to espy this foresaid Peter talking with a certain stranger, a man well stricken in age, with a black sunburned face, a long beard, and a cloak cast homely about his shoulders, whom, by his favor and apparel, forthwith I judged to be a mariner. But the said Peter, seeing me, came unto me and saluted me. And as I was about to answer him, "See you this man," saith he (and therewith he pointed to the man that I saw him talking with before). "I was minded," quoth he, "to bring him straight home to you." "He should have been very welcome to me," said I, "for your sake." "Nay," quoth he, "for his own sake if you knew him, for there is no man this day living that can tell you of so many strange and unknown peoples and countries as this man can. And I know well that you be very desirous to hear of such news." "Then I conjectured not far amiss,"[6] quoth I, "for even at the first sight, I judged him to be a mariner." "Nay," quoth he, "there you were greatly deceived. He has sailed indeed, not as the mariner Palinurus,[7] but as the expert and prudent prince Ulysses.[8] Yea, rather as the ancient and sage philosopher Plato.[9] For this same Raphael Hythloday (for this is his name) is very well learned in the Latin tongue, but profound and excellent in the Greek language, wherein he ever bestowed more study than in the Latin, because he had given himself wholly to the study

Raphael Hythloday.

---

[5] Nôtre Dame is Antwerp's cathedral.

[6] "I conjectured not far amiss" = "I guessed correctly."

[7] Palinurus was Aeneas's pilot in Virgil's *Aeneid,* bk. V, lines 833–61; bk. VI; lines 337–83. He dozed at the helm and fell overboard.

[8] Ulysses in Homer's *The Odyssey* is revealed not just as especially resourceful, but as someone who had traveled widely in his world.

[9] According to Diogenes Laertius (ca. 200–250 C.E.), Plato also had a reputation for traveling extensively around the Mediterranean.

of philosophy. Whereof he knew that there is nothing extant in Latin that is to any purpose, saving a few of Seneca's and Cicero's doings. His patrimony that he was born unto he left to his brethren (for he is a Portugal born), and for the desire that he had to see and know the far countries of the world, he joined himself in company with Amerigo Vespucci, and in the three last voyages of those four that be now in print and abroad in every man's hands, he continued still in his company, saving that in the last voyage he came not home again with him.[10] For he made such means and shift, what by entreatance and what by importune suit,[11] that he got license of Master Amerigo (though it were sore against his will) to be one of the twenty-four which in the end of the last voyage were left in the country of Gulike.[12] He was, therefore, left behind for his mind sake, as one that took more thought and care for traveling than dying, having customably in his mouth these sayings: *He that hath no grave is covered with the sky,*[13] and *the way to heaven out of all places is of like length and distance.*[14] Which fantasy of his (if God had not been his better friend) he had surely bought full dear. But after the departing of Master Vespucci, when he had traveled through and about many countries with five of his companions, Gulikians,[15] at the last by marvelous chance

[10] Amerigo Vespucci (1451–1512), the Florentine explorer who gave his name to the Americas, made four American voyages between 1497 and 1502, the latter two for the King of Portugal. Two Latin accounts of his voyages were published around 1504. See pp. 4, 69*n*4.

[11] "He made such means and shift, what by entreatance and what by importune suit" = "he used every possible means of persuasion and entreaty."

[12] In the original Latin, More speaks only of Hythloday being left behind at a *castello,* or fort. In the letter describing this fourth voyage, which took Vespucci to the coasts of Brazil, the explorer also mentions only a fort, locating it at 18° latitude south of the equator, which would place it about five hundred miles north of present-day Rio de Janeiro. Gulike is a name made up by Robynson for this translation. It might be a pastiche of English and Greek linking the English verb *to gull,* in the sense of "to fool," with the Greek ending *-ike,* meaning "art of" or "science of." Hence "the country of Gulike" would be a land "of the art of fooling." Many of More's own puns in *Utopia* make similar jokes. A second possibility, based on a pastiche of Latin and Greek, links the Latin noun *gula,* which means not only the "throat" or "gullet" but also the "seat of appetite," with the Greek *-ike.* On this reading, the "country of Gulike" would be a land of "the art of pure appetite" or a land "of complete gluttons," arguably a way of representing the cannibalism of the peoples of the region. Most English readers of the day would have immediately registered the sound of the word *gull* in the name and chosen the first of these proposed readings. I thank Professors Walter Englert, Nigel Nicholson, and C. D. C. Reeve of Reed College for their help with this point.

[13] From the Latin poet Lucan's epic *Pharsalia,* bk. 7, line 819.

[14] From Cicero's *Tusculan Disputations,* I.xliii.104.

[15] At this point the original Latin text speaks only of Hythloday being accompanied by "five companions from the fort," who presumably would have been among the twenty-four men Vespucci had left behind, all of whom were "Christian men," according to Vespucci; pointedly, however, More himself does not explicitly mention the Christianity of the twenty-four.

he arrived in Taprobane,[16] from whence he went to Calicut,[17] where he chanced to find certain of his country ships, wherein he returned again to his country, nothing less than looked for."

All this, when Peter had told me, I thanked him for his gentle kindness that he had vouchsafed to bring me to the speech of that man, whose communication he thought should be to me pleasant and acceptable. And therewith I turned me to Raphael. And when we had hailed each other and had spoken these common words that be customably spoken at the first meeting and acquaintance of strangers, we went thence to my house and there in my garden, upon a bench covered with green torves,[18] we sat down talking together. There he told us how that after the departing of Vespucci, he and his fellows that tarried behind in Gulike[19] began by little and little, through fair and gentle speech, to win the love and favor of the people of that country, insomuch that, within short space, they did dwell among them not only harmless, but also occupying with them very familiarly.[20] He told us also that they were in high reputation and favor with a certain great man (whose name and country is now quite out of my remembrance) which of his mere liberality[21] did bear the costs and charges of him and his five companions. And besides that gave them a trusty guide to conduct them in their journey (which by water was in boats and by land in wagons) and to bring them to other princes with very friendly commendations.

Thus after many days' journeys, he said, they found towns and cities and weal publics, full of people governed by good and wholesome laws. For under the line equinoctial,[22] and on both sides of the same as far as the sun doth extend his course, lieth (quoth he) great and wide deserts and wildernesses, parched, burned, and dried up with continual

---

[16]Taprobane is the name used by Greek and Roman writers to designate present-day Sri Lanka. On his fourth voyage, Vespucci had originally set sail for the Indian Ocean, and More may have read Vespucci's description as suggesting that he had actually arrived there rather than in what is now South America.

[17]Calicut is present-day Calcutta, the seaport on the Malabar Coast in Madras, India. The Portuguese first began visiting there in the late 1480s and by 1511 had built a fortified post on the site.

[18]"Torves" = "turfs of grass."

[19]Once again, More's original Latin mentions only those who had stayed behind "at the fort."

[20]"They did dwell among them not only harmless, but also occupying with them very familiarly" = "they not only lived among them free from danger, but did business with them on very friendly terms."

[21]"Mere liberality" = "disinterested generosity."

[22]"Line equinoctial" = "the equator."

and intolerable heat. All things be hideous, terrible, loathsome, and unpleasant to behold; all things out of fashion and comeliness,[23] inhabited with wild beasts and serpents, or, at the least while, with people that be no less savage, wild, and noisome than the very beasts themselves be. But a little farther beyond that, all things begin by little and little to wax pleasant; the air soft, temperate, and gentle; the ground covered with green grass; less wildness in the beasts. At the last shall you come again to people, cities, and towns wherein is continual intercourse and occupying of merchandise and chaffer,[24] not only among themselves and with their borderers, but also with merchants of far countries, both by land and water. "There I had occasion," said he, "to go to many countries on every side, for there was no ship ready to any voyage or journey, but I and my fellows were into it very gladly received." The ships that they found first were made plain, flat, and broad in the bottom, trow-wise.[25] The sails were made of great rushes, or of wickers, and in some places of leather. Afterward they found ships with ridged keels and sails of canvas, yea, and shortly after, having all things like ours. The shipmen also very expert and cunning, both in the sea and in the weather. But he said that he found great favor and friendship among them, for teaching them the feat and use of the lodestone,[26] which to them before that time was unknown, and, therefore, they were wont to be very timorous and fearful upon the sea, nor to venture upon it but only in the summertime. But now they have such a confidence in that stone that they fear not stormy winter, in so doing, farther from care than danger. Insomuch that it is greatly to be doubted, lest that thing, through their own foolish hardiness, shall turn them to evil and harm, which at the first was supposed should be to them good and commodious.[27]

Ships of strange fashions.

The lodestone.

But what he told us that he saw in every country where he came, it were very long to declare. Neither it is my purpose at this time to make rehearsal thereof. But peradventure in another place I will speak of it, chiefly such things as shall be profitable to be known, as in special be those decrees and ordinances that he marked to be well and wittily

---

[23] "Out of fashion and comeliness" = "out of shape and pleasing appearance."
[24] "Continual intercourse and occupying of merchandise and chaffer" = "continual wholesale and retail trade" (*chaffer* refers to retail buying and selling).
[25] "Trow-wise" = "bargelike."
[26] "Lodestone" = "magnetic compass."
[27] "Commodious" = "profitable," "beneficial."

provided and enacted among such peoples as do live together in a civil policy[28] and good order. For of such things did we basely inquire and demand of him, and he likewise very willingly told us of the same. But as for monsters, because they be no news, of them we were nothing inquisitive, for nothing is more easy to be found than be barking Scyllas, ravening Celænos, and Læstrygons, devourers of people, and such like great and incredible monsters.[29] But to find citizens ruled by good and wholesome laws, that is an exceeding rare and hard thing. But as he marked many fond and foolish laws in those newfound lands, so he rehearsed divers acts and constitutions whereby these our cities, nations, countries, and kingdoms may take example to amend their faults, enormities, and errors, whereof in another place, as I said, I will entreat.

Now at this time I am determined to rehearse only that he told us of the manners, customs, laws, and ordinances of the Utopians. But first I will repeat our former communication by the occasion, and, as I might say, the drift whereof he was brought into the mention of that weal public.[30] For when Raphael had very prudently touched divers things that be amiss, some here and some there, yea, very many on both parts, and again had spoken of such wise laws and prudent decrees as be established and used, both here among us and also there among them, as a man so perfect and expert in the laws and customs of every several country, as though into what place soever he came guestwise, there he had led all his life.

Then Peter much marveling at the man, "Surely, Master Raphael," quoth he, "I wonder greatly why you get you not into some king's court? For I am sure there is no prince living that would not be very glad of you as a man not only able highly to delight him with your profound learning, and this your knowledge of countries and peoples, but also meet to instruct him with examples and help him with counsel. And thus doing, you shall bring yourself in a very good case,[31] and also be of ability to help all your friends and kinfolk."

---

[28]"Civil policy" = "organized state," "commonwealth."

[29]These are monsters from Homer's *Odyssey* and Virgil's *Aeneid.* The Scylla, a six-headed sea monster, appears in both: *Odyssey,* bk. 12, lines 73–100, 234–59; *Aeneid,* bk. 3, lines 420–32. Cælenos, one of the bird-women known as Harpies, is mentioned in the *Aeneid,* bk. 3, lines 209–58, and the Læstrygons, a tribe of giant cannibals, are described in the *Odyssey,* bk. 10, lines 76–132.

[30]As noted by J. H. Hexter and commented on in the Introduction, the dialogue breaks off at this point to turn to a discussion of the subject of counsel; it returns to the promised description of Utopian institutions only many pages later. See pp. 29–30, 76*nn*76–78.

[31]"Bring yourself in a very good case" = "become very well off," "become very prosperous."

"As concerning my friends and kinfolk," quoth he, "I pass not greatly for them,[32] for I think I have sufficiently done my part towards them already. For these things, that other men do not depart from until they be old and sick, yea, which they be then very loath to leave when they can no longer keep, those very same things did I, being not only lusty[33] and in good health but also in the flower of my youth, divide among my friends and kinfolk, which I think with this my liberality ought to hold them contented, and not to require nor to look that besides this, I should for their sakes give myself in bondage unto kings." "Nay, God forbid that," quoth Peter. "It is not my mind that you should be in bondage to kings, but as a retainer to them at your pleasure,[34] which surely, I think, is the nighest[35] way that you can devise how to bestow your time fruitfully, not only for the private commodity[36] of your friends and for the general profit of all sorts of people, but also for the advancement of yourself to a much wealthier state and condition than you be now in." "To a wealthier condition," quoth Raphael, "by that means, that my mind standeth clean against? Now I live at liberty after mine own mind and pleasure, which I think very few of these great states and peers of realms can say. Yea, and there be enough of them that sue for great men's friendships and, therefore, think it no great hurt if they have not me, nor three or four such other as I am." "Well, I perceive plainly, friend Raphael," quoth I, "that you be desirous neither of riches nor of power. And, truly, I have in no less reverence and estimation a man of your mind than any of them all that be so high in power and authority. But you shall do as it becometh you, yea, and according to this wisdom, to this high and free courage of yours, if you can find in your heart so to appoint and dispose yourself that you may apply your wit and diligence to the profit of the weal public, though it be somewhat to your own pain and hindrance. And this shall you never so well do nor with so great profit perform, as if you be of some great prince's council and put into his head (as I doubt not but you will) honest opinions and virtuous persuasions. For from the prince, as from a perpetual wellspring, cometh among the people the flood of all that is good or evil. But in you is so perfect learn-

---

[32]"I pass not greatly for them" = "I am not very concerned about providing for them."
[33]"Lusty" = "cheerful."
[34]At this point in the original Latin, More speaks of the difference between being in "servitude" to a master (from the Latin verb *seruio*) and being in the "service" of a king (from the Latin verb *inseruio*), to which Hythloday replies that the difference is but one syllable.
[35]"Nighest" = "nearest."
[36]"Private commodity" = "personal profit," "advantage."

ing that without any experience, and again so great experience, that without any learning you may well be any king's councillor."

"You be twice deceived, Master More," quoth he, "first in me and again in the thing itself, for neither is in me the ability that you force upon me, and if it were never so much, yet in disquieting mine own quietness I should nothing further the weal public. For, first of all, the most part of all princes have more delight in warlike matters and feats of chivalry (the knowledge whereof I neither have nor desire) than in the good feats of peace, and employing much more study how by right or by wrong to enlarge their dominions than how well and peaceably to rule and govern that they have already. Moreover, they that be counselors to kings, every one of them either is of himself so wise indeed that he needeth not, or else he thinketh himself so wise that he will not allow another man's counsel, saving that they do shamefully and flatteringly give assent to the fond and foolish sayings of certain great men, whose favors, because they be in high authority with their prince, by assentation [37] and flattery they labor to obtain. And, verily, it is naturally given to all men to esteem their own inventions best. So both the raven and the ape think their own young ones fairest. Then if a man in such a company, where some disdain and have despite at other men's inventions,[38] and some count their own best, if among such men," I say, "a man should bring forth anything that he hath read done [39] in times past or that he hath seen done in other places, there the hearers fare as though the whole existimation [40] of their wisdom were in jeopardy to be overthrown, and that ever after they should be counted for very dizzards,[41] unless they could in other men's inventions pick out matter to reprehend and find fault at.

"If all other poor helps fail, then this is their extreme refuge. These things, say they, pleased our forefathers and ancestors. Would God we could be so wise as they were, and, as though they had wittily concluded the matter and with this answer stopped every man's mouth, they sit down again. As who should say it were a very dangerous matter if a man in any point should be found wiser than his forefathers were. And yet be we content to suffer the best

Triptakers.[42]

---

[37] "Assentation" = "servile expression of assent."
[38] "Have despite at other men's inventions" = "have contempt for other men's arguments."
[39] "Read done" = "read about being done."
[40] "Existimation" = "estimation."
[41] "Dizzards" = "fools," "blockheads."
[42] "Triptakers" = "faultfinders."

and wittiest of their decrees to lie unexecuted. But if in anything a better order might have been taken than by them was, there we take fast hold, finding therein many faults.

"Many times have I chanced upon such proud, lewd, overthwart, and wayward judgments, yea, and once in England —" "I pray you, Sir," quoth I, "have you been in our country?" "Yea, forsooth," quoth he, "and there I tarried for the space of four or five months together, not long after the insurrection that the western Englishmen made against their king, which by their own miserable and pitiful slaughter was suppressed and ended.[43] In the mean season I was much bound and beholden to the right reverend father John Morton, Archbishop and Cardinal of Canterbury, and at that time also Lord Chancellor of England,[44] a man, Master Peter (for Master More knoweth already that I will say), not more honorable for his authority than for his prudence and virtue. He was of a mean stature and, though stricken in age, yet bear he his body upright. In his face did shine such an amiable reverence[45] as was pleasant to behold, gentle in communication, yet earnest and sage. He had great delight many times with rough speech to his suitors to prove, but without harm, what prompt wit and what bold spirit were in every man. In the which, as in a virtue much agreeing with his nature, so that therewith were not joined impudency,[46] he took great delectation. And the same person, as apt and meet to have an administration in the weal public,[47] he did lovingly embrace. In his speech he was fine, eloquent, and pithy; in the law he had profound knowledge; in wit he was incomparable, and in memory wonderful excellent. These qualities, which in him were by nature singular, he by learning and use had made perfect.[48] The king put much trust in his counsel; the weal public also in a manner leaned upon him when I was there. For even in

Partial judgments.

Cardinal Morton.

[43] Hythloday is referring here to the Cornish Rising of 1497. For discussion, see pp. 34, 74n86.

[44] John Morton (1420?–1500), a supporter of the Lancastrians and then the Tudors in the Wars of the Roses, became Archbishop of Canterbury and Lord Chancellor of England in 1486, near the beginning of Henry VII's reign. He was granted his cardinal's hat, at Henry's request, by Pope Alexander VI in 1493. As a youth, More was in service in Morton's household, and More seems to have held him in considerable affection. See pp. 27, 72n66.

[45] "Amiable reverence" = "friendly concern," "regard."

[46] "So that therewith were not joined impudency" = "so that it was not combined with shameless effrontery."

[47] "As apt and meet to have an administration in the weal public" = "as well suited to having an office in the commonwealth."

[48] "Made perfect" = "had perfected."

the chief of his youth he was taken from school into the court, and there passed all his time in much trouble and business, being continually tumbled and tossed in the waves of divers misfortunes and adversities. And so by many and great dangers he learned the experience of the world, which so being learned cannot easily be forgotten.

"It chanced on a certain day, when I sat at his table, there was also a certain layman cunning in the laws of your realm, who, I cannot tell whereof, taking occasion, began diligently and earnestly to praise that straight and rigorous justice which at that time was there executed upon felons, who as he said, were for the most part twenty hanged together upon one gallows. And, seeing so few escaped punishment, he said he could not choose but greatly wonder and marvel how and by what evil luck it should so come to pass that thieves, nevertheless, were in every place so rife and so rank. 'Nay Sir,' quoth I (for I durst boldly speak my mind before the cardinal), 'marvel nothing hereat, for this punishment of thieves passes the limits of justice and is also very hurtful to the weal public, for it is too extreme and cruel a punishment for theft and yet not sufficient to refrain and withhold men from theft; for simple theft is not so great an offense that it ought to be punished with death; neither there is any punishment so horrible that it can keep them from stealing which have no other craft whereby to get their living. Therefore, in this point not you only, but also the most part of the world, be like evil schoolmasters which be readier to beat than to teach their scholars. For great and horrible punishments be appointed for thieves, whereas much rather provision should have been made that there were some means whereby they might get their living, so that no man should be driven to this extreme necessity, first to steal, and then to die.' 'Yes,' quoth he, 'this matter is well enough provided for already. There be handicrafts, there is husbandry to get their living by, if they would not willing be naught.'[50] 'Nay,' quoth I, 'you shall not escape so. For first of all, I will speak nothing of them that come home out of the wars maimed and lame, as not long ago out of Blackheath field and, a little before that, out of the wars in France.[51] Such, I say, as put their lives in jeopardy for the weal public's or the king's sake, and by reason of weakness and lameness be not able to occupy their old

Of laws not made according to equity.[49]

By what means there might be fewer thieves and robbers.

---

[49] "Laws not made according to equity" = "laws not fairly or rightly made."

[50] "Would not willing be naught" = "would not willingly refuse."

[51] Blackheath, in the county of Kent, is located just south of Greenwich in the vicinity of London. It was the site of the final battle in the Cornish Rising of 1497, mentioned earlier. The hostilities with France, mentioned here, occurred in 1492–93.

crafts, and be too aged to learn new, of them I will speak nothing, forasmuch as wars have their ordinary recourse.

"'But let us consider those things that chance daily before our eyes. First, there is a great number of gentlemen which cannot be content to live idle themselves, like dors,[52] of that which others have labored for, their tenants I mean, whom they poll and shave[53] to the quick by raising their rents (for this only point of frugality do they use, men else through their lavish and prodigal spending, able to bring themselves to very beggary). These gentlemen, I say, do not only live in idleness themselves, but also carry about with them at their tails a great flock or train of idle and loitering servingmen,[55] which never learned any craft whereby to get their livings. These men, as soon as their master is dead or be sick themselves, be incontinent thrust out of doors,[56] for gentlemen had rather keep idle persons than sick men, and many times the dead man's heir is not able to maintain so great a house and keep so many servingmen as his father did. Then in the mean season[57] they that be thus destitute of service either starve for hunger or manfully play the thieves. For what would you have them to do? When they have wandered abroad so long until they have worn threadbare their apparel and also appaired[58] their health, then gentlemen, because of their pale and sickly faces and patched coats, will not take them into service, and husbandmen[59] dare not set them a work, knowing well enough that he is nothing meet[60] to do true and faithful service to a poor man with a spade and a mattock for small wages and hard fare, which, being daintily and tenderly pampered up in idleness and pleasure, was wont with a sword and a buckler[61] by his side to jet through the street with a bragging look[62] and to think himself too good to be any man's mate.'

Idleness, the mother of thieves.

Landlords by the way checked for rent-raising.[54]

Of idle servingmen come thieves.

---

[52]"Dors" = "drones," "lazy idlers."

[53]"Poll and shave" = "plunder and extort." The terms derived originally from tonsuring the heads of monks and friars.

[54]"Landlords by the way checked for rent-raising" = "landlords rebuked in passing for rent-raising."

[55]"Servingmen" = "servants."

[56]"Be incontinent thrust out of doors" = "be straightaway thrown out of the household."

[57]"In the mean season" = "meanwhile."

[58]"Appaired" = "injured."

[59]"Husbandmen" = "farmers."

[60]"Nothing meet" = "not suited," "not fit."

[61]"Buckler" = "shield."

[62]"Bragging look" = "swaggering manner."

"'Nay, by Saint Mary, Sir,' quoth the lawyer, 'not so. For this kind of men must we make most of. For in them, as men of stouter stomachs,[63] bolder spirits, and manlier courages than handicraftsmen and ploughmen be, doth consist the whole power, strength, and puissance[64] of our army when we must fight in battle.' 'Forsooth, Sir, as well you might say,' quoth I, 'that for war's sake you must cherish thieves, for surely you shall never lack thieves, while you have them. No, nor thieves be not the most false and faint-hearted soldiers, nor soldiers be not the cowardliest

Between soldiers and thieves small diversity.

thieves, so well these two crafts agree together. But this fault, though it be much used among you, yet is it not peculiar to you only, but common almost to all nations.

"'Yet France, besides this, is troubled and infected with a much sorer plague. The whole realm is filled and besieged with hired soldiers in peacetime (if that be peace) which be brought in under the same color and pretense that hath persuaded you to keep these idle servingmen. For these wisefools[65] and very archdolts thought the wealth of the whole country herein to consist, if there were ever in a readiness a strong and a sure garrison, specially of old practiced soldiers, for they put no trust at all in men unexercised.[66] And, therefore, they must be forced to seek for war to the end they may ever have practiced soldiers and cunning manslayers, lest that (as it is prettily said of Sallust) their hands and their minds, through idleness or lack of exercise, should wax dull.[67] But how pernicious and pestilent a thing it is to maintain such beasts the Frenchmen, by their own harms, have learned, and the examples of the Romans,

What inconveniences cometh by continual garrisons of soldiers.

Carthaginians, Syrians, and many other countries do manifestly declare. For not only the empire, but also the fields and cities of these by divers occasions have been overrun and destroyed of their own armies beforehand had in a readiness.[68] Now how unnecessary a thing this is. Hereby it may appear that the French soldiers, which from their youth have been practiced and inured in feats of arms, do not crack nor advance themselves to have very often got the upper hand[69] and mastery of your

---

[63] "Stouter stomachs" = "fiercer temperaments."

[64] "Puissance" = "power."

[65] "Wisefools" is the literal translation of the word *Morosophis,* a Latinized form of a compound Greek word, which More used in the original Latin text.

[66] "Unexercised" = "not trained," "not regularly drilled in maneuvers."

[67] From Sallust's *Cataline,* 16.3.

[68] "Of their own armies beforehand had in a readiness" = "by their own standing armies."

[69] "Do not crack nor advance themselves to have very often got the upper hand" = "cannot boast that they have often gotten the upper hand."

new-made and unpracticed soldiers. But in this point I will not use many words lest perchance I may seem to flatter you. No, nor those same handicraftmen of yours in cities, nor yet the rude and uplandish[70] ploughmen of the country, are not supposed to be greatly afraid of your gentlemen's idle servingmen, unless it be such as be not of body or stature correspondent to their strength and courage, or else whose bold stomachs be discouraged through poverty. Thus you may see that it is not to be feared lest they should be effeminated,[71] if they were brought up in good crafts and laborsome works whereby to get their livings, whose stout and sturdy bodies (for gentlemen vouchsafe to corrupt and spill[72] none but picked and chosen men) now, either by reason of rest and idleness, be brought to weakness, or else by too easy and womanly exercises to be made feeble and unable to endure hardness. Truly, howsoever the case standeth, this methinketh is nothing available[73] to the weal public, for war sake, which you never have, but when you will yourselves to keep and maintain an innumerable flock of that sort of men that be so troublesome and noyous[74] in peace, whereof you ought to have a thousand times more regard than of war.

"'But yet this is not only the necessary cause of stealing. There is another which, as I suppose, is proper and peculiar to you Englishmen alone.' 'What is that,' quoth the cardinal? 'Forsooth, my lord,' quoth I, 'your sheep that were wont to be so meek and tame and so small eaters, now, as I hear say, be become so great devourers and so wild that they eat up and swallow down the very men themselves. They consume, destroy, and devour whole fields, houses, and cities. For look in what parts of the realm doth grow the finest and therefore dearest wool. There noblemen and gentlemen, yea, and certain abbots, holy men no doubt, not contenting themselves with the yearly revenues and profits that were wont to grow to their forefathers and predecessors of their lands, nor being content that they live in rest and pleasure nothing profiting, yea, much annoying the weal public, leave no ground for tillage. They enclose all into pastures, they throw down houses, they pluck down towns and leave nothing standing, but only the church to be made a sheephouse.[75] And as though you lost no

> English sheep, devourers of men.

---

[70]"Uplandish" = "boorish."

[71]In More's original Latin, the word is *effoeminentur,* from the verb *effemino* (or *effoemino*), meaning "to deprive of masculine qualities" or "to make womanish."

[72]"Spill" = "ruin."

[73]"Available" = "beneficial."

[74]"Noyous" = "vexatious."

[75]For discussion of enclosure and related processes of agricultural change, see pp. 33–34, 74*n*85.

small quantity of ground by forests, chases, lands, and parks, those good holy men turn all dwelling places and all glebe land [76] into desolation and wilderness.

"'Therefore, that one covetous and insatiable cormorant [77] and very plague of his native country may compass about and enclose many thousand acres of ground together within one pale [78] or hedge, the husbandmen be thrust out of their own, or else either by covin [79] and fraud or by violent oppression, they be put besides it, or by wrongs and injuries they be so wearied that they be compelled to sell all. By one means, therefore, or by other, either by hook or crook, they must needs depart away poor, silly, wretched souls: men, women, husbands, wives, fatherless children, widows, woeful mothers with their young babes, and their whole household small in substance and much in number, as husbandry requireth many hands. Away they trudge, I say, out of their known and accustomed houses, finding no place to rest in. All their household stuff, which is very little worth though it might well abide the sale, yet being suddenly thrust out, they be constrained to sell it for a thing of naught. And when they have wandered abroad till that be spent, what can they then else do but steal, and then justly pardy [80] be hanged, or else go about a-begging? And yet then also they be cast in prison as vagabonds, because they go about and work not, whom no man will set a-work, though they never so willingly proffer themselves thereto. For one shepherd or herdsman is enough to eat up that ground with cattle, to the occupying whereof about husbandry many hands were requisite. And this is also the cause why victuals be now in many places dearer. Yea, besides this the price of wool is so risen that poor folks which were wont to work it and make cloth thereof, be now able to buy none at all. And by this means very many be forced to forsake work and to give themselves to idleness. For after that so much ground was enclosed for pasture, an infinite multitude of sheep died of the rot, such vengeance God took of their inordinate and unsatiable covetousness, send-

Sheepmasters, decayers of husbandry.

The decay of husbandry causeth beggary, which is the mother of vagabonds and thieves.

The cause of dearth of victuals.

What inconvenience cometh of dearth of wool.

---

[76] Glebe land is a portion of land assigned to a clergyman as part of his benefice.

[77] The cormorant has a long history as a symbol of greed, tracing its way, according to Erasmus, back to Aristophanes. See Desiderius Erasmus, *Adages,* trans. R. A. B. Mynors, in *Collected Works of Erasmus,* vol. 33 (Toronto: University of Toronto Press, 1991), pp. 90–91, and vol. 34 (Toronto: University of Toronto Press, 1992), pp. 144–45.

[78] "Pale" = "fence."

[79] "Covin" = "collusion."

[80] "Pardy" = "by God!"

ing among the sheep that pestiferous murrain [81] which much more justly
should have fallen on the sheepmasters' own heads.
And though the number of sheep increase never so
fast, yet the price falleth not one mite, [82] because there
be so few sellers. For they be almost all coming into a few rich men's
hands, whom no need forceth to sell before they lust, [83] and they lust not
before they may sell as dear as they lust. [84]

The cause of dearth of
wool.

"'Now the same cause bringeth in like dearth of the
other kinds of cattle, yea, and that so much the more
because that, after farms plucked down and husbandry
decayed, there is no man that passeth for the breeding of young store. [85]

Dearth of cattle with the
cause thereof.

For these rich men bring not up the young ones of great cattle as they
do lambs. But first they buy them abroad very cheap and afterward,
when they be fatted in their pastures, they sell them again exceedingly
dear, and, therefore, as I suppose, the whole incommodity hereof is not
yet felt, for that they make dearth only in those places where they sell.
But when they shall fetch them away from thence whereby they be bred
faster than they can be brought up, then shall there also be felt great
dearth, store [86] beginning there to fail where the ware is bought. Thus
the unreason-able covetousness of a few hath turned that thing to the
utter undoing of your island, in the which thing the
chief felicity of your realm did consist. For this great
dearth of victuals causeth men to keep as little houses
and as small hospitality as they possibly may, and to put
away their servants. Whither, I pray you, but a-begging, or else (which
these gentle bloods and stout stomachs will soon set their minds unto)
a-stealing?

Dearth of victuals is the
decay of housekeeping,
whereof ensueth beggary
and theft.

"'Now to amend the matter, [87] to this wretched beggary and miserable poverty is joined great wantonness, importunate superfluity, and

---

[81] "Murrain" refers to one of several infectious diseases of sheep and cattle.

[82] A mite is a very small unit of coinage; hence the phrase "not one mite" in present-day
terms might mean "not one penny," or in Robynson's day, when the penny was worth far
more than it is now, "not one farthing."

[83] "Lust" = "desire," "please."

[84] At this point in the original Latin text, More says that although one cannot speak of
these activities of the landlords first as a monopoly, because there is more than one seller,
the trade is held in such few hands that it is an oligopoly. The latter word is a combination
of Greek roots that together mean "few sellers." There is no known ancient Greek instance
of this usage; More seems to have invented it himself for the present purpose. See CW 4,
pp. 68–69.

[85] "There is no man that passeth for the breeding of young store" = "no one is able to
maintain breeding stock."

[86] "Store" = "stock," "supplies."

[87] "Now to amend the matter" = "now to go one better."

excessive riot.[88] For not only gentlemen's servants, but also handicraftsmen, yea, and almost the ploughmen of the country, with all other sorts of people, use much strange and proud newfangledness in their apparel and too much prodigal riot[89] and sumptuous fare at their table.

Excess in apparel and diet, a maintainer of beggary and theft.

Now bawds, queans,[90] whores, harlots, strumpets, brothelhouses, stews and yet another stews,[91] wine taverns, alehouses, and tippling houses, with so many naughty, lewd, and unlawful games as dice, cards, tables,[92] tennis, bowls, quoits,[93] do not all these send the haunters of them straight a-stealing when their money is gone? Cast out these pernicious abominations. Make a law that they, which plucked down farms and towns of husbandry, shall re-edify[94] them, or else yield and uprender[95] the possession thereof to such as will go to the cost of building them anew. Suffer not these rich men to buy up all, to engross and forestall,[96] and with their monopoly[97] to keep the market alone as please them. Let not so many be brought up in idleness; let husbandry and tillage be restored; let clothworking be renewed that there may be honest labors for this idle sort to pass their time in profitably, which hitherto either poverty hath caused to be thieves, or else now be either vagabonds or idle servingmen and shortly will be thieves.

Bawds, whores, wine taverns, alehouses, and unlawful games be very mothers of thieves.

Rich men, engrossers, and forestallers.

"'Doubtless, unless you find a remedy for these enormities, you shall in vain advance yourselves of executing justice upon felons, for this justice is more beautiful in appearance and more flourishing to the show

---

[88]"Great wantonness, importunate superfluity, and excessive riot" = "great extravagance, grievous self-indulgence, and excessive debauchery."

[89]"Prodigal riot" = "wasteful dissipation."

[90]"Queans" = "prostitutes."

[91]A "stew" is a bath house, particularly one used as a brothel. "Stews," in the plural, often refers to a street or district of brothels.

[92]"Tables" = "backgammon."

[93]The game of tennis referred to here is "real tennis," in which a ball is hit with a racket back and forth by two players in an enclosed oblong court. Bowls is played by rolling a round bowl closest to a designated spot on a bowling green. Quoits was a game played by tossing a disk of stone or a ring of iron at a stake placed in the ground.

[94]"Re-edify" = "rebuild."

[95]"Uprender" = "surrender."

[96]"To engross" is to gather something of value — commodities, manufactured goods, lands, etc. — into a single set of hands. To forestall is to buy up goods before they reach the market with a view to enhancing the price.

[97]"Monopoly" derives from the Greek, meaning "single seller." In the original Latin text, all discussions of this subject trace themselves back to Book I of Aristotle's *Politics*, I.10.1259a6–36. For more on this subject, see pp. 37, 74*n*90.

than either just or profitable. For by suffering your
youth wantonly and viciously[98] to be brought up and to
be infected, even from their tender age, by little and
little with vice, then, a God's name,[99] to be punished
when they commit the same faults after being come to man's state, which
from their youth they were ever like to do. In this point, I pray you, what
other thing do you than make thieves and then punish them?'

The corrupt education of youth, a mother of thievery.

"Now as I was thus speaking, the lawyer began to make himself ready
to answer and was determined with himself to use the common fashion
and trade of disputers, which be more diligent in rehearsing than answering, as thinking the memory worthy of the chief praise. 'Indeed, Sir,'
quoth he, 'you have said well, being but a stranger, and one that might
rather hear something of these matters than have any exact or perfect
knowledge of the same, as I will incontinent[100] by open proof make manifest and plain. For first I will rehearse in order all that you have said;
then I will declare wherein you be deceived through lack of knowledge
in all our fashions, manners, and customs; and last of all I will answer
your arguments and confute them every one. First, therefore, I will begin where I promised. Four things you seemed to me —'

"'Hold your peace,' quoth the cardinal, 'for it appeareth that you will make no short answer which
make such a beginning. Wherefore, at this time you
shall not take the pains to make your answer, but keep
it to your next meeting, which I would be right glad that it might be even
tomorrow next, unless either you or Master Raphael have any earnest
let.[101] But now, Master Raphael, I would very gladly hear of you why you
think theft not worthy to be punished with death, or what other punishment you can devise more expedient to the weal public, for I am sure you
are not of that mind that you would have theft escape unpunished. For if
now the extreme punishment of death cannot cause them to leave stealing, then if ruffians and robbers should be sure of their lives, what violence, what fear were able to hold their hands from robbing, which
would take the mitigation of the punishment as a very provocation to the
mischief?'

He is worthily put to flight that is too full of words.

"'Surely my lord,' quoth I, 'I think it not right nor
justice that the loss of money should cause the loss of

That theft ought not to be punished by death.

---

[98] "Wantonly and viciously" = "recklessly and dissolutely."
[99] "A God's name" = "in God's name."
[100] "Incontinent" = "straightway," "immediately."
[101] "Earnest let" = "serious hindrance," "impediment."

man's life. For mine opinion is that all the goods in the world are not able to countervail man's life. But if they would thus say that the breaking of justice and the transgression of the laws is recompensed with this punishment and not the loss of the money, then why may not this extreme and rigorous justice well be called plain injury. For so cruel governance, so strait[102] rules and unmerciful laws   *Strait laws not allowable.* be not allowable, that if a small offense be committed, by and by the sword should be drawn.[103] Nor so stoical ordinances are to be born withal, as to count all offenses of such equality that the killing of a man or the taking of his money from him were both a matter, and the one no more heinous offense than the other, between the which two, if we have any respect to equity, no similitude or equality consisteth.[104] God commandeth us that we shall not kill. And be we then so hasty to kill a man for taking a little money? And if any man would understand killing by this commandment of God to be forbidden after no larger wise than man's constitutions define[105] killing to be lawful, then why may it not likewise by man's constitutions be determined after what sort whoredom, fornication, and perjury may be   *That man's law ought not to be prejudicial to God's* lawful? For whereas, by the permission of God, no man   *law.* hath power to kill neither himself nor yet any other man, then if a law, made by the consent of men concerning slaughter of men, ought to be of such strength, force, and virtue that they which, contrary to the commandment of God, have killed those whom this constitution of man commanded to be killed, be clean quit and exempt out of the bonds and danger of God's commandment,[106] shall it not then by this reason follow that the power of God's commandment shall extend no further than man's law doth define and permit? And so shall it come to pass that in like manner man's constitutions in all things shall determine how far the observation of all God's commandments shall extend. To be short, Moses' law, though it were ungentle and sharp, as a law that was given to bondmen, yea, and them very   *Theft in the old law not punished by death.* obstinate, stubborn, and stiff-necked, yet it punished

---

[102]"Strait" = "strict."

[103]At this point in the original Latin text, More and the accompanying marginal note by Giles and Erasmus refer to the "Manlian edicts" discussed by Livy, VIII.vii.1–22.

[104]The reference to "stoical ordinances" in this sentence is to the ancient Stoic paradox asserting that all crimes are equal, which Cicero describes and criticizes in *De finibus,* 4.9.21–23, 4.27.75, 4.28.77.

[105]"Be forbidden after no larger wise than man's constitutions define" = "be interpreted as extending no further than what human laws decree."

[106]"Be clean quit and exempt out of the bonds and danger of God's commandment" = "are not held guilty of violating God's commandment and are freed from punishment."

theft by the purse and not with death.[107] And let us not think that God, in the new law of clemency and mercy under the which He rules us with fatherly gentleness as His dear children, hath given us great scope and license to the execution of cruelty one upon another.

"'Now ye have heard the reasons whereby I am persuaded that this punishment is unlawful. Furthermore, I think there is nobody that knoweth not how unreasonable, yea, how pernicious a thing it is to the weal public that a thief and a homicide or murderer should suffer equal and like punishment. For the thief, seeing that man that is condemned for theft in no less jeopardy nor judged to no less punishment than him that is convicted of manslaughter, through this cogitation only he is strongly and forcibly provoked and in a manner constrained to kill him whom else he would have but robbed. For the murder being once done, he is in less fear and in more hope that the deed shall not be betrayed or known, seeing the party is now dead and rid out of the way which only might have uttered[108] and disclosed it. But if he chance to be taken and descried,[109] yet he is in no more danger and jeopardy than if he had committed but single felony. Therefore, whiles we go about with such cruelty to make thieves afraid, we provoke them to kill good men.

"'Now, as touching this question: what punishment were more commodious and better? That truly in my judgment is easier to be found than what punishment might be worse. For why should we doubt that to be a good and a profitable way for the punishment of offenders, which we know did in times past so long please the Romans, men in the administration of a weal public most expert, politic, and cunning? Such as among them were convict of great and heinous trespasses,[110] them they condemned into stone quarries and into mines to dig metal, there to be kept in chains all the days of their life. But as concerning this matter, I allow the ordinance of no nation so well as that which I saw, while I traveled abroad about the world, used in Persia among the people that commonly be called the Polylerites,[111]

Marginal notes:

What inconvenience ensueth of punishing theft with death.

Punishing of theft by death causeth the thief to be a murderer.

What lawful punishment may be devised for theft.

How the Romans punished theft.

A worthy and commendable punishment of thieves in the weal public of the Polylerites in Persia.

---

[107] See *Exodus*, 22:1–4.
[108] "Uttered" = "published."
[109] "Taken and descried" = "captured and denounced."
[110] "Trespasses" = "damaging wrongs."
[111] The name of the Polylerites, made up by More, is based on two Greek words, meaning together "much nonsense."

whose land is both large and ample and also well and wittily governed,
and the people in all conditions free and ruled by their own laws, saving
that they pay a yearly tribute to the great king of Persia. But because
they be far from the sea, compassed, and enclosed almost round about
with high mountains and do content themselves with the fruits of their
own land, which is of itself very fertile and fruitful, for this cause neither
they go to other countries nor other come to them. And according to the
old custom of the land, they desire not to enlarge the bounds of their dominions; and those that they have by reason of the high hills be easily
defended; and the tribute which they pay to their chief lord and king
sets them quite free from warfare. Thus their life is commodious rather
than gallant[112] and may better be called happy, or wealthy, than notable or famous. For they be not known as much as by name, I suppose,
saving only to their next neighbors and borders. They that in the land
be attainted and convict[113] of felony make restitution of that which they
stole to the right owner and not (as they do in other
lands) to the king, whom they think to have no more   A privy nip[114] for them
right to the thief-stolen thing than the thief himself   that do otherwise.
hath. But if the thing be lost or made away, then the value of it is paid of
the goods of such offenders, which else remaineth all whole to their
wives and children. And they themselves be condemned to be common
laborers, and, unless the theft be very heinous, they be
neither locked in prison nor fettered in gyves,[115] but be   Thieves condemned to be
untied and go at large, laboring in the common works.   common laborers.
They that refuse labor, or go slowly and slackly to their work, be not only
tied in chains but also pricked forward with stripes.[116] But being diligent
about their work they live without check or rebuke. Every night they be
called in by name and be locked in their chambers. Beside their daily labor, their life is nothing hard or incommodious. Their fare is indifferent
good, borne at the charges of the weal public, because they be common
servants to the commonwealth. But their charges in all places of the land .
is not borne alike, for in some parts that which is bestowed upon them
is gathered of alms.[117] And though that way be uncertain, yet the people
be so full of mercy and pity that none is found more profitable or plentiful. In some places certain lands be appointed hereunto of the revenues

---

[112]"Commodious rather than gallant" = "comfortable rather than grand."
[113]"Attainted and convict" = "accused and found guilty."
[114]"Privy nip" = "private rebuke."
[115]"Gyves" = "shackles."
[116]"Stripes" = "lashes of the whip."
[117]"Gathered of alms" = "from charitable donations."

whereof they be maintained; and in some places every man gives a certain tribute for the same use and purpose. Again, in some parts of the land these servingmen (for so be Servingmen. these damned persons called) do no common work, but as every private man needeth laborers, so he cometh into the marketplace and there hireth some of them for meat and drink and a certain limited wages by the day, somewhat cheaper than he should hire a free man. It is also lawful for them to chastise the sloth of the servingmen with stripes. By this means they never lack work and, besides the gaining of their meat and drink, every one of them bringeth daily something into the common treasury. All and every one of them be appareled in one color. Their heads be not polled [118] or shaven, but rounded a little above the ears, and the tip of one ear is cut off. Every one of them may take meat and drink of their friends, and also a coat of their own color, but to receive money is death, as well to the giver as to the receiver. And no less jeopardy it is for a free man to receive money of a servingman for any manner of cause, and likewise for servingmen to touch weapons. The servingmen of every several shire [119] be distinct and known from other by their several and distinct badges which to cast away is death, as it is also to be seen out of the precinct of their own shire or to talk with a servingman of another shire. And it is no less danger to them for to intend to run away than to do it in deed. Yea, An evil intent esteemed as the deed. and to conceal such an enterprise in a servingman it is death; in a free man servitude. Of the contrary part, to him that openeth and uttereth [120] such counsels be decreed large gifts; to a free man a great sum of money; to a servingman freedom; and to them both forgiveness and pardon of that they were of counsel in that pretense. So that it can never be so good for them to go forward in their evil purpose as by repentance to turn back.

"'This is the law and order in this behalf, as I have showed you. Wherein what humanity is used, how far it is from cruelty, and how commodious it is, you do plainly perceive. Forasmuch as the end of their wrath and punishment intendeth noth- The right end and intent of punishment. ing else but the destruction of vices and saving of men, with so using and ordering them that they cannot choose but be good, and what harm soever they did before, in the residue of their life to make amends for the same. Moreover, it is so little feared that they should turn

---

[118] "Polled" = "cropped."
[119] "Shire" = "county," "administrative division."
[120] "Openeth and uttereth" = "reveals and reports."

again to their vicious conditions that wayfaring men [121] will for their safe-guard choose them to their guides before any other, in every shire changing and taking new, for if they would commit robbery, they have nothing about them meet for that purpose. They may touch no weapons; money found about them should betray the robbery. They should be no sooner taken with the manner, but forthwith they should be punished. Neither they can have any hope at all to escape away by fleeing, for how should a man that in no part of his apparel is like other men fly privily [122] and unknown, unless he would run away naked? Howbeit, so also flying he should be descried by the rounding of his head and his earmark. But it is a thing to be doubted that they will lay their heads together and conspire against the weal public. No, no, I warrant you. For the servingmen of one shire alone could never hope to bring to pass such an enterprise without soliciting, enticing, and alluring the servingmen of many other shires to take their parts, which thing is to them so impossible that they may not as much as speak or talk together or salute one another. No, it is not to be thought that they would make their own countrymen and companions of their counsel [123] in such a matter, which they know well should be jeopardy to the concealer thereof and great commodity and goodness to the opener and detector of the same. Whereas, on the other part, there is none of them all hopeless or in despair to recover again his former state of freedom, by humble obedience, by patient suffering, and by giving good tokens [124] and likelihood of himself that he will ever after that live like a true and an honest man. For every year divers of them be returned to their freedom through the commendation of their patience.'

"When I had thus spoken, saying, moreover, that I could see no cause why this order might not be had in England with much more profit than the justice which the lawyer so highly praised. 'Nay,' quoth the lawyer, 'this could never be so established in England, but that it must needs bring the weal public into great jeopardy and hazard.' And, as he was thus saying, he shook his head and made a wry mouth and so he held his peace. And all that were there present, with one assent, agreed to his saying.

"'Well,' quoth the cardinal, 'yet it were hard to judge without a proof whether this order would do well here or no. But when the sentence of death is given, if then the king should command execution to be deferred and spared and would prove this order and fashion, taking away

[121] "Wayfaring men" = "travelers by road."
[122] "Privily" = "secretly."
[123] "Of their counsel" = "privy to their plans."
[124] "Good tokens" = "good signs," "good evidence."

the privileges of all sanctuaries,[125] if then the proof should declare the thing to be good and profitable, then it were well done that it were established, else the condemned and reprieved persons may as well and as justly be put to death after this proof as when they were first cast. Neither any jeopardy can in the mean space grow hereof. Yea, and me thinketh that these vagabonds may very well be ordered after the same fashion against whom we have hitherto made so many laws and so little prevailed.'

Vagabonds.[126]

"When the cardinal had thus said, then every man gave great praise to my sayings, which a little before they had disallowed. But most of all was esteemed that which was spoken of vagabonds, because it was the cardinal's own addition. I cannot tell whether it were best to rehearse the communication that followed, for it was not very sad.[127] But yet you shall hear it, for there was no evil in it, and partly it pertained to the matter before said.

The wavering judgments of flatterers.

"There chanced to stand by a certain jesting parasite,[128] or scoffer, which would seem to resemble and counterfeit the fool. But he did in such wise counterfeit that he was almost the very same indeed that he labored to represent. He so studied with words and sayings brought forth so out of time and place to make sport and move laughter that he himself was oftener laughed at than his jests were. Yet the foolish fellow brought out now and then such indifferent and reasonable stuff that he made the proverb true which saith: *He that shooteth oft, at the last shall hit the mark.*[129] So that when one of the company said that through my communication a good order was found for thieves, and that the cardinal also had well provided for vagabonds so that only remained some good provision to be made for them that through sickness and age were fallen into poverty and were become so impotent and unwieldy that they were not able to work for their living: 'Tush,' quoth he, 'let me alone with them; you shall see me do well enough with them. For I had rather than any good[130] that this kind of people were driven somewhere out of my sight, they have so sore troubled me many times and oft, when they have with

Sick, aged, impotent persons and beggars.

---

[125] More refers here to the privilege of sanctuary, or immunity from arrest, enjoyed under the law by fugitives from justice when in the precincts of a church or monastery. For discussion, see pp. 40, 44, 75*n*101.

[126] "Vagabonds" = "vagrants," "idle wanderers."

[127] "Not very sad" = "not very serious-minded."

[128] "Parasite" = "toady," "hanger-on."

[129] In the original Latin text, the proverb relates to the throwing of dice; it is derived from Cicero's *De Divinatione* 2.59.121. See CW 4, p. 356.

[130] "For I had rather than any good" = "for more than anything."

their lamentable tears begged money of me, and yet they could never to my mind so tune their song that thereby they ever got of me one farthing. For evermore the one of these two chanced: either that I would not or else that I could not because I had it not. Therefore, now they be waxed wise, for when they see me go by, because they will not leese their labor,[131] they let me pass and say not one word to me. So they look for nothing of me, no, in good sooth no more than if I were a priest or a monk. But I will make a law that all these beggars shall be distributed and bestowed into houses of religion. The men shall be made lay brethren, as they call them, and the women nuns.'

> A common proverb[132] among beggars.

"Hereat the cardinal smiled and allowed it in jest, yea, and all the residue in good earnest. But a certain friar, graduate in divinity,[133] took such pleasure and delight in the jest of priests and monks that he also, being else a man of grizzly[134] and stern gravity, began merrily and wantonly to test and taunt. 'Nay,' quoth he, 'you shall not so be rid and dispatched of beggars unless you make some provision also for us friars.' 'Why,' quoth the jester, 'that is done already, for my lord himself set a very good order for you when he decreed that vagabonds should be kept straight and set to work, for you be the greatest and veriest vagabonds that be.' This jest also, when they saw the cardinal not disprove it, every man took it gladly, saving only the friar, for he (and that no marvel), being thus touched on the quick and hit on the gall,[135] so fret, so fumed and chafed at it, and was in such a rage that he could not refrain himself from chiding, scolding, railing, and reviling. He called the fellow ribald, villain, javel,[136] backbiter, slanderer, and the child of perdition, citing, therewith, terrible threatenings out of Holy Scripture. Then the jesting scoffer began to play the scoffer indeed, and, verily, he was good at it, for he could play a part in that play, no man better. 'Patient yourself, good master friar,' quoth he, 'and be not angry, for Scripture saith: *In your patience you shall save your souls.*'[137] Then the friar (for I will rehearse his own very words): 'No, gallow's wretch, I am not angry,' quoth he, 'or, at the least wise, I do not sin, for the psalmist saith: *Be you angry and sin not.*'[138] Then the cardinal spake

> A merry talk between a friar and a fool.

> Talk qualified according to the person that speaketh.

---

[131]"Leese their labor" = "part with their labor," i.e., "make an extra effort."
[132]"Proverb" = "saying."
[133]"Graduate in divinity" = "holding a university degree from the faculty of theology."
[134]"Grizzly" = "gray," "venerable."
[135]"Hit on the gall" = "struck on a tender or sore point."
[136]"Javel" = "rascal."
[137]Luke 21:19.
[138]Psalms 4:4.

gently to the friar and desired him to quiet himself. 'No, my lord,' quoth he, 'I speak not but of a good zeal as I ought, for holy men had a good zeal. Wherefore it is said: *The zeal of thy house hath eaten me.*[139] And it is sung in the church: *The scorners of Elisha, whiles he went up into the house of God, felt the zeal of the bald,*[140] as peradventure this scorning villain ribald shall feel.' 'You do it,' quoth the cardinal, 'perchance of a good mind and affection, but methinketh you should do, I cannot tell whether more holily, certes[141] more wisely, if you would not set your wit to a fool's wit, and with a fool take in hand a foolish contention.' 'No, forsooth, my lord,' quoth he, 'I should not do more wisely. For Solomon the wise saith: *Answer a fool according to his folly,*[142] like as I do now, and do show him the pit that he shall fall into if he take not heed. For if many scorners of Elisha, which was but one bald man, felt the zeal of the bald, how much more shall one scorner of many friars feel, among whom be many bald men? And we have also the pope's bulls, whereby all that mock and scorn us be excommunicate, suspended, and accursed.' The cardinal, seeing that none end would be made, sent away the jester by a privy beck[143] and turned the communication to another matter. Shortly after, when he was risen from the table, he went to hear his suitors and so dismissed us.

"Look, Master More, with how long and tedious a tale I have kept you, which surely I would have been ashamed to have done, but that you so earnestly desired me and did after such a sort give ear unto it as though you would not that any parcel of that communication should be left out. Which, though I have done somewhat briefly, yet could I not choose but rehearse it for the judgment of them, which, when they had improved and disallowed my sayings, yet incontinent, hearing the cardinal allow them, did themselves also approve the same. So impudently flattering him that they were nothing ashamed to admit, yea, almost in good earnest, his jester's foolish inventions, because that he himself by smiling at them did seem not to disprove them. So that hereby you may right well perceive how little the courtiers would regard and esteem me and my sayings."

"I ensure you, Master Raphael," quoth I, "I took great delectation in hearing you. All things that you said were spoken so wittily and so pleasantly. And methought myself to be in the meantime not only at home in my country, but also through the pleasant remembrance of the cardinal,

---

[139] Psalms 69:9.
[140] The passage relates to a medieval hymn, attributed to Adam of St. Victor, derived from 2 Kings 2:23–24.
[141] "Certes" = "certainly."
[142] Proverbs 26:5.
[143] "Beck" = "signal," "gesture."

in whose house I was brought up of a child, to wax a child again. And, friend Raphael, though I did bear very great love towards you before, yet seeing you do so earnestly favor this man, you will not believe how much my love towards you is now increased. But yet, all this notwithstanding, I can by no means change my mind, but that I must needs believe that you, if you be disposed and can find in your heart to follow[144] some prince's court, shall with your good counsels greatly help and further the commonwealth, wherefore there is nothing more appertaining to your duty, that is to say to the duty of a good man. For whereas your Plato judgeth that weal publics shall by this means attain perfect felicity, either if philosophers be kings, or else if kings give themselves to the study of philosophy,[145] how far, I pray you, shall commonwealths then be from this felicity if philosophers will vouchsafe to entrust kings with their good counsel?"

"They be not so unkind," quoth he, "but they would gladly do it, yea, many have done it already in books that they have put forth, if kings and princes would be willing and ready to follow good counsel. But Plato doubtless did well foresee, unless kings themselves would apply their minds to the study of philosophy, that else they would never thoroughly allow the counsel of philosophers, being themselves before even from their tender age infected and corrupt with perverse and evil opinions, which thing Plato himself proved true in King Dionysius.[146] If I should propose to any king wholesome decrees, doing my endeavor to pluck out of his mind the pernicious original causes of vice and naughtiness, think you not that I should forthwith either be driven away or else made a laughingstock? Well, suppose I were with the French king[147] and there sitting in his council, whiles in that most secret consultation the king himself there being present in his own person, they beat their brains and search the very bottom of their wits to discuss by what craft and means the king may still keep Milan and draw to him again fugitive Naples.[148] And then how to con-

The Frenchmen privily counseled from the desire of Italy.

---

[144]"Follow" = "join."

[145]*Republic,* V.473c–d; for discussion see pp. 9–10.

[146]According to ancient sources, Plato, who reputedly visited Sicily twice during the reign of Dionysius the Younger of Syracuse, had no success in turning him from his tyranny into a philosopher-king.

[147]In 1515, the French king was Francis I.

[148]The references here are to France's Italian wars, begun when Charles VIII (1483–1498) invaded Italy in 1494, pursuing his claim to the kingdom of Naples. Louis XII (1498–1515) followed the same policy. Naples was gained and lost twice in that period, once each by the two kings — in 1495 and 1496, and again in 1501 and 1503. Louis also conquered Milan in 1499, but the Swiss forced the French to leave in 1512. As the passage continues, the

quer the Venetians and how to bring under his jurisdiction all Italy; then how to win the dominion of Flanders, Brabant, and of all Burgundy, with diverse other lands whose kingdoms he had long ago in mind and purpose invaded. Here, whiles one counseleth to conclude a league of peace with the Venetians, so long to endure as shall be thought meet and expedient for their purpose, and to make them also of their counsel, yea, and besides that to give them part of the prey, which afterward, when they have brought their purpose about after their own minds, they may require and claim again, another think- Lance knights.[149] eth best to hire the Germans; another would have the favor of the Swissers won with money; another's advice is to appease the puissant power of the emperor's majesty with gold, as with a most pleasant and acceptable sacrifice; whiles another giveth counsel to make peace with the king of Aragon and to restore unto him his own kingdom of Navarre as a full assurance of peace. Another cometh in with his five eggs[150] and adviseth to hook in the king of Castile with some hope of affinity or alliance and to bring to their part certain peers of his court for great pensions. Whiles they all stay at the chiefest doubt of all, what to do in the meantime with England, and yet agree all in this to make peace with the Englishmen, and with most sure and strong bands to bind that weak and feeble friendship so that they must be called friends and had in suspicion as enemies. And that, therefore, the Scots must be had in a readiness, as it were in a standing, ready at all occasions, in aunters[151] the Englishmen should stir never so little, incontinent to set upon them. And, moreover, privily and secretly (for openly it may not be done by the truce that is taken), privily, therefore, I say to make much of some peer of England that is banished his country, which must claim title to the crown of the realm and affirm himself just inheritance thereof, that by this subtle means they may hold to them the king in whom else they have but small trust and affiance. Here, I say, where so great and high matters be in consultation, where so many noble and wise men counsel their king only to war, here if I, silly man, should rise up and will them to turn over the leaf and learn a new lesson, saying that my counsel is not to meddle with Italy but to tarry still at home, and that the kingdom of

---

advice Hythloday suggests might be given at the council table about possible strategies and potential alliances reflects with great acumen the policy alternatives attempted or considered by the French in the pursuit of their wars in Italy.

[149]The marginal note "Lance knights" refers to the German pikemen or *landesknechte;* in the original Latin editions, the marginal note referred to "Swiss mercenaries."

[150]"Cometh in with his five eggs" = "interrupts fussily with an idle suggestion."

[151]"In aunters" = "in case."

France alone is almost greater than that it may well be governed of one man so that the king should not need to study how to get more. And then should propose unto them the decrees of the people that be called the Achorians,[152] which be situate over against the island of Utopia on the southeast side. These Achorians once made war in their king's quarrel for to get him another kingdom, which he laid claim unto and advanced himself right inheritor to the crown thereof by the title of an old alliance. At the last when they had gotten it and saw that they had even as much vexation and trouble in keeping it as they had in getting it, and that either their new-conquered subjects by sundry occasions were making daily insurrections to rebel against them, or else that other countries were continually with divers inroads and foragings invading them, so that they were ever fighting either for them or against them and never could break up their camps. Seeing themselves in the mean season pilled[153] and impoverished, their money carried out of the realm, their own men killed to maintain the glory of another nation, when they had no war, peace nothing better than war, by reason that their people in war had so inured themselves to corrupt and wicked manners that they had taken a delight and pleasure in robbing and stealing, that through manslaughter they had gathered[154] boldness to mischief, that their laws were had in contempt and nothing set by or regarded, that their king being troubled with the charge and governance of two kingdoms could not, nor was not able, perfectly to discharge his office towards them both, seeing again that all these evils and troubles were endless, as the last laid their heads together and like faithful and loving subjects gave to their king free choice and liberty to keep still the one of these two kingdoms whether he would, alleging that he was not able to keep both, and that they were more than might well be governed of half a king. Forasmuch as no man would be content to take him for his muleteer[155] that keepeth another man's mules besides his, so this good prince was constrained to be content with his old kingdom and to give over the new to one of his friends, who shortly after was violently driven out. Furthermore, if I should declare unto them that all this busy preparance to[156] war, whereby so many nations for his sake should be brought into a troublesome hurly-burly,

A notable example, and worthy to be followed.

---

[152]The name Achorians is derived from Greek roots, meaning "people without a country."

[153]"Pilled" = "plundered, despoiled."

[154]"Gathered" = "added."

[155]"Muleteer" = "mule driver."

[156]"Preparance to" = "preparation for."

when all his coffers were emptied, his treasures wasted and his people destroyed, should at the length through some mischance be in vain and to none effect. And that, therefore, it were best for him to content himself with his own kingdom of France as his forefathers and predecessors did before him, to make much of it, to enrich it and to make it as flourishing as he could, to endeavor himself to love his subjects and again to be beloved of them, willingly to live with them, peaceably to govern them and with other kingdoms not to meddle, seeing that which he hath already is even enough for him, yea, and more than he can well turn him to. This mine advice, Master More, how think you it would be heard and taken?" "So God help me not very thankfully," quoth I.

"Well, let us proceed then," quoth he. "Suppose that some king and his council were together whetting their wits and devising what subtle craft they might invent to enrich the king with great treasures of money.[157] First one counseleth to raise and enhance the valuation of money when the king must pay any, and again to call down[159] the value of coin to less than[160] it is worth when he must receive or gather any. For thus great sums shall be paid with a little money, and where little is due much shall be received. Another counseleth to feign war that when, under this color and pretense the king hath gathered great abundance of money, he may, when it shall please him, make peace with great solemnity and holy ceremonies to blind the eyes of the poor commonalty, as taking pity and compassion, forsooth, upon man's blood, like a loving and a merciful prince. Another putteth the king in remembrance of certain old and moth-eaten laws that of long time have not been in execution, which because no man can remember that they were made, every man hath transgressed. The fines of these laws he counseleth the king to require, for there is no way so profitable, nor more honorable, as the which hath a show and color of justice. Another adviseth him to forbid many things under great penalties and fines, especially such things as is for the people's profit not be used, and afterward to dispense for money with them, which by this prohibition sustain loss and damage, for by this means the favor of the

[margin note:] Enhancing and imbasing[158] of coins.

[margin note:] Counterfeit wars.

[margin note:] The renewing of old laws.

[margin note:] Restraints.

---

[157]The policies satirically discussed in this paragraph mention devices for raising money that monarchs in Europe, and especially the English kings Edward IV and Henry VII, used to enhance their treasures.

[158]"Imbasing" = "debasing."

[159]"Call down" = "debase," "devalue."

[160]In Robynson's original, the word given is *them,* a printer's error for *than.*

people is won and profit riseth two ways. First by taking forfeits of them whom covetousness of gains hath brought in danger of this statute, and also by selling privileges and licenses, Selling of licenses. which the better that the prince is, forsooth, the dearer he selleth them, as one that is loath to grant to any private person anything that is against the profit of his people and, therefore, may sell none but at an exceeding dear price. Another giveth the king counsel to endanger[161] unto his grace the judges of the realm, that he may have them ever on his side and that they may in every matter dispute and reason for the king's right. Yea, and further to call them into his palace and to require them there to argue and discuss his matters in his own presence. So there shall be no matter of his so openly wrong and unjust wherein one or other of them, either because he will have something to allege and object or that he is ashamed to say that which is said already, or else to pick a thank[162] with his prince, will not find some hole open to set a snare in, wherewith to take the contrary part in a trip.[163] Thus whiles the judges cannot agree amongst themselves, reasoning and arguing of that which is plain enough and bringing the manifest truth in doubt, in the mean season the king may take a fit occasion to understand the law as shall most make for his advantage, whereunto all other, for shame or for fear, will agree. Then the judges may be bold to pronounce on the king's side, for he that giveth sentence for the king cannot be without a good excuse. For it shall be sufficient for him to have equity on his part, or the bare words of the law, or a written and wrested understanding of the same (or else, with which good and just judges is of greater force than all laws be) the king's indisputable prerogative.

"To conclude, all the counselors agree and consent together with the rich Crassus that no abundance of The saying of rich Crassus. gold can be sufficient for a prince which must keep and maintain an army.[164] Furthermore, that a king, though he would, can do nothing unjustly, for all that all men have, yea, also the men themselves be all his, and that every man hath so much of his own as the king's gentleness hath not taken from him. And that it shall be most for the king's advantage that his subjects have very little or nothing in their pos-

---

[161] "To endanger" = "to subject to the absolute control."

[162] "Pick a thank" = "curry favor."

[163] "Will not find some hole open to set a snare in, wherewith to take the contrary part in a trip" = "will find a way to set a verbal trap in order to support his monarch in pursuing a bad policy or blunder."

[164] Derived from Cicero's *De Officiis*, I.viii.25. Crassus was a member, along with Caesar and Pompey, of the First Triumvirate.

session as whose safeguard doth herein consist, that his people do not wax wanton and wealthy through riches and liberty, because where these things be, there men be not wont patiently to obey hard, unjust, and unlawful commandments. Whereas, on the other part, need and poverty doth hold down and keep under stout courages and maketh them patient perforce, taking from them bold and rebelling stomachs. Here again, if I should rise up and boldly affirm that all these counsels be to the king dishonor and reproach, whose honor and safety is more and rather supported and upholden by the wealth and riches of his people than by his own treasures, and if I should declare that the commonality chooseth their king for their own sake and not for his sake, to the intent that through his labor and study they might all live wealthily safe from wrongs and injuries and that, therefore, the king ought to take more care for the wealth of his people than for his own wealth, even as the office and duty of a shepherd is, in that he is a shepherd, to feed his sheep rather than himself.

"For as touching this, that they think the defense and maintenance of peace to consist in the poverty of the people, the thing itself showeth that they be far out of the way. For where shall a man find more wrangling, quarreling, Poverty, the mother of debate and decay of realms. brawling, and chiding than among beggars who be more desirous of new mutations and alterations than they that be not content with the present state of their life? Or, finally, who be bolder stomached to bring all in a hurly-burly (thereby trusting to get some windfall) than they that have now nothing to lose? And if any king were so smally regarded and so lightly esteemed, yea, so behated[165] of his subjects that other ways he could not keep them in awe, but only by open wrongs, by polling and shaving, and by bringing them to beggary, surely it were better for him to forsake his kingdom than to hold it by this means, whereby though the name of the king be kept, yet the majesty is lost, for it is against the dignity of a king to have rule over beggars, but rather over rich and wealthy men.

"Of this mind was the hardy and courageous Fabricius when he said that he had rather be a ruler of rich A worthy saying of Fabricius. men than be rich himself.[166] And, verily, one man to live in pleasure and wealth whiles all others weep and smart for it, that is the part not of a king, but of a tailor. To be short, as he is a foolish physician

---

[165] "Behated" = "detested."
[166] From Plutarch's *Moralia*, 194F; the remark is given by Plutarch to Manius Curius Denatatus, a colleague of Gaius Fabricius Luscinus at the time of Rome's war against Pyrrhus, King of Epirus (280–75 B.C.E.).

that cannot cure his patient's disease unless he cast him in another sickness, so he that cannot amend the lives of his subjects, but by[167] taking from them the wealth and commodity of life, he must needs grant that he knoweth not the feat how to govern men. But let him rather amend his own life, renounce unhonest pleasures and forsake pride, for these be the chief vices that cause him to run in the contempt or hatred of his people. Let him live of his own, hurting no man. Let him do cost[168] not above his power. Let him restrain wickedness. Let him prevent vices and take away the occasions of offenses, by well ordering his subjects and not suffering wickedness to increase, afterwards to be punished. Let him not be too hasty in calling again laws which a custom hath abrogated, especially such as have been long forgotten and never lacked nor needed. And let him never, under the cloak and pretense of transgression, take such fines and forfeits as no judge will suffer a private person to take as unjust and full of guile.

"Here if I should bring forth before them the law of the Macarians,[169] which be not far distant from Utopia, whose king, the day of his coronation, is bound by a solemn oath that he shall never at any time have in his treasure above a thousand pound of gold or silver. They say a very good king, which took more care for the wealth and commodity of his country than[170] for the enriching of himself, made this law to be a stop and a bar to kings from heaping and hoarding up so much money as might impoverish their people. For he foresaw that this sum of treasure would suffice to support the king in battle against his own people, if they should chance to rebel, and also to maintain his wars against the invasions of his foreign enemies. Again, he perceived the same stock of money to be too little and unsufficient to encourage and enable him wrongfully to take away other men's goods, which was the chief cause why the law was made. Another cause was this: He thought that by this provision his people should not lack money, wherewith to maintain their daily occupying and chaffer. And seeing the king could not choose but lay out and bestow all that came in above the prescript[171] sum of his stock, he thought he would seek no occasions to do his subjects injury. Such a king shall be feared of evil men and loved of good men. These, and such other infor-

A strange and notable law of the Macarians.

---

[167] Robynson's original text has *be,* a printer's error for *by.*

[168] "Do cost" = "be at expense."

[169] The name Macarian is derived from a Greek word meaning "happy" or "blessed."

[170] At this point in Robynson's original text, the printer erred in adding the word *the,* which has here been deleted.

[171] "Prescript" = "prescribed."

mations, if I should use among men wholly inclined and given to the contrary part, how deaf hearers think you should I have?" "Deaf hearers doubtless," quoth I, "and in good faith no marvel. And to be plain with you, truly, I cannot allow that such communication shall be used, or such counsel given, as you be sure shall never be regarded nor received. For how can so strange informations be profitable, or how can they be beaten into their heads, whose minds be already prevented with clean contrary persuasions? This school philosophy[172] is not unpleasant among friends in familiar communication, but in the councils of kings where great matters be debated and reasoned with great authority, these things have no place." "That is it which I meant," quoth he, "when I said philosophy had no place among kings."

School philosophy in the consultations of princes hath no place.

"Indeed," quoth I, "this school philosophy hath not, which thinketh all things meet for every place. But there is another philosophy more civil which knoweth, as you would say, her own stage, and thereafter ordering and behaving herself in the play that she hath in hand, playeth her part accordingly with comeliness, uttering nothing out of due order and fashion. And this is the philosophy that you must use.[173] Or else, whiles a comedy of Plautus is playing and the vile bondmen scoffing and trifling among themselves, if you should suddenly come upon the stage in a philosopher's apparel and rehearse out of Octavia the place wherein Seneca disputeth with Nero, had it not been better for you to have played the dumb person than by rehearsing that which served neither for the time nor place to have made such a tragical comedy or gallimaufry?[175] For by bringing in other stuff that nothing appertaineth to the present matter, you must needs mar and pervert the play that is in hand, though the stuff that you bring be much better. What part soever you have taken upon you, play that as well as you can and make the best of it, and do not, therefore, disturb and bring out of order the whole matter, because that another which is merrier and better cometh to your remembrance.

A fine and a fit similitude.

A dumb place.[174]

---

[172] By "school philosophy" (*philosophia scholastica* in the original Latin), More intends the sort of academic philosophy discussed and debated in the universities, i.e., scholastic philosophy.

[173] See Cicero, *Orator*, xxxv.123. For discussion of this important passage, see pp. 12–13, 70–71nn29–34.

[174] In the original Latin text, the marginal note is given in Greek meaning "a part without words." CW 4, pp. 98–99.

[175] "Gallimaufry" = "hodgepodge."

"So the case standeth in a commonwealth, and so it is in the consultations of kings and princes. If evil opinions and naughty persuasions[176] cannot be utterly and quite plucked out of their hearts, if you cannot even as you would remedy vices which use and custom hath confirmed, yet for this cause you must not leave and forsake the commonwealth. You must not forsake the ship in a tempest because you cannot rule and keep down the winds. No, nor you must not labor to drive into their heads new and strange informations, which you know well shall be nothing regarded with them that be of clean contrary minds. But you must with a crafty wile and subtle train study and endeavor yourself, as much as in you lieth, to handle the matter wittily and handsomely for the purpose, and that which you cannot turn to good so to order it that it be not very bad, for it is not possible for all things to be well unless all men were good, which I think will not be yet these good many years."

"By this means," quoth he, "nothing else will be brought to pass, but whiles that I go about to remedy the madness of others, I should be even as mad as they, for if I would speak things that be true, I must needs speak such things, but as for to speak false things, whether that be a philosopher's part or no I cannot tell; truly it is not my part. Howbeit, this communication of mine, though peradventure it may seem unpleasant to them, yet can I not see why it should seem strange or foolishly newfangled. If so be that I should speak those things that ──────────── Plato feigneth[177] in his weal public or that the Utopians *The Utopian weal public.* do in theirs, these things though they were (as they be ──────────── indeed) better, yet they might seem spoken out of place. Forasmuch as here amongst us, every man hath his possessions several to himself, and there all things be common. But what was in my communication contained that might not, and ought not, in anyplace to be spoken? Saving that to them which have thoroughly decreed and determined with themselves to run headlongs the contrary way, it cannot be acceptable and pleasant because it calleth them back and showeth them the jeopardies. Verily, if all things that evil and vicious manners have caused to seem inconvenient and naughty should be refused[178] as things unmeet and reproachful, then we must among Christian people wink at the most part of all those things which Christ taught us, and so straitly forbade them to be winked at, that those things also which He whispered in the ears of his disciples, He commanded to be proclaimed in open houses. And

---

[176]"Naughty persuasions" = "bad or nasty beliefs."
[177]"Feigneth" = "devised."
[178]"Refused" = "rejected."

yet the most part of them is more dissident[179] from the manners of the world nowadays than my communication was. But preachers, sly and wily men, following your counsel (as I suppose) because they saw men evil willing to frame their manners to Christ's rule, they have wrested and wried[180] his doctrine, and, like a rule of lead,[181] have applied it to men's manners that by some means at the least way, they might agree together. Whereby I cannot see what good they have done, but that men may more sickerly[182] be evil. And I truly should prevail even as little in kings' councils. For either I must say otherways than they say, and then I were as good to say nothing, or else I must say the same that they say, and (as Mitio saith in Terence) help to further their madness.[183] For that crafty wile and subtle train[184] of yours, I cannot perceive to what purpose it serveth, wherewith you would have me to study and endeavor myself, if all things cannot be made good, yet to handle them wittily and handsomely for the purpose, that as far forth as is possible they may not be very evil, for there is no place to dissemble in nor to wink in. Naughty counsels must be openly allowed and very pestilent decrees must be approved. He shall be counted worse than a spy, yea, almost as evil as a traitor that with a faint heart doth praise evil and noisome decrees.

"Moreover, a man can have no occasion to do good, chancing into the company of them which will sooner pervert a good man than be made good themselves, through whose evil company he shall be marred, or else, if he remain good and innocent, yet the wickedness and folly of others shall be imputed to him and laid in his neck. So that it is impossible with that crafty wile and subtle train to turn anything to better. Wherefore, Plato by a goodly similitude declareth why wise men refrain to meddle in the commonwealth, for when they see the people swarm into the streets and daily wet to the skin with rain, and yet cannot persuade them to go out of the rain and to take their houses, knowing well that if they should go out to them, they should nothing prevail nor win ought by it, but with them be wet also in the rain, they do keep themselves within their houses, being content that they be safe themselves, seeing they cannot remedy the folly of the people.[185] Howbeit, doubtless, Master More (to speak truly as my mind giveth me), where possessions be

---

[179]"Dissident" = "at variance."
[180]"Wried" = "twisted."
[181]See Aristotle, *Nicomachean Ethics,* 5.10.1137b30–32.
[182]"Sickerly" = "certainly," "decidedly."
[183]From Terence, *Adelphi/The Brothers,* Act 1, lines 145–47.
[184]"Train" = "course of action."
[185]See Plato, *Republic,* 6.496d–e.

private, where money beareth all the stroke,[186] it is hard and almost impossible that there the weal public may justly be governed and prosperously flourish. Unless you think thus, that justice is there executed where all things come into the hands of evil men or that prosperity there flourisheth where all is divided among a few, which few, nevertheless, do not lead their lives very wealthily,[187] and the residue live miserably, wretchedly, and beggarly. Wherefore, when I consider with myself and weigh in my mind the wise and godly ordinances of the Utopians, among whom with very few laws all things be so well and wealthily ordered, that virtue is had in price and estimation, and, yet, all things being there common, every man hath abundance of everything. Again, on the other part, when I compare with them so many nations ever making new laws, yet none of them all well and sufficiently furnished with laws, where every man calleth that he hath gotten his own proper and private goods, where so many new laws daily made be not sufficient for every man to enjoy, defend, and know from another man's that which he calleth his own, which thing the infinite controversies in the law, daily rising, never to be ended, plainly declare to be true. These things (I say) when I consider with meself,[188] I hold well with Plato and do nothing marvel that he would make no laws for them that refused those laws, whereby all men should have and enjoy equal portions of wealths and commodities. For the wise man did easily foresee this to be the one and only way to the wealth of a commonalty, if equality of all things should be brought in and established, which I think is not possible to be observed where every man's goods be proper and peculiar to himself. For where every man under certain titles and pretenses draweth and plucketh[189] to himself as much as he can, so that a few divide among themselves all the whole riches, be there never so much abundance and store, there to the residue is left lack[190] and poverty. And for the most part it chanceth that this latter sort is more worthy to enjoy that state of wealth than the other be, because the rich men be covetous, crafty, and unprofitable.[191] On the other part, the poor be lowly, simple, and by their daily labor more profitable to the commonwealth than to themselves. Thus I do fully persuade meself that no equal and just distribution of things can be made, nor that perfect wealth shall

Plato willed all things in a commonwealth to be common.

---

[186] "Beareth all the stroke" = "has the greatest authority."
[187] "Wealthily" = "in a wholesome and happy way."
[188] "Meself" = "myself."
[189] "Plucketh" = "gathers."
[190] "Lack" = "want," "starvation."
[191] "Unprofitable" = "not beneficial to the community's welfare."

ever be among men, unless this propriety[192] be exiled and banished. But so long as it shall continue, so long shall remain among the most and best part of men the heavy and inevitable burden of poverty and wretchedness which, as I grant that it may be somewhat eased, so I utterly deny that it can wholly be taken away. For if there were a statute made that no man should possess above a certain measure of ground and that no man should have in his stock above a prescript and appointed sum of money, if it were by certain laws decreed that neither the king should be of too great power, neither the people too haut[193] and wealthy, and that offices should not be obtained by inordinate suit[194] or by bribes and gifts, that they should neither be bought nor sold, nor that is should be needful for the offices to be at any cost or charge in their offices, for so occasion is given to them by fraud and ravin[195] to gather up their money again, and by reason of gifts and bribes the offices be given to rich men, which should rather have been executed of wise men, by such laws, I say, like as sick bodies that be desperate and past cure, be wont with continual good cherishing[196] to be kept and botched up[197] for a time, so these evils also might be lightened and mitigated. But that they may be perfectly cured and brought to a good and upright state, it is not to be hoped for whiles every man is master of his own to himself. Yea, and whiles you go about to do your cure of one part, you shall make bigger the sore of another part, so the help of one causeth another's harm, forasmuch as nothing can be given to anyone, unless it be taken from another."

"But I am of a contrary opinion," quoth I, "for methinketh that men shall never there live wealthily where all things be common.[198] For how can there be abundance of goods, or of anything, where every man withdraweth his hand from labor? Whom the regard of his own gains driveth not to work, but the hope that he hath in other men's travails maketh him slothful. Then when they be pricked with poverty and yet no man can by any law or right defend that for his own which he hath gotten with the labor of his own hands, shall not there of necessity be continual sedition and bloodshed? Especially the authority and reverence of magistrates

---

[192]"Propriety" = "property" (from the Latin *proprietas,* referring to ownership and what is properly one's own).

[193]"Haut" = "high," "lofty."

[194]"Inordinate suit" = "excessive petitioning or importuning."

[195]"Ravin" = "robbery."

[196]"Cherishing" = "nursing."

[197]"Botched up" = "patched up."

[198]"More's" arguments here derive from Aristotle, *Politics,* 2.1–4.1260b25–1262b36. For discussion, see pp. 11, 70nn24–28.

being taken away, which, what place it may have with such men among whom is no difference, I cannot devise."[199]

"I marvel not," quoth he, "that you be of this opinion. For you conceive in your mind either none at all, or else a very false image and similitude of this thing. But if you had been with me in Utopia and had presently seen their fashions and laws, as I did, which lived there five years and more, and would never have comen thence[200] but only to make that new land known here, then doubtless you would grant that you never saw people well ordered, but only there." "Surely," quoth Master Peter, "it shall be hard for you to make me believe that there is better order in that new land than is here in these countries that we know, for good wits be as well here as there. And I think our commonwealths be ancienter than theirs, wherein long use and experience hath found out many things commodious for man's life. Besides that, many things here among us have been found by chance, which no wit could ever have devised."

"As touching the ancientness," quoth he, "of commonwealths, then you might better judge if you had read the histories and chronicles of that land, which, if we may believe, cities were there before men were here. Now what thing soever hitherto by wit hath been devised or found by chance, that might be as well there as here. But I think, verily, though it were so that we did pass them in wit, yet in study, in travail, and in laborsome endeavor they far pass us. For (as their chronicles testify) before our arrival there, they never heard anything of us whom they call the ultraequinoctials, saving that once about 1,200 years ago a certain ship was lost by the isle of Utopia which was driven thither by tempest. Certain Romans and Egyptians were cast on land, which after that they never went thence. Mark now what profit they took of this one occasion through diligence and earnest travail. There was no craft nor science within the empire of Rome whereof any profit could rise, but they either learned it of these strangers, or else of them taking occasion to search for it, found it out. So great profit was it to them that ever any went thither from hence. But if any like chance before this hath brought any man from thence hither that is as quite out of remembrance, as this also perchance in time to come shall be forgotten that ever I was there. And like as they quickly, almost at the first meeting, made their own whatsoever is among us wealthily devised, so I suppose it would be long before we would receive anything that among them is better instituted than among us. And this, I suppose, is the chief cause why their com-

[199] "Devise" = "guess."
[200] "Would never have comen thence" = "would never have left."

monwealths be wiselier governed and do flourish in more wealth than ours, though we neither in wit nor riches be their inferiors."

"Therefore, gentle Master Raphael," quoth I, "I pray you and beseech you describe unto us the island. And study not to be short, but declare largely in order their grounds, their rivers, their cities, their people, their manners, their ordinances, their laws, and to be short all things that you shall think us desirous to know. And you shall think us desirous to know whatsoever we know not yet." "There is nothing," quoth he, "that I will do gladlier, for all these things I have fresh in mind. But the matter requireth leisure." "Let us go in, therefore," quoth I, "to dinner. Afterward we will bestow the time at our pleasure." "Content," quoth he, "be it." So we went in and dined. When dinner was done, we came into the same place again and sat us down upon the same bench, commanding our servants that no man should trouble us. Then I and Master Peter Giles desired Master Raphael to perform his promise. He, therefore, seeing us desirous and willing to harken to him, when he had sit still and paused a little while musing and bethinking himself, thus he began to speak.

The end of the First Book.

THE SECOND BOOK

of the communication of Raphael Hythloday, concerning the best state of a commonwealth containing the description of Utopia, with a large declaration of the politic government and of all the good laws and orders of the same island.

The island of Utopia containeth in breadth in the middle part of it (for there it is broadest) two hun- dred miles, which breadth continueth through the most part of the land, saving that by little and little it cometh in and waxeth narrower towards both the ends, which fetching about a circuit or compass of five hundred miles, do fashion the whole island like to the new moon. Between these two corners the sea runneth in, dividing them asunder by the distance of eleven miles or thereabouts, and there surmounteth into a large and wide sea, which by reason that the land on every side compasseth it about and sheltereth it from the winds, is not

The site and fashion of the new island Utopia.

rough nor mounteth not with great waves, but almost floweth quietly, not much unlike a great standing pool, and maketh well-nigh all the space within the belly[1] of the land in manner of a haven, and to the great commodity of the inhabitants receiveth in ships towards every part of the land. The forefronts or frontiers of the two corners, what with fords and shelves and what with rocks, be very jeopardous and dangerous. In the middle distance between them both standeth up above the water a great rock, which, therefore, is nothing perilous because it is in sight. Upon the top of this rock is a fair and a strong tower builded,[2] which they hold with a garrison of men. Other rocks there be lying hid under the water, which, therefore, be dangerous. The channels be known only to themselves, and, therefore, it seldom chanceth that any stranger unless he be guided by an Utopian can come into this haven, insomuch that they themselves could scarcely enter without jeopardy, but that their way is directed and ruled by certain landmarks standing on the shore. By turning, translating,[3] and removing these marks into other places they may destroy their enemies' navies, be they never so many. The outside or utter[4] circuit of the land is also full of havens, but the landing is so surely fenced, what by nature and what by workmanship of man's hand, that a few defenders may drive back many armies.

A place naturally fenced needeth but one garrison.

A politic device in changing of landmarks.

Howbeit, as they say and as the fashion of the place itself doth partly show, it was not ever compassed about with the sea. By King Utopus,[5] whose name as conqueror the island beareth (for before his time it was called Abraxa),[6] which also brought the rude and wild people to that excellent perfection in all good fashions, humanity, and civil gentleness wherein they now go beyond all the people of the world, even at his first arriving and entering upon the land, forthwith obtaining the victory,

The island of Utopia so named of King Utopus.

---

[1] "Belly" = "interior."

[2] "Builded" = "built."

[3] "Translating" = "carrying from one place to another."

[4] "Utter" = "outer."

[5] There is no mention of Utopus being a king in the original Latin. In the body of the text, Utopus is referred to only by his name; in the accompanying marginal note, supplied by Erasmus and Giles, he is referred to as a *dux,* the Latin word for someone who leads, especially a military commander. See pp. 20, 72nn57–58.

[6] "Abraxa" derives from the Greek *Abraxas,* the name given by the second-century Greek gnostic Basilides to the highest of the 365 heavens that he posited; the Greek letters in the name add up numerologically to 365.

caused fifteen miles space of uplandish[7] ground, where the sea had no passage, to be cut and digged up, and so brought the sea round about the land. He set to this work not only the inhabitants of the island (because they should not think it done in contumely and despite) but also all his own soldiers. Thus the work, being divided into so great a number of workmen, was with exceeding marvelous speed dispatched, insomuch

Many hands make light work.

that the borderers, which at the first began to mock and to jest at this vain enterprise, then turned their derision to marvel at the success and to fear.

There is in the island fifty-four large and fair cities or shire towns,[8] agreeing all together in one tongue, in like manners, institutions, and laws. They be all set and situate alike, and in all points fashioned alike, as far forth as the place or plot suffereth. Of these cities, they that be nighest together be twenty four miles asunder.

Cities in Utopia.

Similitude causeth concord.

A mean distance between city and city.

Again there is none of them distant from the next above one day's journey afoot.

There come yearly to Amaurote out of every city three old men wise and well-experienced, there to entreat and debate of the common matters of the land. For this city (because it standeth just in the midst of the island and is, therefore, most meet for the ambassadors of all parts of the realm) is taken for the chief and head city. The precincts and bounds of the shires be so commodiously appointed out and set forth for the cities that none of them

The distribution of lands.

all hath of any side less than twenty miles of ground, and of some side also much more as of that part where the cities be of farther distance asunder. None of the cities desire to enlarge the bounds and limits of their shire, for they count

But this nowadays is the ground of all mischief.

themselves rather the good husbands than the owners of their lands.

They have in the country in all parts of the shire houses or farms builded, well appointed, and furnished with all sorts of instruments and tools belonging to husbandry. These houses be inhabited of the citizens which come thither to dwell by course. No household or farm in the coun-

Husbandry and tillage chiefly and principally regarded and advanced.

try has fewer than fifteen persons, men and women, besides two bondmen, which be all under the rule and order of the good man and the good

---

[7]"Uplandish" = "hilly."

[8]Fifty-four is also the total number of English and Welsh counties plus London, which had the status of a county in its own right.

wife of the house, being both very sage, discreet, and ancient persons. And every thirty farms or families have one head ruler which is called a Philarch,[9] being as it were a head bailiff.[10] Out of every one of these families or farms cometh every year into the city, twenty persons which have continued two years before in the country. In their place so many fresh be sent thither out of the city, who, of them that have been there a year already and be therefore expert and cunning[11] in husbandry, shall be instructed and taught. And they the next year shall teach other. This order is used for fear that either scarceness of victuals or some other like incommodity should chance, through lack of knowledge, if they should be altogether new and fresh and inexpert in husbandry. This manner and fashion of yearly changing and renewing the occupiers of husbandry, though it be solemn and customably used to the intent that no man shall be constrained against his will to continue long in that hard and sharp kind of life, yet many of them have such a pleasure and delight in husbandry that they obtain a longer space of years.

These husbandmen plow and till the ground, and breed up cattle, and provide and make ready wood, which they carry to the city either by land or by water, as they may most conveniently. They bring up a great multitude of pullen[12] and that by a marvelous policy, for the hens do not sit upon the eggs, but by keeping them in a certain equal heat they bring life into them and hatch them. The chickens, as soon as they come out of the shell, follow men and women instead of the hens. They bring up very few horses, nor none but very fierce ones, and that for no other use or purpose but only to exercise their youth in riding and feats of arms. For oxen be put to all the labor of plowing and drawing, which they grant to be not so good as horses at a sudden brunt[13] and (as we say) at a dead lift,[14] but yet they hold opinion that oxen will abide and suffer much more

The duties of men of husbandry.

A strange fashion in hatching and bringing up pullen.

The use of horses.

The use of oxen.

[9] "Philarch" derives from a Greek word meaning "head of a tribe."

[10] Robynson supplied *bailiff* on his own in an effort to clarify the role of the Philarch. In England, the word *bailiff* could refer to the chief administrative officer or magistrate in a district within one of the counties or to one of the officers of justice serving under a sheriff or to the agent or steward of the lord of a manor. None of these functions quite fits what Hythloday says about the Philarch. Since the bailiff of a manor had special responsibility for supervising the husbandry of a farm, Robynson appears to be drawing an analogy with this sort of activity.

[11] "Cunning" = "expert," "knowledgeable."

[12] "Pullen" = "poultry."

[13] "Sudden brunt" = "quick spurt."

[14] "At a dead lift" = "at pulling a dead weight."

labor, pain, and hardness than horses will. And they think that oxen be not in danger and subject unto so many diseases, and that they be kept and maintained with much less cost and charge, and finally that they be good for meat when they be past labor.

They sow corn [15] only for bread. For their drink is either wine made of grapes, or else of apples or pears, or else it is clear water, and many times mead made of honey [16] or licorice sod [17] in water, for thereof they have great store. And though they know certainly (for they know it perfectly indeed) how much victuals the city with the whole country or shire round about it doth spend, yet they sow much more corn and breed up much more cattle than serveth for their own use, parting the overplus among their borderers. Whatsoever necessary things be lacking in the country, all such stuff they fetch out of the city, where without any exchange they easily obtain it of the magistrates of the city, for every month many of them go into the city on the holy day. When their harvest day draweth near and is at hand, then the Philarchs, which be the head officers and bailiffs of husbandry, send word to the magistrates of the city what number of harvest men is needful to be sent to them out of the city. The which company of harvest men being ready at the day appointed, almost in one fair day dispatcheth all the harvest work.

Bread and drink.

A great discretion in sowing of corn.

Mutual help quickly dispatcheth.

Of the Cities and Namely of Amaurote

As for their cities, who so knoweth one of them, knoweth them all. They be all so like one to another, as far forth as the nature of the place permitteth. I will describe, therefore, to you one or other of them, for it skilleth not greatly [18] which; but which rather than Amaurote? Of them all this is the worthiest and of most dignity, for the residue knowledge it for the head city because there is the council house. Nor to me any of them all is better beloved, as wherein I lived five whole years together.

The city of Amaurote standeth upon the side of a low hill in fashion almost four-square, for the breadth of it beginneth a little beneath the top of the hill and still

The description of Amaurote, the chief city in Utopia.

---

[15] "Corn" = "cereal grain."
[16] Mead is an alcoholic drink made from fermented honey.
[17] "Sod" = "boiled."
[18] "It skilleth not greatly" = "it makes little difference."

continueth by the space of two miles, until it come to the river of Anyder.
The length of it, which lieth by the river's side, is some-
what more. The river of Anyder rises four and twenty   The description of the
                                                         river of Anyder.
miles above Amaurote out of a little spring, but being
increased by other small rivers and brooks that run into it, and among
other two somewhat big ones, before the city it is half a mile broad and
farther broader, and forty miles beyond the city it falleth into the ocean
sea. By all that space that lieth between the sea and the city, and certain
miles also above the city, the water ebbeth and floweth six hours together with a swift tide. When the sea floweth in, for the
length of thirty miles it filleth all the Anyder with salt   The very like in England
                                                               in the river Thames.
water and driveth back the fresh water of the river, and
somewhat further it changeth the sweetness of the fresh water with salt-
ness. But a little beyond that the river waxeth sweet and runneth forby[19]
the city fresh and pleasant, and when the sea ebbeth and goeth back
again the fresh water followeth it almost even to the very fall into the sea.
There goeth a bridge over the river made not of piles
or of timber, but of stonework with gorgeous and sub-   Herein also doth London
                                                          agree with Amaurote.[20]
stantial arches at that part of the city that is farthest
from the sea, to the intent that ships may pass along forby all the side
of the city without let.[21] They have also another river which indeed is not
very great, but it runneth gently and pleasantly, for it riseth even out of
the same hill that the city standeth upon and runneth down a slope
through the midst of the city into Anyder.[22] And because it riseth a little
without the city, the Amaurotians have enclosed the head spring of it
with strong fences and bulwarks and so have joined it
to the city. This is done to the intent that the water   The use of fresh water.
should not be stopped nor turned away or poisoned if
their enemies should chance to come upon them. From thence the water is derived and conveyed down in canals of brick divers ways into the
lower parts of the city. Where that cannot be done, by reason that the
place will not suffer it, there they gather the rainwater in great cisterns,
which doth them as good service. The city is com-
passed about with a high and thick stone wall full of   The defense of town
                                                          walls.
turrets and bulwarks. A dry ditch, but deep and broad

---

[19]"Forby" = "near," "beside."
[20]Many of the parallels would have been readily recognized by More's English readers,
but in many ways Amaurote represents an idealized London, especially in regard to its
cleanness and orderliness.
[21]"Without let" = "without hindrance."
[22]The London parallel is the stream known as the Fleet.

and overgrown with bushes, briars and thorns, goeth about three sides or quarters of the city. To the fourth side the river itself serveth for a ditch.

The streets be appointed and set forth very com- Streets.
modious and handsome, both for carriage and also
against the winds. The houses be of fair and gorgeous Buildings and houses.
building, and on the street side they stand joined to-
gether in a long row through the whole street without any partition or
separation. The streets be twenty feet broad. On the
back side of the houses, through the whole length of To every dwelling house a garden plot adjoining.
the street, lie large gardens enclosed round about with
the back part of the streets. Every house hath two doors, one into the
street and a postern door on the backside into the garden. These doors
be made with two leaves, never locked nor bolted, so easy to be opened
that they will follow the least drawing of a finger and
shut again alone. Who so will may go in, for there is This gear smelleth of Plato, his community.[23]
nothing within the houses that is private, or any man's
own. And every tenth year they change their houses by lot.

They set great store by their gardens. In them they have vineyards, all
manner of fruit, herbs, and flowers, so pleasant, so well furnished, and
so finely kept that I never saw thing more fruitful nor
better trimmed in any place. Their study and diligence The commodity of gardens is commended also of Virgil.[24]
herein cometh not only of pleasure, but also of a certain
strife and contention that is between street and street
concerning the trimming, husbanding, and furnishing of their gardens,
every man for his own part. And, verily, you shall not lightly find in all
the city anything that is more commodious, either for the profit of the citizens or for pleasure. And, therefore, it may seem that the first founder
of the city minded nothing so much as these gardens. For they say that
King Utopus[25] himself, even at the first beginning appointed and drew
forth the platform[26] of the city into this fashion and figure that it hath
now, but the gallant garnishing and the beautiful setting forth of it,
whereunto he saw that one man's age would not suffice, that he left to his
posterity. For their chronicles, which they keep written with all diligent
circumspection, containing the history of 1,760 years even from the first

[23] See Plato, *Republic,* V.416d. The marginal note here is a rough translation of the one supplied by Erasmus and Giles for the original Latin editions.
[24] See Virgil, *Georgics,* IV.116–48. Again, this marginal note translates the one supplied in the original Latin editions.
[25] There is no mention of the title *king* in the original Latin text; Utopus appears in this place only by his name.
[26] "Platform" = "topographical plan."

conquest of the island, record and witness that the houses in the beginning were very low and, like homely cottages or poor shepherd houses,
made at all adventures[27] of every rude piece of timber that came first to
hand, with mud walls and ridged roofs, thatched over with straw. But
now the houses be curiously builded after a gorgeous and gallant sort,
with three stories one over another. The outsides of the walls be made
either of hard flint[28] or of plaster, or else of brick, and the inner sides be
well strengthened with timber work. The roofs be plain and flat, covered
with a certain kind of plaster that is of no cost, and yet so tempered that
no fire can hurt or perish it and withstandeth the violence of the weather
better than any lead. They keep the wind out of their
windows with glass, for it is there much used, and some   Glazed or canvased
                                                            windows.
here also with fine linen cloth dipped in oil or amber,
and that for two commodities, for by this means more light cometh in
and the wind is better kept out.

Of the Magistrates

Every thirty families or farms choose them yearly an officer, which in
their old language is called the Syphogrant, and by a newer name
the Philarch. Every ten Syphogrants, with all their thirty families, be
under an officer which was once called the Tranibore,
now the chief Philarch.[29] Moreover, as concerning the   A Tranibore in the Uto-
                                                            pians' tongue signifieth a
election of the prince,[30] all the Syphogrants, which be   head or chief peer. A mar-
                                                            velous strange fashion
in number two hundred, first be sworn to choose him   in choosing magistrates.
whom they think most meet and expedient. Then by a
secret election they name prince one of those four whom the people before named unto them, for out of the four quarters of the city there be

---

[27]"At all adventures" = "at random," "without regard to the consequences."

[28]"Hard flint" = "strong stonework."

[29]The meanings of these names are somewhat obscure. Syphogrant may derive from
Greek roots meaning "wise old men." Another possibility is that its main root relates to the
Greek word meaning "of the sty" and that the name itself should be translated as "warden
of the sty," a pun on *steward* in English. Tranibore may derive from Greek roots meaning
"master eater." It has been suggested that both names relate to the system of governance
that operated at London's Inns of Court, where there were stewards and where the senior
lawyers were known as "Benchers" because of the role they played in instructing prospec-
tive barristers in the law while at table. In the original Latin text, the "chief Philarch" mentioned by Robynson is given as the "protophylarch," the only time this term is used in the
book. See CW 4, pp. 122, 398–99.

[30]In the original Latin text, the word here is *princeps,* which means literally "first
leader."

four chosen, out of every quarter one to stand for the election, which be put up to the council. The prince's office continueth all his lifetime, unless he be deposed or put down for suspicion of tyranny. They choose the Tranibores yearly, but lightly they change them not. All the other officers be but for one year. The Tranibores every third day, and sometimes if need be oftener, come into the council house with the prince. Their counsel is concerning the commonwealth. If there be any controversies among the commoners, which be very few, they dispatch and end them by and by. They take every two Syphogrants to them in council,[31] and every day a new couple. And it is provided that nothing touching the commonwealth shall be confirmed and ratified, unless it has been reasoned of and debated three days in the council before it be decreed. It is death to have any consultation for the commonwealth out of the council or the place of the common election. This statute, they say, was made to the intent that the prince and Tranibores might not easily conspire together to oppress the people by tyranny and to change the state of the weal public. Therefore, matters of great weight and importance be brought to the election house of the Syphogrants, which open the matter to their families. And afterward, when they have consulted among themselves, they show their devise to the council.[32] Sometime the matter is brought before the council of the whole island. Furthermore, this custom also the council useth to dispute or reason of no matter the same day that it is first proposed or put forth, but to defer it to the next sitting of the council. Because that no man, when he hath rashly there spoken that cometh to his tongue's end, shall then afterward rather study for reasons wherewith to defend and maintain his first foolish sentence than for the commodity of the commonwealth, as one rather willing the harm or hindrance of the weal public than any loss or diminution óf his own existimation, and as one that would be ashamed (which is a very foolish shame) to be counted anything at the first overseen in the matter, who at the first ought to have spoken rather wisely than hastily or rashly.

Marginal notes:

Tyranny in a well-ordered weal public utterly to be abhorred.

Suits and controversies between party and party forthwith to be ended which nowadays of a set purpose be unreasonably delayed.

Against hasty and rash decrees or statutes.

A custom worthy to be used these days in our councils and parliaments.

---

[31] "They take every two Syphogrants to them in council" = "they rotate the Syphogrants in the council two at a time."

[32] "They show their devise to the council" = "they show what they have worked out to the council."

Of Sciences, Crafts, and Occupations

Husbandry is a science common to them all in general, both men and women, wherein they be all expert and cunning. In this they be all instructed even from their youth, partly in their schools with traditions and precepts and partly in the country nigh the city, brought up as it were in playing, not only beholding the use of it, but by occasion of exercising their bodies practicing it also. Besides husbandry, which (as I said) is common to them all, every one of them learneth one or other several and particular science as his own proper craft. That is most commonly either clothworking in wool or flax, or masonry, or the smith's craft or the carpenter's science, for there is none other occupation that any number to speak of doth use there. For their garments, which throughout all the island be of one fashion (saving that there is a difference between the man's garment and the woman's, between the married and the unmarried), and this one continueth forevermore unchanged, seemly and comely to the eye, no less to the moving and wielding of the body, also fit both for winter and summer. As for these garments (I say) every family maketh their own. But of the other foresaid crafts every man learneth one, and not only the men, but also the women. But the women, as the weaker sort, be put to the easier crafts, as to work wool and flax. The more laborsome sciences be committed to the men. For the most part every man is brought up in his father's craft, for most commonly they are naturally thereto bent and inclined. But if a man's mind stand to any other, he is by adoption put into a family of that occupation, which he doth most fantasy,[33] whom not only his father, but also the magistrates, do diligently look to that he be put to a discreet and an honest householder. Yea, and if any person when he hath learned one craft be desirous to learn another, he is likewise suffered[34] and permitted. When he hath learned both, he occupieth whether he will, unless the city have more need of the one than of the other.

    The chief and almost the only office of the Syphograts is to see and take heed that no man sit idle, but that every one apply his own craft with earnest dili-

Husbandry or tillage practiced of all estates, which nowadays is reject unto a few of the basest sort.

Sciences or occupations should be learned for necessity's sake, and not for the maintenance of riotous excess and wanton pleasure.

Similitude in apparel.

No citizen without a science.

To what occupation everyone is naturally inclined, that let him learn.

Idle persons to be driven out of the weal public.

---

[33] "Fantasy" = "fancy," "take a liking to."
[34] "Suffered" = "tolerated," "allowed."

gence. And yet for all that, not to be wearied from early in the morning to late in the evening with continual work like laboring and toiling beasts. For this is worse than the miserable and wretched condition of bondmen, which nevertheless is almost everywhere the life of workmen and artificers, saving in Utopia. For they, dividing the day and the night into twenty-four just [35] hours, appoint and assign only six of those hours to work before noon,

A moderation in the labor and toil of artificers.

upon the which they go straight to dinner. And after dinner, when they have rested two hours, then they work three hours and upon that they go to supper. About eight of the clock in the evening (counting one of the clock at the first hour after noon) they go to bed; eight hours they give to sleep. All the void [36] time, that is between the hours of work, sleep, and meat that they be suffered to bestow, every man as he liketh best himself, not to the intent that they should misspend this time in riot or slothfulness, but, being then licensed from the labor of their own occupations, to bestow the time well and thriftily upon some other science as shall please them. For it is a solemn custom there to have lectures daily early in the morning, where to be present they only be constrained that be namely chosen and appointed to learning.[37] Howbeit, a great multitude of every sort of

The study of good literature.

people, both men and women, go to hear lectures, some one and some another as every man's nature is inclined. Yet, this notwithstanding, if any man had rather bestow this time upon his own occupation (as chanceth in many whose minds rise not in the contemplation of any science liberal),[38] he is not letted nor prohibited, but is also praised and commended as profitable to the commonwealth.

After supper they bestow one hour in play: in summer in their gardens, in winter in their common halls

Playing after supper.

where they dine and sup. There they exercise themselves in music or else in honest and wholesome communication. Diceplay and such other foolish and pernicious games they know not, but they use two games not much unlike the

But nowadays dice-play is the pastime of princes.

chess. The one is the battle of numbers, wherein one number stealeth away another. The other is wherein vices fight with virtues, as it were in battle array or a set field, in the which game is very properly showed both the strife and

Plays or games also profitable.

---

[35]"Just" = "exactly the same in length," "equally long."

[36]"Void" = "unfilled," "unassigned."

[37]"Where to be present they only be constrained that be namely chosen and appointed to learning" = "where all that is necessary to be in attendance is that one be distinguished, chosen, and ordained for learning."

[38]"Any science liberal" = "any of the liberal arts."

discord that vices have among themselves, and again their unity and concord against virtues; and also what vices be repugnant to what virtues; with what power and strength they assail them openly; by what wiles and subtlety they assault them secretly; with what help and aid the virtues resist and overcome the puissance of the vices; by what craft they frustrate their purposes; and finally by what sleight[39] or means the one getteth the victory.

But here lest you be deceived, one thing you must look more narrowly upon. For seeing they bestow but six hours in work,[40] perchance you may think that the lack of some necessary things hereof may ensue. But this is nothing so. For that small time is not only enough, but also too much for the store and abundance of all things that be requisite either for the necessity or commodity of life. The which thing you also shall perceive if you weigh and consider with yourselves how great a part of the people in other countries liveth idle. First, almost all women,[41] which be the half of the whole number, or else, if the women be somewhere occupied, there most commonly in their stead the men be idle. Besides this, how great and how idle a company is there of priests and religious men, as they call them? Put thereto all rich men, especially all landed men, which commonly be called gentlemen and noblemen. Take into this number also their servants. I mean all that flock of stout bragging rush-bucklers.[42] Join to them also sturdy and valiant beggars, cloaking their idle life under the color of some disease or sickness, and truly you shall find them much fewer than you thought, by whose labor all these things are wrought that in men's affairs are now daily used and frequented.

The kinds and sorts of idle people: Women.

Priests and religious men; rich men and landed men.

Servingmen.

Sturdy and valiant beggars.

---

[39]"Sleight" = "strategy," "tactics."

[40]The mention of "six hours in work" is carried over from More's original Latin text. It is clearly an error, since the Utopian workday included two periods of labor, i.e., six hours before the midday meal and three hours before the evening meal. Nevertheless the nine-hour total is well below the twelve- to fourteen- and even sixteen-hour days put in by ordinary farmers and craftsmen in More's era.

[41]In suggesting that "almost all women" in sixteenth-century English or European society were idle, Hythloday, or More himself, must have been thinking only of the wives and daughters of men in the professions, such as lawyers, or in the gentry and nobility, where women engaged in child-rearing and household management but not in the productive labor of their husbands and fathers. In virtually all other social ranks in More's day, in the city as well as in the countryside, women took a heavy share of the burden of work necessary to supply the household's domestic needs and to participate in market activities.

[42]"Rush-bucklers" = "swashbucklers," "swaggering ruffians."

Now consider with yourself, of these few that do work, how few are occupied in necessary works, for where money beareth all the swing,[43] there many vain and superfluous occupations must needs be used to serve only for riotous superfluity and unhonest pleasure. For the same multitude that now is occupied in work, if they were divided into so few occupations as the necessary use of nature requireth, in so great plenty of things as then of necessity would ensue, doubtless the prices would be too little for the artificers to maintain their livings. But if all these that be now busied about unprofitable occupations, with all the whole flock of them that live idly and slothfully, which consume and waste everyone of them more of these things that come by other men's labor than two of the workmen themselves do, if all these (I say) were set to profitable occupations, you easily perceive how little time would be enough, yea, and too much to store us with all things that may be requisite either for necessity or for commodity, yea, or for pleasure, so that the same pleasure is true and natural.

Wonderful, wittily spoken.

And this in Utopia the thing itself maketh manifest and plain, for there in all the city, with the whole country or shire adjoining to it, scarcely five hundred persons of all the whole number of men and women that be neither too old nor too weak to work, be licensed and discharged from labor. Among them be the Syphogrants (who though they be by the laws exempt and privileged from labor) yet they exempt not themselves, to the intent they may the rather by their example provoke others to work. The same vacation from labor do they also enjoy to whom the people, persuaded by the commendation of the priests and secret election of the Syphogrants, have given a perpetual license from labor to learning. But if any one of them prove not according to the expectation and hope of him conceived, he is forthwith plucked back to the company of artificers. And, contrariwise, often it chanceth that a handicraftsman doth so earnestly bestow his vacant and spare hours in learning and through diligence so profiteth therein that he is taken from his handy occupation and promoted to the company of the learned. Out of this order of the learned be chosen ambassadors, priests, Tranibores, and finally the prince himself, whom they in their old tongue call Barzanes,[44] and by a newer name, Adamus.[45] The residue of the

Not as much as the magistrates live idly.

Only learned men called to offices.

---

[43] "Beareth all the swing" = "has full sway."

[44] "Barzanes" derives from the Greek, meaning "son of Zeus."

[45] In the original Latin text, the name is given as Ademus, which is derived from the Greek, meaning "peopleless."

people being neither idle nor yet occupied about unprofitable exercises, it may be easily judged in how few hours how much good work by them may be done and dispatched towards those things that I have spoken of.

This commodity they have also above other, that in the most part of necessary occupations they need not so much work as other nations do. For first of all the building or repairing of houses asketh everywhere so many men's continual labor, be- How to avoid excessive cost in building. cause that the unthrifty heir suffereth the houses that his father builded in continuance of time to fall in decay. So that which he might have upholden[46] with little cost, his successor is constrained to build it again anew to his great charge. Yea, many times also the house that stood one man in much money,[47] another is of so nice and so delicate a mind that he setteth nothing by it.[48] And it being neglected and, therefore, shortly falling into ruin, he buildeth up another in another place with no less cost and charge. But among the Utopians, where all things be set in good order and the commonwealth in a good stay,[49] it very seldom chanceth that they choose a new plot to build an house upon. And they do not only find speedy and quick remedies for present faults, but also prevent them that be like to fall. And by this means their houses continue and last very long with little labor and small reparations, insomuch that this kind of workmen sometimes have almost nothing to do, but that they be commanded to hew timber at home and to square and trim up stoves,[50] to the intent that if any work chance, it may the speedilier rise.

Now, sir, in their apparel, mark (I pray you) how few How to lessen the charge in apparel. workmen they need. First of all, while they be at work they be covered homely[51] with leather or skins that will last seven years. When they go forth abroad they cast upon them a cloak, which hideth the other homely apparel. These cloaks throughout the whole island be all of one color and that is the natural color of wool. They, therefore, do not only spend much less woolen cloth than is spent in other countries, but also the same standeth them in much less cost. But linen cloth is made with less labor and is, therefore, had more in use. But in linen cloth only whiteness, in woolen only cleanliness is regarded. As for the small-

---

[46] "Upholden" = "maintained."
[47] "That stood one man in much money" = "that cost one man much money to maintain."
[48] "Setteth nothing by it" = "expends nothing on it."
[49] "In a good stay" = "well buttressed," "well supported."
[50] "Stoves" = "staves."
[51] "Homely" = "plainly," "simply."

ness or fineness of the thread, that is nothing passed for.[52] And this is the cause wherefore in other places four or five cloth gowns of divers colors and as many silk coats are not enough for one man. Yea, and if he be of the delicate and nice sort, ten be too few, whereas there one garment will serve a man most commonly two years. For why should he desire more? Seeing if he had them, he should not be the better hapt[53] or covered from cold, neither in his apparel any whit the comelier.

Wherefore, seeing they are all exercised in profitable occupations and that few artificers in the same crafts be sufficient, this is the cause that, plenty of all things being among them, they do sometimes bring forth an innumerable company of people to amend the highways if any be broken. Many times also, when they have no such work to be occupied about, an open proclamation is made that they shall bestow fewer hours in work, for the magistrates do not exercise their citizens against their wills in unneedful labors. For why in the institution of that weal public, this end is only and chiefly pretended and minded, that what time may possibly be spared from the necessary occupations and affairs of the commonwealth, all that the citizens should withdraw from the bodily service to the free liberty of the mind and garnishing of the same, for herein they suppose the felicity of this life to consist.

Of Their Living and Mutual Conversation [54] Together

But now will I declare how the citizens use themselves one towards another; what familiar occupying and entertainment[55] there is among the people; and what fashion they use in the distribution of everything. First, the city consisteth of families; the families most commonly are made of kindreds, for the women, when they be married at a lawful age, they go into their husbands' houses.[56] But the male children, with all the whole male offspring,[57] continue still in their own family and be governed of the eldest and ancientest father, unless he dote for age,[58] for

---

[52] "Nothing passed for" = "for which there is no equal."

[53] "Hapt" = "cloaked," "clothed."

[54] "Conversation" = "society."

[55] "Occupying and entertainment" = "trafficking and manner of social behavior."

[56] From the context, the term *kindred* is meant to refer to a patrilocal, and seemingly a patrilineal, descent group in which women not only leave the households of their fathers on marriage to join and become members of the families of their husbands, but also in which the children of these marriages trace their lineage in the male line.

[57] The original Latin text speaks in this place of the male grandchildren, as well as the male children, remaining in the household of the oldest father.

[58] "Dote for age" = "be in his dotage."

then the next to him in age is placed in his room. But to

The number of citizens.

the intent the prescript number of the citizens should
neither decrease nor above measure increase, it is ordained that no family which in every city be six thousand in the whole,
besides them of the country, shall at once have fewer children of the age
of fourteen years or thereabout than ten or more than sixteen, for of children under this age no number can be prescribed or appointed. This
measure or number is easily observed and kept, by putting them that in
fuller families be above the number into families of smaller increase. But
if chance be that in the whole city the store increase above the just number, therewith they fill up the lack of other cities. But if so be that the
multitude throughout the whole island pass and exceed the due number, then they choose out of every city certain citizens and build up a
town under their own laws in the next land where the inhabitants have
much waste [59] and unoccupied ground, receiving also of the same country people to them if they will join and dwell with them. They thus joining and dwelling together do easily agree in one fashion of living, and
that to the great wealth of both the peoples. For they so bring the matter about by their laws that the ground, which before was neither good
nor profitable for the one nor for the other, is now sufficient and fruitful enough for them both. But if the inhabitants of that land will not
dwell with them to be ordered by their laws, then they drive them out of
those bounds which they have limited and appointed out for themselves.
And if they resist and rebel, then they make war against them, for they
count this the most just cause of war, when any people holdeth a piece
of ground void and vacant to no good nor profitable use, keeping others
from the use and possession of it, which notwithstanding by the law of
nature ought thereof to be nourished and relieved. If any chance do so
much diminish the number of any of their cities that it cannot be filled
up again without the diminishing of the just number of the other cities
(which they say chanced but twice since the beginning of the land
through a great pestilent plague), then they fulfill and make up the number with citizens fetched out of their own foreign towns, for they had
rather suffer their foreign towns to decay and perish than any city of
their own island to be diminished.

But now again to the conversation of the citizens
among themselves. The eldest (as I said) ruleth the

So might we well be
discharged and eased
of the idle company of
servingmen.

family. The wives be ministers to their husbands, the
children to their parents, and, to be short, the younger
to their elders. Every city is divided into four equal parts or quarters. In

[59] "Waste" = "uncultivated land."

the midst of every quarter there is a marketplace of all manner of things. Thither the works of every family be brought into certain houses, and every kind of thing is laid up several in barns or storehouses. From hence the father of every family or every householder fetcheth whatsoever he and his have need of and carrieth it away with him without money, without exchange,[60] without any gage, pawn, or pledge.[61] For why should anything be denied unto him? Seeing there is abundance of all things, and that it is not to be feared lest any man will ask more than he needs. For why should it be thought that that man would ask more than enough, which is sure never to lack? Certainly in all kinds of living creatures either fear of lack doth cause covetousness and ravin, or in man only pride, which counteth it a glorious thing to pass and excel others in the superfluous and vain ostentation of things. The which kind of vice among the Utopians can have no place.

The cause of covetousness and extortion.

Next to the marketplaces that I spake of stand meat markets,[62] whither be brought not only all sorts of herbs and the fruits of trees with bread, but also fish and all manner of four-footed beasts and wild fowl that be man's meat. But first the filthiness and ordure thereof is clean washed away in the running river without the city in places appointed meet for the same purpose. From thence the beasts be brought in, killed, and clean washed by the hands of their bondmen, for they permit not their free citizens to accustom themselves to the killing of beasts, through the use whereof they think clemency the gentlest affection of our nature by little and little to decay and perish. Neither they suffer anything that is filthy, loathsome, or uncleanly to be brought into the city, lest the air by the stench thereof, infected and corrupt, should cause pestilent diseases. Moreover, every street hath certain great large halls set in equal distance one from another, every one known by a several name.[63] In these halls dwell the Syphogrants, and to every one of the same halls be appointed thirty families, on either side, fifteen. The stewards of every hall at a certain hour come into the meat markets where they receive meat according to the number of their halls.

Of the slaughter of beasts we have learned manslaughter.

Filth and ordure bring the infection of pestilence into cities.

---

[60] By "exchange," Robynson appears to mean a written promise to pay so much in currency for the item, i.e., a "bill of debt," not a "bill of exchange" in the strict sense, which would require the transaction to take place in the currencies of different places.

[61] "Without any gage, pawn, or pledge" = "without leaving anything of value on deposit."

[62] "Meat markets" = "food markets."

[63] "By a several name" = "by its own particular name."

But first and chiefly of all, respect is had to the sick that be cured[64] in the hospitals. For in the circuit of the city, a little without the walls, they have four hospitals,

Care, diligence, and attendance about the sick.

so big, so wide, so ample, and so large that they may seem four little towns, which were devised of that bigness partly to the intent the sick, be they never so many in number, should not lie to throng and strait,[65] and therefore uneasily and incommodiously, and partly that they which were taken and holden with contagious diseases, such as be wont by infection to creep from one to another, might be laid apart far from the company of the residue. These hospitals be so well appointed and with all things necessary to health, so furnished and, moreover, so diligent attendance through the continual presence of cunning physicians is given, that though no man is sent thither against his will, yet not withstanding there is no sick person in all the city that had not rather lie there than at home in his own house.

When the steward of the sick hath received such meats as the physicians have prescribed, then the best is equally divided among the halls according to the company of every one, saving that there is had a respect to the prince, the bishop, the Tranibores, and to ambassadors and all strangers, if there be any, which be very few and seldom. But they also when they be there have certain several houses appointed and prepared for them. To these halls at the set hours of dinner and supper cometh all the whole Syphogranty or ward, warned by the noise of a brazen trumpet, except such as be sick in the hospitals or else in their own houses.

Howbeit, no man is prohibited or forbid after the halls be served to fetch home meat out of the market to his own house, for they know that no man will do it without a cause reasonable. For though no man be pro-

Every man is at his liberty so that nothing is done by compulsion.

hibited to dine at home, yet no man doth it willingly because it is counted a point of small honesty.[66] And also it were a folly to take the pain to dress[67] a bad dinner at home when they may be welcome to good and fine fare so nigh handy at the hall.

In this hall all vile service, all slavery and drudgery, with all laborsome toil and base business is done by bondmen. But the women of every family, by course, have the office and charge of cookery for seething[68] and dressing the meat

Women both dress and serve the meat.

---

[64]"Cured" = "cared for."
[65]"To throng and strait" = "in distress and privation."
[66]"Small honesty" = "little decency."
[67]"Dress" = "prepare."
[68]"Seething" = "boiling," "stewing."

and ordering all things thereto belonging. They sit at three tables or more, according to the number of their company. The men sit upon the bench next the wall, and the women against them on the other side of the table, that if any sudden evil should chanceth to them, as many times happeneth to women with child, they may rise without trouble or disturbance of anybody and go thence to the nursery.

The nurses [69] sit several alone with their young suck- | Nurses.
lings in a certain parlor appointed and deputed to the same purpose, never without fire and clean water, nor yet without cradles, that when they will they may lay down the young infants and at their pleasure take them out of their swathing clothes [70] and hold them to the fire and refresh them with play. Every mother is nurse to her own child, unless either death or sickness be the let. [71] When that chanceth, the wives of the Syphogrants quickly provide a nurse, and that is not hard to be done, for they that can do it proffer themselves to no service so gladly as to that, because that there | Nothing sooner provoketh men to well doing than praise and commendation.
this kind of pity is much praised, and the child that is nourished ever after taketh his nurse for his own natural mother. Also among the nurses sit all the children that be under the age of five years. All the other children of both kinds, as well boys as girls, that are under the age of marriage | The education of young children.
do either serve at the tables or else, if they be too young thereto, yet they stand by with marvelous [72] silence. That which is given to them from the table they eat, and other several dinnertime they have none.

The Syphogrant and his wife sit in the midst of the high table, forasmuch as that is counted the honorablest place and because from thence all the whole company is in their sight, for that table standeth overthwart the over end of the hall. [73] To them are joined two of the ancientest and eldest, for at every table they sit four at a mess. But if there be a church standing in that Syphogranty or ward, then the priest and his wife sitteth with the Syphogrant, as chief in the company. On both sides of them sit young men and next unto them again old men. And thus throughout all

---

[69] By "nurses" is meant wet nurses, i.e., women who suckle infants, but as the next sentence makes clear, Utopian mothers normally breast-feed their own children. In England in More's day, the children of more prosperous families often were put out to be nursed by poor women for a fee.

[70] "Swathing clothes" = "swaddling clothes."

[71] "Be the let" = "prevents her."

[72] "Marvelous" = "admirable."

[73] "Overthwart the over end of the hall" = "across the upper end of the hall" (i.e., the end away from the entrance door).

the house equal of age be set together and yet be mixed and matched with unequal ages. This, they say, was ordained to the intent that the sage gravity and reverence of the elders should keep the youngers from wanton license of words and behaviors, forasmuch as nothing can be so secretly spoken or done at the table, but either they that sit on the one side or on the other must needs perceive it. The dishes be not set down in order from the first place, but all the old men (whose places be marked with some special token to be known) are first served of their meat and then the residue equally. The old men divide their dainties[74] as they think best to the younger on each side of them. Thus the elders be not defrauded of their due honor, and, nevertheless, equal commodity cometh to everyone.

The young mixed with their elders.

Old men regarded and reverenced.

They begin every dinner and supper of reading something that pertaineth to good manners and virtue, but it is short because no man shall be grieved therewith. Hereof the elders take occasion of honest communication, but neither sad nor unpleasant. Howbeit, they do not spend all the whole dinnertime themselves with long and tedious talks, but they gladly hear also the young men, yea, and purposely provoke them to talk to the intent that they may have a proof of every man's wit and towardness or disposition to virtue, which commonly in the liberty of feasting doth show and utter itself.

This nowadays is observed in our universities.

Talk at the table.

Their dinners be very short, but their suppers are somewhat longer, because that after dinner followeth labor; after supper, sleep and natural rest, which they think to be of more strength and efficacy to wholesome and healthful digestion.

This is repugnant to the opinion of our physicians.

No supper is passed without music, nor their banquets lack no conceits nor junkets.[75] They burn sweet gums and spices or perfumes and pleasant smells, and sprinkle about sweet ointments and waters, yea, they leave nothing undone that maketh for the cheering of the company, for they be much inclined to this opinion, to think no kind of pleasure forbidden whereof cometh no harm. Thus, therefore, and after this sort they live together in the city, but in the country they that dwell alone far from any neighbors do dine and sup at home in their

Music at the table.

Pleasure without harm not discommendable.

---

[74]"Dainties" = "delicacies."
[75]"Conceits nor junkets" = "fancy sweets or cakes."

own houses, for no family there lacketh any kind of victuals, as from whom cometh all that the citizens eat and live by.

Of Their Journeying or Traveling Abroad, with Divers Other Matters Cunningly Reasoned and Wittily Discussed

But if any be desirous to visit either their friends dwelling in another city or to see the place itself, they easily obtain license of their Syphogrants and Tranibores, unless there be some profitable let.[76] No man goeth out alone but a company is sent forth together with their prince's letters, which do testify that they have license to go that journey and prescribeth also the day of their return. They have a wagon given them with a common bondman which driveth the oxen and taketh charge of them. But unless they have women in their company, they send home the wagon again as an impediment and a let. And though they carry nothing forth with them, yet in all their journey they lack nothing, for wheresoever they come, they be at home. If they tarry in a place longer than one day, then there everyone of them falleth to his own occupation and be very gently[77] entertained of the workmen and companies of the same crafts. If any man, of his own head and without leave, walk out of his precinct and bounds,[78] taken without the prince's letters, he is brought again for a fugitive or a runaway with great shame and rebuke and is sharply punished. If he be taken in that fault again, he is punished with bondage. If any be desirous to walk abroad into the fields or into the country that belongeth to the same city that he dwelleth in, obtaining the goodwill of his father and the consent of his wife, he is not prohibited. But into what part of the country soever he cometh he hath no meat given him until he have wrought out his forenoon's task or dispatched so much work as there is wont to be wrought before supper. Observing this law and condition, he may go whither he will within the bounds of his own city, for he shall be no less profitable to the city than if he were within it. Now you see how little liberty they have to loiter; how they can have no cloak or pretense to idleness.[79] There be neither wine taverns, nor alehouses, nor stews, nor any occasion for vice or wicked-

O holy commonwealth, and of Christians to be followed.

---

[76]"Let" = "obstruction."

[77]"Gently" = "genteelly," i.e., courteously or obligingly, as one gentleman would treat another.

[78]"Out of his precinct and bounds" = "out of his own home territory."

[79]"Cloak or pretense to idleness" = "excuse or pretext for idleness."

ness, no lurking corners,[80] no places of wicked councils or unlawful assemblies. But they be in the present sight and under the eyes of every man, so that of necessity they must either apply their accustomed labors or else recreate themselves with honest and laudable pastimes.

This fashion and trade of life, being used among the people, it cannot be chosen but that they must of necessity have store and plenty of all things. And seeing they be all thereof partners equally, therefore, can no man there be poor or needy. In the council of Amaurote, whither, as I said, every city sendeth three men apiece yearly, as soon as it is perfectly known of what things there is in every place plenty, and again what things be scant in any place, incontinent the lack of the one is performed and filled up with the abundance of the other.[81] And this they do freely without any benefit,[82] taking nothing again of them to whom the things are given, but those cities that have given of their store to any other city that lacketh, requiring nothing again of the same city, do take such things as they lack of another city to which they gave nothing. So the whole island is as it were one family or household. But when they have made sufficient provision of store for themselves (which they think not done until they have provided for two years following, because of the uncertainty of the next year's proof)[83] then of those things whereof they have abundance, they carry forth into other countries great plenty, as grain, honey, wool, flax, wood, madder,[84] purple dyed fells,[85] wax, tallow, leather, and living beasts. And the seventh part of all these things, they give frankly[86] and freely to the poor of that country. The residue they sell at a reasonable and mean[87] price. By this trade of traffic or merchandise they bring into their own country not only great plenty of gold and silver, but also all such things as they lack at home, which is almost nothing but iron. And by reason they have

Equality is the cause that every man hath enough.

A commonwealth is nothing else but a great household.

The traffic and merchandise of the Utopians.

---

[80] "Lurking corners" = "hiding places."

[81] "Incontinent the lack of the one is performed and filled up with the abundance of the other" = "the shortage in one place is immediately met from the abundant supplies in the others."

[82] "Without any benefit" = "without any material recompense or pecuniary gain."

[83] "Uncertainty of the next year's proof" = "uncertainty of next year's results," i.e., next year's harvest.

[84] "Madder" is a reddish dyestuff made from the root of a herbaceous climbing plant.

[85] "Fells" are animal skins or hides from which the hair has been removed.

[86] "Frankly" = "without reserve."

[87] "Mean" = "moderate."

long used this trade, now they have more abundance of these things than any man will believe.

Now, therefore, they care not whether they sell for ready money, or else upon trust to be paid at a day and to have the most part in debts. But in so doing they never follow the credence of private men, but the assurance or warrantise[88] of the whole city by instruments and writings made in that behalf accordingly. When the day of payment is come and expired, the city gathereth up the debt of the private debtors and putteth it into the common box, and so long hath the use and profit of it until the Utopians', their creditors, demand it. The most part of it they never ask, for that thing which is to them no profit to take it from other to whom it is profitable, they think it no right nor conscience. But if the case so stand that they must lend part of that money to another people, then they require their debt, or when they have war. For the which purpose only they keep at home all the treasure which they have to be helped and succored by it either in extreme jeopardies or in sudden dangers, but especially and chiefly to hire therewith, and that for unreasonable great wages, strange soldiers. For they had rather put strangers in jeopardy than their own countrymen, knowing that for money enough their enemies themselves many times may be bought and sold, or else through treason be set together by the ears among themselves. For this cause they keep an inestimable treasure, but yet not as a treasure, but so they have it and use it, as in good faith I am ashamed to show, fearing that my words shall not be believed. And this I have more cause to fear, for that I know how difficultly and hardily I meself would have believed another man telling the same if I had not presently seen it with mine own eyes. For it must needs be that how far a thing is dissonant and disagreeing from the guise and trade[89] of the hearers, so far shall it be out of their belief. Howbeit, a wise and indifferent esteemer of things will not greatly marvel perchance, seeing all their other laws and customs do so much differ from ours, if the use also of gold and silver among them be applied rather to their own fashions than to ours. I mean in that they occupy[90] not money

In all things and above all things to their continuity they have an eye.

By what policy money may be in less estimation.

It is better either with money or by policy to avoid war than with much loss of man's blood to fight.

A fine wit.

---

[88] "Warrantise" = "binding guarantee."
[89] "Guise and trade" = "habit and way of life."
[90] "Occupy" = "use."

themselves, but keep it for that chance, which, as it may happen, so it may be that it shall never come to pass. In the meantime gold and silver whereof money is made, they do so use, as none of them doth more esteem it than the very nature of the thing deserveth. And then who doth not plainly see how far it is under iron, as without the which men can no better live than without fire and water. Whereas to gold and silver nature hath given no use that we may not well lack, if that the folly of men had not set it in higher estimation for the rareness sake. But of the contrary part, nature, as a most tender and loving mother, hath placed the best and most necessary things open abroad, as the air, the water, and the earth itself, and hath removed and hid farthest from us vain and unprofitable things. Therefore, if these metals among them should be fast[91] locked up in some tower, it might be suspected that the prince and the council (as the people is ever foolishly imagining) intended by some subtlety to deceive the commons and to take some profit of it to themselves. Furthermore, if they should make thereof plate and such other finely and cunningly wrought stuff, if at any time they should have occasion to break it and melt it again therewith to pay their soldiers' wages, they see and perceive very well that men would be loath to part from those things that they once began to have pleasure and delight in. To remedy all this they have found out a means which, as it is agreeable to all their other laws and customs, so it is from ours, where gold is so much set by and so diligently kept, very far discrepant and repugnant,[92] and, therefore, uncredible,[93] but only to them that be wise.[94] For whereas they eat and drink in earthen and glass vessels, which indeed be curiously and properly made and yet be of very small value, of gold and silver they make commonly chamber pots and other vessels that serve for most vile uses, not only in their common halls but in every man's private house. Furthermore, of the same metals they make great chains, fetters, and gyves wherein they tie their bondmen. Finally, whosoever for any offense be infamed, by their ears hang rings of gold, upon their fingers they wear rings of gold, and about their necks chains of gold, and, in conclusion, their heads be tied about with gold. Thus by all means possible they procure to have gold and silver among them in reproach and infamy. And these metals, which

Gold worse than iron as touching the necessary use thereof.

O wonderful contumely of gold.

Gold, the reproachful badge of infamed persons.

---

[91] "Fast" = "securely."
[92] "Very far discrepant and repugnant" = "very dissimilar and divergent."
[93] "Uncredible" = "incredible," "beyond belief."
[94] "But only to them that be wise" = "except for those that have experienced it."

other nations do as grievously and sorrowfully forgo as in a manner their own lives, if they should altogether and at once be taken from the Utopians, no man there would think that he had lost the worth of one farthing. They gather also pearls by the seaside and diamonds and carbuncles[95] upon certain rocks, and yet they seek not for them, but, by chance finding them, they cut and polish them and therewith they deck their young infants, which like as in the first years of their childhood, they make much and be fond and proud of such ornaments, so when they be a little more grown in years and discretion, perceiving that none but children do wear such toys and trifles, they lay them away even of their own shamefastness, without any bidding of their parents, even as our children, when they wax big, do cast away nuts, brooches, and puppets.[96]

Gems and precious stones, toys for young children to play withal.

Therefore, these laws and customs, which be so far different from all other nations, how divers fantasies also and minds they do cause, did I never so plainly perceive as in the ambassadors of the Anemolians.[97] These ambassadors came to Amaurote whiles I was there, and because they came to entreat of great and weighty matters, those three citizens apiece out of every city were come thither before them. But all the ambassadors of the next countries, which had been there before and knew the fashions and manners of the Utopians, among whom they perceived no honor given to sumptuous apparel, silks to be contemned, gold also to be infamed and reproachful,[98] were wont to come thither in very homely and simple array. But the Anemolians, because they dwell far thence and had very little acquaintance with them, hearing that they were all appareled alike and that very rudely and homely, thinking them not to have the things which they did not wear, being therefore more proud than wise, determined in the gorgeousness of their apparel to represent very gods and with the bright shining and glittering of their gay clothing to dazzle the eyes of the silly poor Utopians. So there came in three ambassadors with one hundred servants all appareled in changeable[99] colors, the most of them in silks; the ambassadors themselves (for at home in their own

A very pleasant tale.

---

[95] "Carbuncles" = "precious stones."

[96] In the original Latin text, the words given by Robynson as "nuts, brooches, and puppets," are *nucas, bullas, & pupas,* referring in sequence to worthless objects cast upon the ground, as in our game of marbles (*nux*), trinkets or amulets hung about the children's necks (*bulla*), and finally to children's dolls (*pupa*).

[97] The name Anemolian derives from Greek, meaning "windy" in the sense of being full of empty words.

[98] "Infamed and reproachful" = "defamed and scorned."

[99] "Changeable" = "varying," "various."

country they were noblemen) in cloth of gold with great chains of gold, with gold hanging at their ears, with gold rings upon their fingers, with brooches and aglets[100] of gold upon their caps which glittered full of pearls and precious stones; to be short, trimmed and adorned with all those things which among the Utopians were either the punishment of bondmen, or the reproach of infamed persons, or else trifles for young children to play withal.

Therefore, it would have done a man good at his heart to have seen how proudly they displayed their peacocks' feathers, how much they made of their painted sheaths,[101] and how loftily they set forth and advanced themselves when they compared their gallant apparel with the poor raiment of the Utopians, for all the people were swarmed forth into the streets. And, on the other side, it was no less pleasure to consider how much they were deceived and how far they missed of their purpose, being contrary ways taken than they thought they should have been, for to the eyes of all the Utopians, except very few which had been in other countries for some reasonable cause, all that gorgeousness of apparel seemed shameful and reproachful,[102] insomuch that they most reverently saluted the vilest and most abject of them for lords, passing over the ambassadors themselves without any honor, judging them by their wearing of golden chains to be bondmen. Yea, you should have seen children also that had cast away their pearls and precious stones, when they saw the like sticking upon the ambassadors' caps, dig and push their mothers under the sides, saying thus to them: "Look, ——————— Mother, how great a lubber[103] doth yet wear pearls and   O witty head. precious stones as though he were a little child still." ——————— But the mother, yea, and that also in good earnest, "Peace, Son," saith she, "I think he be some of the ambassadors' fools." Some found fault at their golden chains as to no use nor purpose, being so small and weak that a bondman might easily break them, and again so wide and large that when it pleased him, he might cast them off and run away at liberty whether he would.

But when the ambassadors had been there a day or two and saw so great abundance of gold so lightly esteemed, yea, in no less reproach than it was with them in honor,[104] and besides that more gold in the

---

[100] "Aglets" = "spangles."
[101] "Painted sheaths" = "showy exteriors."
[102] "Reproachful" = "worthy of reproach."
[103] "Lubber" = "lout," "oafish fellow."
[104] "In no less reproach than it was with them in honor" = "as little valued by the Utopians as it was highly honored by the Anemolians."

chains and gyves of one fugitive bondman than all the costly ornaments of them three was worth, they began to abate their courage[105] and for very shame laid away all that gorgeous array whereof they were so proud. And specially when they had talked familiarly with the Utopians and had learned all their fashions and opinions, for they marvel that any men be so foolish as to have delight and pleasure in the doubtful glistering[106] of a little trifling stone which may behold any of the stars or else the sun itself. Or that any man is so mad as to count himself the

Doubtful he calleth it, either in consideration and respect of counterfeit stones, or else he calleth doubtful very little worth.

nobler for the smaller or finer thread of wool, which selfsame wool (be it now in never so fine a spun thread) a sheep did once wear, and yet was she all that time no other thing than a sheep. They marvel also that gold, which of the own nature is a thing so unprofitable, is now among all people in so high estimation that man himself, by whom, yea, and for the use of whom it is so much set by, is in much less estimation than the gold itself. In so much that a lumpish blockheaded churl,[107] and which hath no more wit than an ass, yea, and as full of naughtiness[108] as of folly, shall have nevertheless

A true saying and a witty.

many wise and good men in subjection and bondage only for this, because he hath a great heap of gold, which if it should be taken from him by any fortune or by some subtle wile and cautel[109] of the law (which no less than fortune doth both raise up the low and pluck down the high) and be given to the most vile slave and abject drivel[110] of all his household, then shortly after he shall go into the service of his servant as an augmentation or overplus beside his money.[111]

But they much more marvel at and detest the madness of them which to those rich men, in whose debt and danger they be not, do give almost divine honors for none other consideration but because they be rich,

How much more wit is in the heads of the Utopians than of the common sort of Christians.

and yet knowing them to be such niggish penny-fathers[112] that they be sure as long as they live not the worth of one farthing of that heap of gold shall come to them.

---

[105]"Courage" = "haughtiness," "pride."
[106]"Glistering" = "brilliance."
[107]"Churl" = "country bumpkin."
[108]"Naughtiness" = "wickedness."
[109]"Wile and cautel" = "deceitful stratagem or trick."
[110]"Drivel" = "drudge," "lowly laborer."
[111]"Then shortly after he shall go into the service of his servant as an augmentation or overplus beside his money" = "then he shall enter the employ of his former servant as though he was an appendage to the coins." Robynson's text has *nor* in place of *or.*
[112]"Niggish penny-fathers" = "niggardly or stingy misers."

These and such like opinions have they conceived partly by education, being brought up in that commonwealth whose laws and customs
be far different from these kinds of folly, and partly by good literature
and learning. For though there be not many in every city which be exempt and discharged of all other labors and appointed only to learning,
that is to say, such in whom even from their very childhood they have
perceived a singular towardness, a fine wit, and a mind apt to good learning, yet all in their childhood be instructed in learning, and the better
part of the people, both men and women, throughout all
their whole life do bestow in learning those spare hours   The studies and literature
which we said they have vacant from bodily labors.   among the Utopians.
They be taught learning in their own native tongue, for it is both copious
in words and also pleasant to the ear, and for the utterance of a man's
mind very perfect and sure. The most part of all that side of the world
useth the same language, saving that among the Utopians it is finest
and purest, and according to the diversity of the countries it is diversely
altered.

Of all these philosophers, whose names be here famous in this part of
the world to us known, before our coming thither, not as much as the
fame of any of them was common among them. And yet
in music, logic, arithmetic, and geometry they have   Music, logic, arithmetic,
found out in a manner all that our ancient philosophers   geometry.
have taught. But as they in all things be almost equal to our old ancient
clerks,[113] so our new logicians in subtle inventions have far passed and
gone beyond them. For they have not devised one of all
those rules of restrictions, amplifications, and supposi-   In this place seemeth to
tions, very wittily invented in the small logicals, which   be a nipping taunt.[114]
here our children in every place do learn. Furthermore, they were never
yet able to find out the second intentions, insomuch that none of them
all could ever see man himself in common, as they call him, though he
be (as you know) bigger than ever was any giant, yea, and pointed to of
us even with our finger.

But they be in the course of the stars and the movings of the heavenly spheres very expert and cunning.   Astronomy.
They have also wittily excogitated[115] and devised instruments of divers
fashions, wherein is exactly comprehended and contained the movings
and situations of the sun, the moon, and of all the other stars which ap-

---

[113]"Clerks" = "learned men."
[114]"In this place seemeth to be a nipping taunt" = "in these remarks there seems to be
rebuking sarcasm."
[115]"Excogitated" = "thought out."

pear in their horizon. But as for the amities and dissensions[116] of the planets and all that deceitful divination by the stars, they never as much as dreamed thereof. Rains, winds, and other courses of tempests they know before by certain tokens, which they have learned by long use and observation. But of the causes of all these things and of the ebbing, flowing, and saltiness of the sea, and finally of the original beginning and nature of heaven and of the world, they hold partly the same opinions that our old philosophers hold and partly, as our philosophers vary among themselves, so they also, whiles they bring new reasons of things, do disagree from all them and yet among themselves in all points they do not accord. In that part of philosophy which entreateth of manners and virtue, their reasons and opinions agree with ours. They dispute of the good qualities of the soul, of the body, and of fortune and whether the name of goodness may be applied to all these or only to the endowments and gifts of the soul. They reason of virtue and pleasure, but the chief and principal question is in what thing, be it one or more, the felicity of man consisteth. But in this point they seem almost too much given and inclined to the opinion of them which defend pleasure, wherein they determine either all or the chiefest part of man's felicity to rest.[118] And (which is more to be marveled at) the defense of this so dainty and delicate an opinion, they fetch even from their grave, sharp, bitter, and rigorous religion. For they never dispute of felicity or blessedness, but they join unto the reasons of philosophy certain principles taken out of religion, without the which to the investigation of true felicity they think reason of itself weak and unperfect. Those principles be these and such like: that the soul is immortal and by the bountiful goodness of God ordained to felicity; that to our virtues and good deeds rewards be appointed after this life and to our evil deeds punishments.[119] Though these be pertaining to

Yet among Christians this gear[117] is highly esteemed these days.

Natural philosophy is a knowledge most uncertain.

Moral philosophy.

The order of good things.

The ends of good things.

The Utopians hold opinion that felicity consisteth in honest pleasure.

The principles of philosophy grounded upon religion.

The theology of the Utopians.

The immortality of the soul, whereof these days certain Christians be in doubt.

---

[116] "Amities and dissensions" = "harmonies and conflicts."

[117] "Gear" = "rubbish."

[118] The focus on pleasure associates one party among the Utopians with the ancient Epicurean thinkers of Greece and Rome.

[119] These ideas have an affinity with those of Saint Thomas Aquinas, who sought to establish the principles of natural religion that could be known through reason alone.

religion, yet they think it meet that they should be believed and granted by proofs of reason. But if these principles were condemned and disannulled,[120] then without any delay they pronounce no man to be so foolish which would not do all his diligence and endeavour to obtain pleasure by right or wrong, only avoiding this inconvenience, that the less pleasure should not be a let or hindrance to the bigger, or that he labored not for that pleasure, which would bring after it displeasure, grief, and sorrow, for they judge it extreme madness to follow sharp and painful virtue, and not only to banish the pleasure of life, but also willingly to suffer grief without any hope of profit thereof ensuing. For what profit can there be if a man, when he hath passed over all his life unpleasantly, that is to say, miserably, shall have no reward after his death?

As every pleasure ought not to be embraced, so grief is not to be pursued but for virtue's sake.

But now, sir, they think not felicity to rest in all pleasure, but only in that pleasure that is good and honest and that hereto, as to perfect blessedness our nature is allured and drawn even of virtue,[121] whereto only they that be of the contrary opinion do attribute felicity, for they define virtue to be life ordered according to nature, and that we be hereunto ordained of God, and that he doth follow the course of nature, which, in desiring and refusing things, is ruled by reason. Furthermore, that reason doth chiefly and principally kindle in men the love and veneration of the divine majesty of whose goodness it is that we be, and that we be in possibility to attain felicity. And that secondarily it both stirreth and provoketh us to lead our life out of care in joy and mirth, and also moveth us to help and further all others in respect of the society of nature to obtain and enjoy the same. For there was never man so earnest and painful a follower of virtue and hater of pleasure that would so enjoin you labors, watchings, and fastings,[123] but he would also exhort you to ease, lighten, and relieve to your power the lack and misery of others, praising the same as

In this definition of virtue they agree with the Stoics.[122]

The work and effect of reason in man.

Aquinas, however, recognized the transcendent importance of revelation in providing access to truths that reason itself could not gain. The Utopians seem to have no such conception, at least not before they learn of Christianity from Hythloday and his companions.

[120]"Disannulled" = "canceled."

[121]"Allured and drawn even of virtue" = "attracted to and equated with virtue."

[122]This discussion distinguishes a second group of Utopians who, in agreeing with the Stoics, opposed the Epicurean ideas about happiness discussed in the previous paragraph. From the discussion that follows, it seems that the Epicurean views had the greater weight among most Utopians.

[123]"Labors, watchings, and fastings" = "contemplative efforts, vigils, and fasts."

a deed of humanity and pity. Then if it be a point of humanity for man to bring health and comfort to man, and especially (which is a virtue most peculiarly belonging to man) to mitigate and assuage the grief of others and, by taking from them the sorrow and heaviness of life, to restore them to joy, that is to say, to pleasure, why may it not then be said that nature doth provoke every man to do the same to himself? For a joyful life, that is to say, a pleasant life, is either evil and, if it be so, then thou shouldst not only help no man thereto, but rather, as much as in thee lieth, withdraw all men from it as noisome and hurtful, or else if thou not only mayst, but also of duty art bound to procure it to others, why not chiefly to thyself, to whom thou art bound to show as much favor and gentleness as to other?

But nowadays some there be that willingly procure unto themselves painful griefs, as though therein rested some high point of religion, whereas rather the religiously disposed person, if they happen to hie[124] either by chance or else by natural necessity, ought patiently to receive and suffer them.

For when nature biddeth thee to be good and gentle to other, she commandeth thee not to be cruel and ungently[125] to thyself. Therefore, even very nature (say they) prescribeth to us a joyful life, that is to say, pleasure as the end of all our operations, and they define virtue to be life ordered according to the prescript of nature. But in that that nature doth allure and provoke men one to help another to live merrily (which surely she doth not without a good cause, for no man is so far above the lot of man's state or condition that nature doth cark[126] and care for him only, which equally favoreth all that be comprehended under the communion of one shape, form, and fashion), verily, she commandeth thee to use diligent circumspection that thou do not so seek for thine own commodities, that thou procure others' incommodities. Wherefore, their opinion is that not only convenants and bargains made among private men ought to be well and faithfully fulfilled, observed,

Bargains and laws.

and kept, but also common laws, which either a good prince hath justly published, or else the people, neither oppressed with tyranny, neither deceived by fraud and guile, hath by their common consent constituted and ratified concerning the partition of the commodities of life, that is to say, the matter of pleasure. These laws not offended, it is wisdom that thou look to thine own wealth, and to do the same for the commonwealth is no less than thy duty if thou bearest any reverent love or any natural zeal and affection to thy native country. But to go about to let another man of his pleasure whiles thou procurest thine own, that is open

[124] "Hie" = "hasten."
[125] "Ungently" = "rough."
[126] "Cark" = "burden."

wrong. Contrariwise, to withdraw something from thyself to give to other, that is a point of humanity and gentleness, which never taketh away so much commodity as it bringeth *The mutual recourse of kindness.* again. For it is recompensed with the return of benefits and the conscience of the good deed, with the remembrance of the thankful love and benevolence of them to whom thou hast done it, doth bring more pleasure to thy mind than that which thou hast withholden from thyself could have brought to thy body. Finally (which to a godly disposed and a religious mind is easy to be persuaded), God recompenseth the gift of a short and small pleasure with great and everlasting joy.

Therefore, the matter diligently weighed and considered, thus they think that all our actions, and in them the virtues themselves, be referred at the last to pleasure as their end *The definition of pleasure.* and felicity. Pleasure they call every motion and state of the body or mind wherein man hath naturally delectation. Appetite they join to nature, and that not without a good cause, for like as not only the senses, but also right reason, coveteth whatsoever is naturally pleasant, so that it may be gotten without wrong or injury, not letting or debarring a greater pleasure, nor causing painful labor, even so those things that men by vain imagination do feign against nature to be pleasant (as though it lay in their power to *False and counterfeit pleasures.* change the things as they do the names of things), all such pleasures they believe to be of so small help and furtherance to felicity that they count them a great let and hinderance. Because that in whom they have once taken place, all his mind they possess with a false opinion of pleasure, so that there is no place left for true and natural delectations. For there be many things which of their own nature contain no pleasantness; yea, the most part of them much grief and sorrow, and yet, through the perverse and malicious flickering enticements of lewd and unhonest[127] desires, be taken not only for special and sovereign pleasures, but also be counted among the chief causes of life. In this counterfeit kind of pleasure they put them that I spake of before, which the better gowns they have on, the bet- *The error of them that esteem themselves the more for apparel's sake.* ter men they think themselves. In the which thing they do twice err, for they be no less deceived in that they think their gown the better than they be, in that they think themselves the better. For if you consider the profitable use of the garment, why should wool of a finer spun thread be thought better than the wool of a

---

[127] "Lewd and unhonest" = "vulgar and unseemly."

coarse spun thread? Yet they, as though the one did pass the other by nature and not by their mistaking, advance themselves, and think the price of their own persons thereby greatly increased. And, therefore, the honor, which in a coarse gown they durst not have looked for, they require, as it were of duty, for their finer gown's sake. And if they be passed by without reverence, they take it displeasantly [128] and disdainfully.

And again is it not a like madness to take a pride in vain and unprofitable honors? For what natural or true *Foolish honors.* pleasure dost thou take of another man's bare head or bowed knees? [129] Will this ease the pain of thy knees or remedy the frenzy of thy head? In this image of counterfeit pleasure, they be of a marvelous madness which, for the opinion of nobility, rejoice much in their own conceit, because it was their fortune to come of such ancestors, whose stock of long time hath been *Vain nobility.* counted rich (for now nobility is nothing else), specially rich in lands. And though their ancestors left them not one foot of land, or else they themselves have pissed it against the walls,[130] yet they think themselves not the less noble therefore of one hair.

In this number also they count them that take plea- *Pleasure in precious* sure and delight (as I said) in gems and precious stones *stones most foolish.* and think themselves almost gods if they chance to get an excellent one, specially of that kind which in that time of their own countrymen is had in highest estimation. For one kind of stone keepeth not his price still in all countries and at all times. Nor they buy them not, but taken out of the gold *The opinion and fancy of* and bare;[131] no nor so neither until they have made *people doth augment and* *diminish the price and* the seller to swear that he will warrant and assure it to *estimation of precious* be a true stone and no counterfeit gem. Such care they *stones.* take lest a counterfeit stone should deceive their eyes instead of a right stone. But why shouldst thou not take even as much pleasure in beholding a counterfeit stone, which thine eye cannot discern from a right stone? They should both be of like value to thee, even as to the blind man. What shall I say of them that *Beholders of treasure,* *not occupying the same.* keep superfluous riches to take delectation only in the beholding and not in the use or occupying thereof? Do they take true

---

[128] "Displeasantly" = "disagreeably."

[129] This passage mocks the signs of deference typically shown by inferiors to superiors in More's day, namely doffing the hat and, sometimes, kneeling.

[130] "Pissed it against the walls" = "squandered it."

[131] "But taken out of the gold and bare" = "unless they are taken out of their settings and exposed fully to view."

pleasure, or else be they deceived with false pleasure? Or of them that be in a contrary vice, hiding the gold which they shall never occupy nor peradventure never see more? And whiles they take care lest they shall lose it, do lose it indeed. For what is it else when they hide it in the ground, taking it both from their own use and perchance from all other men's also? And yet thou, when thou hast hid thy treasure, as one out of all care, hopest for joy. The which treasure, if it should chance to be stolen and thou ignorant of the theft shouldst die ten years after, all that ten years' space that you livest after thy money was stolen, what matter was it to thee whether it had been taken away or else safe as thou leftest it? Truly both ways like profit came to thee.

Hiders of treasure.

A pretty fiction and a witty.

To these so foolish pleasures they join dicers, whose madness they know by hearsay and not by use; hunters also, and hawkers.[132] For what pleasure is there (say they) in casting the dice upon a table, which thou hast done so often that, if there were any pleasure in it, yet the oft use might make thee weary thereof? Or what delight can there be, and not rather displeasure, in hearing the barking and howling of dogs? Or what greater pleasure is there to be felt when the dog followeth an hare than when a dog followeth a dog? For one thing is done in both, that is to say, running, if thou hast pleasure therein. But if the hope of slaughter and the expectation of tearing in pieces the beast doth please thee, thou shouldst rather be moved with pity to see a silly innocent hare murdered of a dog: the weak of the stronger, the fearful of the fierce, the innocent of the cruel and unmerciful. Therefore, all this exercise of hunting, as a thing unworthy to be used of free men, the Utopians have rejected to[133] their butchers, to the which craft (as we said before) they appoint their bondmen. For they count hunting the lowest, the vilest, and most abject part of butchery, and the other parts of it more profitable and more honest, as bringing much more commodity in that they kill beasts only for necessity, whereas the hunter seeketh nothing but pleasure of the silly and woeful[134] beasts' slaughter and murder. The which pleasure in beholding death they think doth rise in the very beasts, either of a cruel affection of mind or else to be changed in continuance of time into cruelty by long use of so cruel a pleasure. These, therefore, and all such like, which be innumerable though the common

Dice-play.

Hunting and hawking.

Hunting, the basest part of butchery among the Utopians, and yet this is now the exercise of most noblemen.

---

[132] "Hawkers" = "falconers," "men engaged in the art of falconry."
[133] "Rejected to" = "cast off to."
[134] "Silly and woeful" = "helpless and miserable or unfortunate."

sort of people doth take them for pleasures, yet they, seeing there is no natural pleasantness in them, do plainly determine them to have no affinity with true and right pleasure. For as touching that they do commonly move the sense with delectation (which seemeth to be a work of pleasure) this does nothing diminish their opinion. For not the nature of the thing, but their perverse and lewd custom is the cause hereof, which causeth them to accept bitter or sour things for sweet things, even as women with child, in their vitiate and corrupt taste,[135] think pitch and tallow sweeter than any honey. Howbeit, no man's judgment, depraved and corrupt either by sickness or by custom, can change the nature of pleasure, more than it can do the nature of other things.

They make divers kinds of pleasures, for some they attribute to the soul and some to the body. To the soul they give intelligence and that delectation that cometh of the contemplation of truth. Hereunto is joined the pleasant remembrance of the good life past. The pleasure of the body they divide into two parts. The first is when delectation is sensibly felt and perceived, which many times chanceth by the renewing and refreshing of those parts which our natural heat drieth up. This cometh by meat and drink. And sometimes whiles those things be expulsed and voided, whereof is in the body overgreat abundance. This pleasure is felt when we do our natural easement, or when we be doing the act of generation, or when the itching of any part is eased with rubbing or scratching. Sometimes pleasure riseth exhibiting to any member nothing that it desireth, nor taking from it any pain that it feeleth, which nevertheless tickleth and moveth our senses with a certain secret efficacy, but with a manifest motion turneth them to it, as is that which cometh of music.

The kinds of true pleasures.

The pleasures of the body.

The second part of bodily pleasure, they say, is that which consisteth and resteth in the quiet and upright state of the body, and that, truly, is every man's own proper health intermingled and disturbed with no grief. For this, if it be not letted nor assaulted with no grief, is delectable of itself, though it be moved with no external or outward pleasure, for though it be not so plain and manifest to the sense, as the greedy lust[136] of eating and drinking, yet nevertheless many take it for the chiefest pleasure. All the Utopians grant it to be a right sovereign[137] pleasure and, as you would say, the foundation and ground of all pleasures, as which even alone is able

Bodily health.

---

[135]"Vitiate and corrupt taste" = "impaired and distorted sense of taste."
[136]"Greedy lust" = "insatiable appetite."
[137]"Right sovereign" = "truly supreme."

to make the state and condition of life delectable and pleasant, and it being once taken away, there is no place left for any pleasure. For to be without grief, not having health, that they call insensibility and not pleasure.

The Utopians have long ago rejected and condemned the opinion of them which said that steadfast and quiet health (for this question also hath been diligently debated among them) ought not, therefore, to be counted a pleasure, because they say it cannot be presently and sensibly perceived and felt by some outward motion. But of the contrary part now they agree almost all in this, that health is a most sovereign pleasure. For seeing that in sickness (say they) is grief, which is a mortal enemy to pleasure even as sickness is to health, why should not then pleasure be in the quietness of health? For they say it maketh nothing to this matter whether you say that sickness is a grief or that in sickness is grief, for all cometh to one purpose. For whether health be a pleasure itself, or a necessary cause of pleasure as fire is of heat, truly, both ways it followeth that they cannot be without pleasure that be in perfect health. Furthermore, whiles we eat (say they) then health, which began to be appaired,[138] fighteth by the help of food against hunger. In the which fight, whiles health by little and little getteth the upper hand, that same proceeding and (as ye would say) that onwardness to the wont strength ministereth that pleasure, whereby we be so freshed.[139] Health, therefore, which in the conflict is joyful, shall it not be merry when it hath gotten the victory? But as soon as it hath recovered the pristinate[140] strength, which thing only in all the fight it coveted, that it incontinent be astonied?[141] Nor shall it not know nor embrace thy[142] own wealth and goodness? For where it is said health cannot be felt, this, they think, is nothing true. For what man waking, say they, feeleth not himself in health, but he that is not? Is there any man so possessed with stonish[143] insensibility or with lethargy, that is to say, the sleeping sickness, that he will not grant health to be acceptable to him and delectable?

But what other thing is delectation than that which by another name is called pleasure? They embrace

Delectation.

---

[138] "Appaired" = "impaired."

[139] "That onwardness to the wont strength ministereth that pleasure, whereby we be so freshed" = "that our advancement to the wished-for healthiness imparts pleasure in its own right, by which we be so refreshed."

[140] "Pristinate" = "pristine," "former," "original."

[141] "It incontinent be astonied" = "it is immediately rendered powerless."

[142] Robynson's original has *the* in this place, apparently a printer's error.

[143] "Stonish" = "stonelike."

chiefly the pleasures of the mind, for them they count
the chiefest and most principal of all. The chief part of
them they think doth come of the exercise of virtue and
conscience of good life. Of these pleasures that the body ministereth,
they give the preeminence to health. For the delight of eating and drinking, and whatsoever hath any like pleasantness, they determine to be
pleasures much to be desired, but no other ways than for health's sake.
For such things of their own proper nature be not so pleasant, but in that
they resist sickness privily stealing on. Therefore, like as it is a wise
man's part rather to avoid sickness than to wish for medicines, and
rather to drive away and put to flight careful griefs than to call for comfort, so it is much better not to need this kind of pleasure than thereby
to be eased of the contrary grief. The which kind of pleasure if any man
take for his felicity, that man must needs grant that then he shall be in
most felicity, if he live that life which is led in continual hunger, thirst,
itching, eating, drinking, scratching, and rubbing. The which life how
not only foul and unhonest, but also how miserable and wretched it is,
who perceiveth not? These doubtless be the basest pleasures of all, as
unpure and unperfect, for they never come but accompanied with their
contrary griefs. As with the pleasure of eating is joined hunger, and that
after no very equal sort. For of these two, the grief is both the more ve-
hement and also of longer continuance, for it beginneth before the pleasure and endeth not until the pleasure die with it, wherefore such pleasures they think not greatly to be set by, but in that they are necessary.
Howbeit, they have delight also in these, and thankful knowledge [144] the
tender love of mother nature, which with most pleasant delectation al-
lureth her children to that, to the necessary use whereof they must from
time to time continually be forced and driven. For how wretched and
miserable should our life be if these daily griefs of hunger and thirst
could not be driven away, but with bitter potions and sour medicines, as
the other diseases be, wherewith we be seldomer troubled. But beauty,
strength, nimbleness, these as peculiar and pleasant
gifts of nature they make much of. But those pleasures
that be received by the ears, the eyes, and the nose,
which nature willeth to be proper and peculiar to man (for no other living creature doth behold the fairness and the beauty of the world, or is
moved with any respect of savors,[145] but only for the diversity of meats,

The pleasures of the mind.

The gifts of nature.

---

[144] "Thankful knowledge" = "gratefully acknowledge."
[145] "Moved with any respect of savors" = "moved by consideration of differing aromas and tastes of foods."

neither perceiveth the concordant and discordant distances of sounds and tunes), these pleasures, I say, they accept and allow as certain pleasant rejoicings of life. But in all things this cautel[146] they use, that a less pleasure hinder not a bigger, and that the pleasure be no cause of displeasure, which they think to follow of necessity if the pleasure be unhonest. But yet to despise the comeliness of beauty, to waste the bodily strength, to turn nimbleness into sloughishness,[147] to consume and make feeble the body with fasting, to do injury to health and to reject the pleasant motions of nature, unless a man neglect these commodities whiles he doth with a fervent zeal procure the wealth of others or the common profit, for the which pleasure foreborn,[148] he is in hope of a greater pleasure at God's hand else for a vain shadow of virtue, for the wealth and profit of no man, to punish himself or to the intent he may be able courageously to suffer adversity, which perchance shall never come to him, this to do they think it a point of extreme madness and a token of a man cruelly minded towards himself and unkind towards nature, as one so disdaining to be in her danger that he renounceth and refuseth all her benefits.

This is their sentence and opinion of virtue and pleasure, and they believe that by man's reason none can be found truer than this, unless any godlier be inspired into man from heaven. Wherein, whether they believe well or no, neither the time doth suffer us to discuss, neither it is now necessary, for we have taken upon us to show and declare their lores[149] and ordinances, and not to defend them. But this thing I believe verily: howsoever these decrees be, that there is in no place of the world neither a more excellent people neither a more flourishing commonwealth. They be light and quick of body, full of activity and nimbleness, and of more strength than a man would judge them by their stature, which for all that is not too low. And though their soil be not very fruitful nor their air very wholesome, yet against the air they so defend them with temperate diet, and so order and husband their ground with diligent travail, that in no country is greater increase and plenty of corn and cattle, nor men's bodies of longer life and subject or apt to fewer diseases. There, therefore, a man may see well and diligently exploited and furnished not only those things which husbandmen do commonly in other countries, as by craft and cunning

Mark this well.

The wealth and description of the Utopians.

---

[146]"Cautel" = "stratagem."
[147]"Sloughishness" = "sluggishness."
[148]"Foreborn" = "shunned."
[149]"Lores" = "precepts," "doctrines."

to remedy the barrenness of the ground, but also a whole wood by the hands of the people plucked up by the roots in one place and set again in another place. Wherein was had regard and consideration, not of plenty, but of commodious carriage,[150] that wood and timber might be nigher to the sea, or the rivers, or the cities, for it is less labor and business to carry grain far by land than wood.

The people be gentle, merry, quick, and fine-witted, delighting in quietness and, when need requireth, able to abide and suffer much bodily labor. Else they be not greatly desirous and fond of it, but in the exercise and study of the mind they be never weary. When they had heard me speak of the Greek litera-ture or learning (for in Latin there was nothing that I *The utility of the Greek tongue.* thought they would greatly allow besides historians and poets), they made wonderful earnest and importunate suit unto me that I would teach and instruct them in that tongue and learning. I began, therefore, to read unto them, at the first truly more because I would not seem to refuse the labor than that I hoped that they would anything profit therein. But when I had gone forward a little, I perceived incontinent by their diligence that my labor should not be bestowed in vain, for they began so easily to fashion their letters, so *A wonderful aptness to learning in the Utopians.* plainly to pronounce the words, so quickly to learn by heart, and so surely to rehearse the same that I marveled at it, saving that the most part of them were fine and chosen wits and of ripe age,[151] picked out of the company of the *But now most block-headed asses are set to learning, and most preg-nant wits corrupt with pleasures.* learned men, which not only of their own free and vol-untary will, but also by the commandment of the coun-cil, undertook to learn this language. Therefore, in less than three years' space there was nothing in the Greek tongue that they lacked. They were able to read good authors without any stay, if the book were not false.[152] This kind of learning, as I suppose, they took so much the sooner because it is somewhat alliant[153] to them. For I think that this nation took their beginning of the Greeks because their speech, which in all other points is not much unlike the Persian tongue, keepeth divers signs and tokens of the Greek language in the names of their cities and of their magistrates.

They have of me (for when I was determined to enter into my fourth voyage, I cast into the ship in the stead of merchandise a pretty fardel[154]

[150] "Commodious carriage" = "ease of transportation."
[151] "Of ripe age" = "mature in years."
[152] "False" = "filled with scribe's or printer's errors."
[153] "Alliant" = "akin."
[154] "Pretty fardel" = "good-sized package or collection."

of books because I intended to come again rather never than shortly), they have, I say, of me the most part of Plato's works, more of Aristotle's, also Theophrastus of plants[155] but in divers places (which I am sorry for) unperfect. For whiles we were a-shipboard, a marmoset chanced upon the book as it was negligently laid by, which wantonly playing therewith plucked out certain leaves and tore them in pieces. Of them that have written the grammar, they have only Lascaris, for Theodorus I carried not with me,[156] nor never a dictionary but Hesichius and Dioscorides.[157] They set great store by Plutarch's books, and they be delighted with Lucian's merry conceits and jests.[158] Of the poets, they have Aristophanes, Homer, Euripides, and Sophocles in Aldus small print.[159] Of the historians they have Thucydides, Herodotus, and Herodian.[160] Also my companion, Tricius Apinatus,[161] carried with him physic books, certain small works of Hippocrates, and Galen's *Microtechne,* the which book they have in great estimation.[162] For though there is almost no nation under heaven that hath less need of physic than they, yet this not withstanding, physic is

Physic highly regarded.

---

[155]Theophrastus, a pupil and successor of Aristotle, was the author, among other texts, of two works on plants, one a description and classification and the other a physiology of plant life.

[156]Constantine Lascaris (d. 1493 or 1500) was a member of a Byzantine noble family with imperial ancestors, who after the fall of Constantinople in 1453 came to reside in Milan under the protection of its duke; his grammar in four books was published in Milan in 1475. The rival grammar of Theodorus of Gaza (c. 1400–1475), another Byzantine scholar living in exile in Italy, was first published in Venice in 1495.

[157]Hesichius was one (or perhaps both) of two dictionary writers who lived in Alexandria and Miletus in the fifth and sixth centuries C.E. His lexicon was first published in Venice in 1514, just before More undertook the writing of *Utopia.* Dioscorides Pedanus, an army physician under Claudius and Nero in the first-century Roman Empire, wrote a systematic account of plants and pharmacology, not a dictionary; his work was first published in Venice in 1499.

[158]Plutarch (c. 50–120 C.E.) was best known in More's era for his *Moralia,* works on ethics. For the significance of Lucian of Samosata (c. 120–180 C.E.) to More, see p. 7.

[159]Aldus Manutius (1449–1515), the Venetian printer, was especially noted, and is here honored at the time of his death, for his publication of Greek texts. His edition of Aristophanes appeared in 1498, his Homer after October 1504, his Euripides in 1504, and his Sophocles in 1502. For a time, Erasmus had lived with him.

[160]Thucydides the Athenian and Herodotus of Halicarnassus are the well-known Greek historians of the fifth century B.C.E. Herodian of Syria (c. 175–250 C.E.) wrote a much less famous history of the Roman emperors from Marcus Aurelius to Gordian III, covering the years 180–238 C.E.

[161]The name, referring to "trifles and toys," derives from Martial's *Epigrams,* XIV.1.

[162]In More's day, Hippocrates of Cos, a contemporary of Socrates in the fifth century B.C.E., and Galen of Pergamum (129?–199 C.E.), were the best known and most highly regarded writers on "physic," or medicine, of the ancient world. Galen's *Microtechne,* also known as the *Ars Medica,* had wide circulation during the Middle Ages as well as during the Renaissance.

nowhere in greater honor because they count the knowledge of it among the goodliest and most profitable parts of philosophy. For whiles they by the help of this philosophy search out the secret mysteries of nature, they think themselves to receive thereby not only wonderful great pleasure, but also to obtain great thanks and favor of the author and maker thereof, whom they think, according to the fashion of other artificers, to have set forth the marvelous and gorgeous frame of the world for man with great affection intentively to behold, whom only he hath made of wit and capacity to consider and understand the excellency of so great a work. And, therefore, he beareth (say they) more goodwill and love to the curious and diligent beholder and viewer of his work and marveler at the same than he doth to him, which like a very brute beast without wit and reason or as one without sense or moving hath no regard to so great and so wonderful a spectacle.

The contemplation of nature.

The wits, therefore, of the Utopians, inured and exercised in learning, be marvelous quick in the inventions of feats helping anything to the advantage and wealth of life. Howbeit, two feats they may thank us for, that is the science of imprinting and the craft of making paper. And yet not only us but chiefly and principally themselves. For when we showed to them Aldus, his print in books of paper, and told them of the stuff whereof paper is made and of the feat of graving[163] letters, speaking somewhat more than we could plainly declare (for there was none of us that knew perfectly either the one or the other), they forthwith very wittily conjectured the thing. And whereas before they wrote only in skins, in barks of trees, and in reeds, now they have attempted to make paper and to imprint letters. And though at the first it proved not all of the best, yet by often assaying the same they shortly got the feat of both, and have so brought the matter about that, if they had copies of Greek authors, they could lack no books. But now they have no more than I rehearsed before, saving that by printing of books they have multiplied and increased the same into many thousands of copies. Whosoever cometh thither to see the land, being excellent in any gift of wit or through much and long journeying well experienced and seen in the knowledge of many countries (for the which cause we were very welcome to them), him they receive and entertain wondrous gently and lovingly, for they have delight to hear what is done in every land, howbeit very few merchantmen come thither. For what should they bring thither unless it were iron, or else gold and silver, which they had rather carry

---

[163] "Graving" = "carving."

home again? Also such things as are to be carried out of their land, they think it more wisdom to carry that gear forth themselves than that others should come thither to fetch it, to the intent they may the better know the outlands on every side of them and keep in ure [164] the feat and knowledge of sailing.

Of Bondmen, Sick Persons, Wedlock, and Divers Other Matters

They neither make bondmen of prisoners taken in battle, unless it be in battle that they fought themselves, nor of bondmen's children, nor, to be short, of any such as they can get out of foreign countries though he were there a bondman, but either such as among themselves for heinous offenses be punished with bondage, or else such as in the cities of other lands for great trespasses be condemned to death. And of this sort of bondman they have most store. For many of them they bring home sometimes paying very little for them, yea, most commonly getting them for gramercy.[165] These sorts of bondmen they keep not only in continual work and labor, but also in bands.[166] But their own men they handle hardest, whom they judge more desperate and to have deserved greater punishment, because they being so godly brought up to virtue in so excellent a commonwealth could not for all that be refrained from misdoing. Another kind of bondman they have when a vile drudge [167] being a poor laborer in another country doth choose of his own free will to be a bondman among them. These they entreat and order honestly and entertain almost as gently as their own free citizens, saving that they put them to a little more labor as thereto accustomed. If any such be disposed to depart thence (which seldom is seen), they neither hold him against his will neither send him away with empty hands.

A marvelous equity of this nation.

The sick (as I said) they see to with great affection and let nothing at all pass concerning either physic or good diet whereby they may be restored again to their health. Such as be sick of incurable diseases they comfort with sitting by them, with talking with them, and, to be short, with all manner of helps that may be. But if the disease be not only incurable but also full of continual pain and anguish, then the priests and the magistrates exhort the man, seeing he is not able to do any duty of life and, by

Of them that be sick.

---

[164] "In ure" = "in practice," "in use."
[165] "For gramercy" = "for a thank-you."
[166] "Bands" = "chains," "shackles."
[167] "Vile drudge" = "lowly, base, or menial laborer."

overliving his own death, is noisome and irksome to others and grievous to himself, that he will determine with himself no longer to cherish that pestilent and painful disease. And seeing his life is to him but a torment, that he will not be unwilling to die, but rather take a good hope to him and either dispatch himself out of that painful life, as out of a prison or a rack of torment, or else suffer himself willingly to be rid out of it by others. And in so doing they tell him he shall do wisely, seeing by his death he shall lose no commodity, but end his pain. And because in that act he shall follow the counsel of the priests, that is to say, of the interpreters of God's will and pleasure, they show him that he shall do like a godly and a virtuous man. They that be thus persuaded finish their lives willingly, either with hunger or else die in their sleep without any feeling of death. But they cause none such to die against his will, nor they use no less diligence and attendance about him, believing this to be an honorable death. Else he that killeth himself before that the priests and the council have allowed the cause of his death, him as unworthy either to be buried or with fire to be consumed, they cast unburied into some stinking marsh.[168]

Voluntary death.

The woman is not married before she be eighteen years old. The man is four years older before he marry. If either the man or the woman be proved to have actually offended before their marriage with another, the party that so hath trespassed is sharply punished, and both the offenders be forbidden ever after in all their life to marry, unless the fault be forgiven by the prince's pardon. But both the good man and the good wife of the house where that offense was committed, as being slack and negligent in looking to their charge, be in danger of great reproach and infamy. That offense is so sharply punished because they perceive that, unless they be diligently kept from the liberty of this vice, few will join together in the love of marriage, wherein all the life must be led with one, and also all the griefs and displeasures coming therewith patiently be taken and borne.

Of wedlock.

Furthermore, in choosing wives and husbands they observe earnestly and straitly a custom which seemed to us very fond and foolish. For a sad and honest matron showeth the woman, be she maid or widow, naked to the wooer. And likewise a sage and discreet man exhibiteth the wooer naked to the woman.[169] At this custom we laughed and disallowed it as foolish.

Though not very honestly, yet not unwisely.

---

[168] For discussion of the significance of this passage on suicide, see p. 18.
[169] This practice parallels the one described in Plato's *Laws*, VI.771e–772a.

But they, on the other part, do greatly wonder at the folly of all other nations which in buying a colt,[170] whereas a little money is in hazard, be so chary and circumspect, that though he be almost all bare, yet they will not buy him unless the saddle and all the harness be taken off, lest under those coverings be hid some gall or sore. And yet in choosing a wife, which shall be either pleasure or displeasure to them all their life after, they be so reckless that all the residue of the woman's body being covered with clothes, they esteem her scarcely by one handbreadth (for they can see no more but her face), and so to join her to them not without great jeopardy of evil agreeing together, if anything in her body afterward should chance to offend and mislike them. For all men be not so wise as to have respect to the virtuous conditions of the party, and the endowments of the body cause the virtues of the mind more to be esteemed and regarded, yea, even in the marriages of wise men. Verily, so foul deformity may be hid under those coverings that it may quite alienate and take away the man's mind from his wife, when it shall not be lawful for their bodies to be separate again. If such deformity happen by any chance after the marriage is consummate and finished, well, there in no remedy but patience. Every man must take his fortune well a worth.[171] But it were well done that a law were made whereby all such deceits might be eschewed and avoided beforehand.

And this were they constrained more earnestly to look upon, because they only of the nations in that part of the world be content every man with one wife apiece. And matrimony is there never broken but by death, except adultery break the bond or else the intolerable wayward manners of either party. For if either of them find themself for any such cause grieved, they may by the license of the council change and take another, but the other party liveth ever after in   Divorcement. infamy and out of wedlock. Howbeit, the husband to put away his wife for no other fault but for that some mishap is fallen to her body, this by no means they will suffer. For they judge it a great point of cruelty that anybody in their most need of help and comfort should be cast off and forsaken and that old age, which both bringeth sickness with it and is a sickness itself, should unkindly and unfaithfully be dealt withal. But now and then it chanceth, whereas the man and the woman cannot well agree between themselves, both of them finding other with whom they hope to live more quietly and merrily, that they, by the full

---

[170]The reference to a "colt" in this context is probably More's private and personal pun: His first wife, who had died in 1511, was Jane Colt, the daughter of John Colt, a gentleman of Newhall in the county of Essex.
[171]"Take his fortune well a worth" = "accept his fate as chance provides."

consent of them both, be divorced asunder and married again to others. But that not without the authority of the council which agreeth to no divorces before they and their wives have diligently tried and examined the matter. Yea, and then also they be loath to consent to it because they know this to be the next way to break love between man and wife, to be in easy hope of a new marriage.

Breakers of wedlock be punished with most grievous bondage. And if both the offenders were married, then the parties which in that behalf have suffered wrong, being divorced from the avoutrers,[172] are married together if they will or else to whom they lust. But if either of them both do still continue in love toward so unkind a bedfellow, the use of wedlock[173] is not to them forbidden if the party faultless be disposed to follow in toiling and drudgery the person which for that offense is condemned to bondage. And very oft it chanceth that the repentance of the one and the earnest diligence of the other doth so move the prince with pity and compassion that he restoreth the bond person from servitude to liberty and freedom again. But if the same party be taken eftsoons[174] in that fault, there is no other way but death.

To other trespasses no prescript punishment is appointed by any law, but according to the heinousness of the offense, or contrary, so the punishment is moderated by the discretion of the council. The husbands chastise their wives and the parents their children, unless they have done any so horrible an offense that the open punishment thereof maketh much for the advancement of honest manners. But most commonly the most heinous faults be punished with the incommodity of bondage, for that they suppose to be to the offenders no less grief and to the commonwealth more profit than if they should hastily put them to death and so make them quite out of the way. For there cometh more profit of their labor than of their death, and by their example they fear other the longer from like offenses.[176] But if they, being thus used, do rebel and kick again, then, forsooth, they be slain as desperate and wild beasts whom neither prison nor chain could restrain and keep under.

> The discerning[175] of punishment put to the discretion of the magistrates.

---

[172] "Avoutrers" = "adulterers."

[173] "Use of wedlock" = "continuation in a married state."

[174] "Eftsoons" = "again," "a second time."

[175] "Discerning" = "distinguishing," "determining."

[176] "And by their example they fear other the longer from like offenses" = "and their continuing presence in the community is a more effective deterrent for similar crimes." The punishment of enslavement for crimes, harsh as it is, represents a mitigation of harshness of the criminal law in England as it was practiced in More's day, when the only punishment available for felony was execution.

But they which take their bondage patiently be not left all hopeless. For after they have been broken and tamed with long miseries, if then they show such repentance as thereby it may be perceived that they be sorrier for their offenses than for their punishment, sometimes by the prince's prerogative, and sometimes by the voice and consent of the people, their bondage either is mitigated or else clean released and forgiven. He that moveth to avoutry[177] is in no less danger and jeopardy than if he had committed avoutry indeed. For in all offenses they count the intent and pretensed purpose as evil as the act or deed itself, thinking that no let ought to excuse him that did his best to have no let.

Motion to avoutry punished.

They have singular delight and pleasure in fools. And as it is a great reproach to do to any of them hurt or injury, so they prohibit not to take pleasure of foolishness, for that, they think, doth much good to the fools. And if any man be so sad and stern that he cannot laugh neither at their words nor at their deeds, none of them be committed to his tuition,[178] for fear lest he would not entreat them gently and favorably enough to whom they should bring no delectation (for other goodness in them is none), much less any profit should they yield him. To mock a man for his deformity or for that he lacketh any part or limb of his body is counted great dishonesty and reproach, not to him that is mocked but to him that mocketh, which unwisely doth embraid[179] any man of that as a vice that was not in his power to eschew.

Pleasure of fools.

Also, as they count and reckon very little wit to be in him that regardeth not natural beauty and comeliness, so to help the same with paintings[180] is taken for a vain and a wanton pride, not without great infamy. For they know even by very experience that no comeliness of beauty doth so highly commend and advance the wives in the conceit[181] of their husbands as honest conditions and lowliness.[182] For as love is oftentimes won with beauty, so it is not kept, preserved, and continued but by virtue and obedience. They do not only fear their people from doing evil by punishments, but also allure them to virtue with rewards of honor. Therefore, they set up in the marketplace the images of notable men and of such as have been great and

Counterfeit beauty.

Sin punished and virtue rewarded.

---

[177]"Avoutry" = "adultery."
[178]"Tuition" = "education."
[179]"Embraid" = "mock."
[180]"Paintings" = "cosmetics."
[181]"Conceit" = "estimation."
[182]"Lowliness" = "humility."

bountiful benefactors to the commonwealth for the perpetual memory of their good acts, and also that the glory and reknown of the ancestors may fire and provoke their posterity to virtue. He that inordinately and ambitiously desireth promotions is left all hopeless for ever attaining any promotion as long as he liveth.

The inordinate desire of honors condemned.

They live together lovingly, for no magistrate is either haughty or fearful.[183] Fathers they be called, and like fathers they use themselves. The citizens (as it is their duty) willingly exhibit unto them due honor without any compulsion. Nor the prince himself is not known from the other by princely apparel or a robe of state, nor by a crown or diadem royal, or cap of maintenance,[184] but by a little sheaf of corn carried before him. And so a taper of wax is borne before the bishop, whereby only he is known.

Magistrates honored.

They have but few laws, for to people so instruct and institute[185] very few do suffice. Yea, this thing they chiefly reprove among other nations, that innumerable books of laws and expositions upon the same be not sufficient. But they think it against all right and justice that men should be bound to those laws which either be in number more than be able to be read or else blinder and darker than that any man can well understand them.

Few laws.

Furthermore, they utterly exclude and banish all attorneys, proctors, and sergeants-at-the-law,[186] which craftily handle matters and subtly dispute of the laws. For they think it most meet that every man should plead his own matter and tell the same tale before the judge that he would tell to his man of law.[187] So shall there be less circumstance of words, and the truth shall sooner come to light, whiles the judge with a discreet judgment doth weigh the words of him whom no lawyer hath instruct with deceit, and whiles he helpeth and beareth out simple wits against the false and

The multitude of lawyers superfluous.

---

[183] "No magistrate is either haughty or fearful" = "no official is either full of pride or a source of terror."

[184] A "cap of maintenance" was a cap signifying the dignity and authority of an office-holder; since Henry VII, one has been borne before the kings and queens of England at their coronations.

[185] "So instruct and institute" = "so educated and disciplined."

[186] In this context, the term "attorney" signifies an agent to whom is delegated the responsibility to plead for others in the law courts. "Proctor" is a general term for a deputy or proxy who stands in for others in managing their personal or business affairs, including representing his client or principal in legal matters. In England, the term "sergeants-at-law" designates, quite specifically, the members of a superior order among barristers, figures who often pleaded for the Crown and from whom the royal judges were chosen.

[187] "Man of law" = "lawyer."

malicious circumventions of crafty children. This is hard to be observed in other countries in so infinite a number of blind and intricate[188] laws. But in Utopia every man is a cunning lawyer, for as (I said) they have very few laws, and the plainer and grosser[189] that any interpretation is, that they allow as most just.

For all laws (say they) be made and published only to the intent that by them every man should be put in remembrance of his duty. But the crafty and subtle interpretation of them (forasmuch as few can attain thereto) can put very few in that remembrance, whereas the simple, the plain, and gross[190] meaning of the laws is open to every man. Else as touching the vulgar sort of the people which be both most in number and have most need to know their duties, were it not as good for them that no law were made at all, as when it is made, to bring so blind an interpretation upon it that without great wit and long arguing no man can discuss it? To the finding out whereof neither the gross judgment[191] of the people can attain, neither the whole life of them that be occupied in working for their livings can suffice thereto.

The intent of laws.

These virtues of the Utopians have caused their next neighbors and borderers, which live free and under no subjection (for the Utopians long ago have delivered many of them from tyranny), to take magistrates of them, some for a year and some for five years' space, which, when the time of their office is expired, they bring home again with honor and praise and take new again with them into their country. These nations have undoubtedly very well and wholesomely provided for their commonwealths. For seeing that both the making and marring of the weal public doth depend and hang upon the manners of the rulers and magistrates, what officers could they more wisely have chosen than those which cannot be led from honesty by bribes (for to them that shortly after shall depart thence into their own country, money should be unprofitable), nor yet be moved either with favor or malice towards any man, as being strangers and unacquainted with the people? The which two vices of affection and avarice, where they take place in judgments, incontinent they break justice, the strongest and surest bond of a commonwealth. These peoples which fetch their officers and rulers from them, the Utopians call their fellows, and other to whom they have been beneficial, they call their friends.

---

[188]"Blind and intricate" = "obscure and perplexingly complicated."
[189]"Grosser" = "easier to comprehend."
[190]"Gross" = "obvious," "common."
[191]"Gross judgment" = "common opinion."

As touching leagues,[192] which in other places between country and country be so often concluded, broken, and renewed, they never make none with any nation. For to what
purpose serve leagues, say they? As though nature had not set sufficient
love between man and man. And who so regardeth not nature, think you
that he will pass for words?[193] They be brought into this opinion chiefly
because that, in those parts of the world, leagues between princes are
wont to be kept and observed very slenderly.[194] For here in Europa,[195]
and especially in these parts where the faith and religion of Christ
reigneth, the majesty of leagues is everywhere esteemed holy and invio-
lable, partly through the justice and goodness of princes, and partly at
the reverence and motion of the head bishops,[196] which like as they
make no promise themselves, but they do very religiously perform the
same, so they exhort all princes in anywise to abide by their promises,
and them that refuse or deny so to do, by their pontifical[197] power and
authority they compel thereto. And surely they think well that it might
seem a very reproachful thing if in the leagues of them which by a peculiar name are called faithful, faith should have no place. But in that
newfound part of the world, which is scarcely so far from us beyond the
line equinoctial as our life and manners be dissident from theirs, no trust
or confidence is in leagues.

But the more and holier ceremonies the league is knit up with, the
sooner it be broken by some cavillation[198] found in the words, which
many times of purpose be so craftily put in and placed that the bands[199]
can never be so sure nor so strong, but they will find some hole open
to creep out at and to break both league and truth. The which crafty

Of leagues.

[192]"Leagues" = "military, political, or commercial convenants, agreements, treaties, or alliances."

[193]"That he will pass for words" = "that he will be moved by mere words."

[194]"Slenderly" = "to a small degree," "perfunctorily."

[195]"Europa" = "Europe." The original Latin text also uses *Europa,* reflecting classical Greek and Roman usage. On the history of the idea of Europe and renewed significance for Christian humanists in the Renaissance, see Denys Hay, *Europe: The Emergence of an Idea,* rev. ed. (Edinburgh: Edinburgh University Press, 1968).

[196]In the original Latin text, the reference here is to popes, or "supreme pontiffs," not generically to "head bishops"; CW 4, p. 196. The point is somewhat ironical since Pope Alexander VI (d. 1503) and his successor Pope Julius II (d. 1513) were notorious for their duplicity in foreign affairs. However, for a Protestant like Robynson, the evident endorsement of papal authority was unacceptable, even in 1556 under Queen Mary I, who had restored England's formal ties to Rome.

[197]"Pontifical" = "episcopal."

[198]"Cavillation" = "frivolous or quibbling objections."

[199]"Bands" = "bonds."

dealing, yea, the which fraud and deceit, if they should know it to be practiced among private men in their bargains and contracts, they would incontinent cry out at it with an open mouth and a sour countenance as an offense most detestable and worthy to be punished with a shameful death, yea, even very they that advance themselves authors[200] of like counsel given to princes. Wherefore it may well be thought, either that all justice is but a base and a low virtue, and which availeth itself far under the high dignity of kings,[201] or, at the leastwise, that there be two justices, the one meet for the inferior sort of the people, going afoot and creeping low by the ground and bound down on every side with many bands, because it shall not run at rovers;[202] the other a princely virtue, which like as it is of much higher majesty than the other poor justice, so also it is of much more liberty as to the which nothing is unlawful that it lusteth after. These manners of princes (as I said), which be there so evil keepers of leagues, cause the Utopians, as I suppose, to make no leagues at all, which perchance would change their mind if they lived here. Howbeit, they think that though leagues be never so faithfully observed and kept, yet the custom of making leagues was very evil begun. For this causeth men (as though nations which be separate asunder, by the space of a little hill or a river, were coupled together by no society or bond of nature)[203] to think themselves born adversaries and enemies one to another, and that it were lawful for the one to seek the death and destruction of the other, if leagues were not, yea, and that after the leagues be accorded, friendship doth not grow and increase. But the license of robbing and stealing doth still remain, as far forth as, for lack of foresight and advisement in writing the words of the league, any sentence or clause to the contrary is not therein sufficiently comprehended. But they be of a[204] contrary opinion: that is, that no man ought to be

[200]"Even very they that advance themselves authors" = "truthfully even those who put themselves forward as the authors."

[201]"Availeth itself far under the high dignity of kings" = "takes profit for itself in contradiction to the high purposes and public duties of monarchs."

[202]"Run at rovers" = "without definite aim or object."

[203]This mention of nations separated by "a little hill or a river" recalls the troubled relations between England and Scotland in the medieval period and More's own day. The most recent event in this ongoing conflict had occurred in 1513, when the Scots were defeated by the earl of Surrey at the battle of Flodden in Northumberland; the Scottish king, three bishops, eleven earls, fifteen lords, and thousands of common soldiers were slain. In this instance, the Scottish king, James IV, a Stuart, was in league with Louis XII of France.

[204]At this place, Robynson's original text has "a of," a printer's error that is corrected here.

counted an enemy which hath done no injury; and that the fellowship of nature is a strong league; and that men be better and more surely knit together by love and benevolence than by convenants of leagues, by hearty affection of mind than by words.

Of Warfare

War or battle, as a thing very beastly and yet to no kind of beasts in so much use as to man,[205] they do detest and abhor. And contrary to the custom almost of all other nations, they count nothing so much against glory as glory gotten in war. And therefore, though they do daily practice and exercise themselves in the discipline of war, and not only the men but also the women upon certain appointed days, lest they should be to seek[206] in the feat of arms if need should require, yet they never go to battle but either in the defense of their own country, or to drive out of their friends' land the enemies that have invaded it, or by their power to deliver from the yoke and bondage of tyranny some people that be therewith oppressed, which thing they do of mere pity and compassion. Howbeit, they send help to their friends, not ever in their defense, but sometimes also to requite and revenge injuries before to them done. But this they do not unless their counsel and advice in the matter be asked whiles it is yet new and fresh. For if they find the cause probable, and if the contrary part[207] will not restore again such things as be of them justly demanded, then they be the chief authors and makers of the war, which they do not only as oft as by inroads and invasions of soldiers' preys and booties be driven away,[208] but then also much more mortally when their friends' merchants in any land, either under the pretense of unjust laws or else by the wresting and wrong understanding of good laws, do sustain an unjust accusation under the color of justice.

Neither the battle which the Utopians fought for the Nephelogetes against the Alaopolitanes,[209] a little before our time, was made for any other cause but that the Nephelogete merchantmen, as the Utopians

---

[205]"As to man" = "as it is to humans."

[206]"Lest they should be to seek" = "lest they should be lacking training."

[207]"Contrary part" = "opponents."

[208]"Which they do not only as oft as by inroads and invasions of soldiers' preys and booties be driven away" = "which they undertake not only when an invasion has plundered the goods of their friends."

[209]"Nephelogetes" derives from Greek roots meaning "people born from the clouds" or "cloud people." "Alaopolitanes" derives from Greek roots meaning "citizens of a people-less land."

thought, suffered wrong of the Alaopolitanes, under the pretense of right. But whether it were right or wrong, it was with so cruel and mortal war revenged, the countries round about joining their help and power to the puissance and malice of both parties that most flourishing and wealthy peoples, being some of them shrewdly shaken and some of them sharply beaten, the mischiefs were not finished nor ended until the Alaopolitanes at the last were yielded up as bondmen into the jurisdiction of the Nephelogetes, for the Utopians fought not this war for themselves. And yet the Nephelogetes before the war, when the Alaopolitanes flourished in wealth, were nothing to be compared with them. So eagerly the Utopians prosecute the injuries done to their friends, yea, in money matters, and not their own likewise. For if they by covin or guile be wiped besides their goods,[210] so that no violence be done to their bodies, they wreak their anger by abstaining from occupying[211] with that nation until they have made satisfaction. Not for because[212] they set less store by their own citizens than by their friends, but that they take the loss of their friends' money more heavily than the loss of their own. Because that their friends' merchantmen, for as much as that they lose is their own private goods, sustain great damage by the loss. But their own citizens lose nothing but of the common goods, and of that which was at home plentiful and almost superfluous, else had it not been sent forth. Therefore, no man feeleth the loss, and for this cause they think it too cruel an act to revenge that loss with the death of many, the incommodity of the which loss no man feeleth neither in his life nor yet in his living. But if it chance that any of their men in any other country be maimed or killed, whether it be done by a common or a private council, knowing and trying out the truth of the matter by their ambassadors, unless the offenders be rendered unto them in recompense of the injury, they will not be appeased, but incontinent they proclaim war against them. The offenders yielded, they punish either with death or with bondage. They be not only sorry, but also ashamed to ———————— achieve the victory with bloodshed, counting it great   Victory dear bought. folly to buy precious wares too dear. They rejoice and ———————— avaunt[213] themselves if they vanquish and oppress their enemies by craft and deceit. And for that act they made a general triumph, and as if the matter were manfully handled, they set up a pillar of stone in the place

---

[210]"If they by covin or guile be wiped besides their goods" = "if by collusion or deceit they should also be cheated of their goods."

[211]"Occupying" = "trading."

[212]"Not for because" = "Not because."

[213]"Avaunt" = "commend."

where they so vanquished their enemies in token of the victory. For then they glory, then they boast and crack[214] that they have played the men, indeed, when they have so overcome, as no other living creature but only man could, that is to say, by the might and puissance of wit. For with bodily strength (say they) bears, lions, boars, wolves, dogs, and other wild beasts do fight. And as the most part of them do pass us in strength and fierce courage, so in wit and reason we be much stronger than they all. Their chief and principal purpose in war is to obtain that thing which, if they had before obtained, they would not have moved battle. But if that be not possible, they take so cruel vengeance of them which be in the fault that ever after they be afraid to do the like.

This is their chief and principal intent, which they immediately and first of all prosecute and set forward. But yet so, that they be more circumspect in avoiding and eschewing jeopardies than they be desirous of praise and renown. Therefore, immediately after that war is once solemnly denounced,[215] they procure many proclamations signed with their own common seal to be set up privily at one time in their enemy's land in places most frequented. In these proclamations they promise great rewards to him that will kill their enemy's prince and somewhat less gifts, but them very great also, for every head of them whose names be in the said proclamations contained. They be those whom they count their chief adversaries next unto the prince. Whatsoever is prescribed unto him that killeth any of the proclaimed persons, that is doubled to him that bringeth any of the same to them alive, yea, and to the proclaimed persons themselves, if they will change their minds and come into them, taking their parts, they proffer the same great rewards with pardon and surety of their lives. Therefore, it quickly cometh to pass that their enemies have all other men in suspicion and be unfaithful and mistrusting among themselves one to another, living in great fear and in no less jeopardy. For it is well known that divers times the most part of them (and specially the prince himself) hath been betrayed of them in whom they put their most hope and trust, so that there is no manner of act nor deed that gifts and rewards do not enforce men unto, and in rewards they keep no measure. But remembering and considering into how great hazard and jeopardy they call them, endeavor themselves to recompense the greatness of the danger with the great benefits. And, therefore, they promise not only wonderful great abundance of gold, but also lands of great revenues lying in most safe places among their friends.

---

[214] "Crack" = "brag."
[215] "Denounced" = "declared," "announced."

And their promises they perform faithfully without any fraud or covin. This custom of buying and selling adversaries among other people is disallowed as a cruel art of a base and cowardish [216] mind. But they in this behalf think themselves much praiseworthy, as who likewise men by this means dispatch great wars without any battle or skirmish. Yea, they count it also a deed of pity and mercy because that by the death of a few offenders the lives of a great number of innocents, as well of their own men as also of their enemies, be ransomed and saved, which in fighting should have been slain. For they do no less pity the base and common sort of their enemy's people than they do their own, knowing that they be driven and enforced to war against their wills by the furious madness of their princes and heads. If by none of these means the matter go forward, as they would have it, then they procure occasions of debate and dissension to be spread among their enemies, as by bringing the prince's brother or some of the noblemen in hope to obtain the kingdom. If this way prevail not, then they rise up the people that be next neighbors and borderers to their enemies, and them they set in their necks under the color of some old title of right, such as kings do never lack. To them they promise their help and aid in their war, and, as for money, they give them abundance. But of their own citizens they send to them few or none, whom they make so much of and love so entirely that they would not be willing to change any of them for their adversary's prince.

But their gold and silver, because they keep it all for this only purpose, they lay it out frankly and freely, as who should live even as wealthily if they had bestowed it every penny. Yea, and besides their riches which they keep at home, they have also an infinite treasure abroad, by reason that (as I have said before) many nations be in their debt. Therefore, they hire soldiers out of all countries and send them to battle, but chiefly of the Zapoletes. [217] This people is five hundred miles from Utopia eastward. They be hideous, savage, and fierce, dwelling in wild woods and high mountains, where they were bred and brought up. They be of an hard nature, able to abide and sustain heat, cold, and labor, abhorring from all delicate dainties, [218] occupying no husbandry nor tillage of the

---

[216] "Cowardish" = "cowardly."

[217] "Zapoletes" is derived from Greek, meaning "busy sellers." The marginal note supplied by Erasmus and Giles in 1516 identifies them with the Swiss. As indicated in The First Book, the Swiss were especially notable for the service they provided as mercenaries during More's era. This note was omitted by Froben, who was Swiss himself, from the 1518 Basel editions of *Utopia,* one of which may therefore have been the text used by Robynson for his translation.

[218] "Abhorring from all delicate dainties" = "shunning all finery."

ground, homely and rude both in the building of their houses and in their apparel, given unto no goodness, but only to the breeding and bringing up of cattle. The most part of their living is by hunting and stealing. They be born only to war, which they diligently and earnestly seek for, and when they have gotten it, they be wondrous glad thereof. They go forth of their country in great companies together, and whosoever lacketh soldiers, there they proffer their service for small wages. This is only the craft that they have to get their living. They maintain their life by seeking their death. For them whom with they be in wages they fight hardily, fiercely, and faithfully, but they bind themselves for no certain time. But upon this condition they enter into bonds that the next day they will take part with the other side for greater wages, and the next day after that, they will be ready to come back again for a little more money. There be few wars thereaway wherein is not a great number of them in both parties. Therefore, it daily chanceth that nigh kinsfolk which were hired together on one part, and there very friendly and familiarly used themselves one with another, shortly after being separate and contrary parts, run one against another enviously and fiercely, and forgetting both kindred and friendship thrust their swords one in another. And that for none other cause but that they be hired of contrary princes for a little money, which they do so highly regard and esteem that they will easily be provoked to change parts for a halfpenny more wages by the day. So quickly they have taken a smack in covetousness,[219] which for all that is to them no profit, for they that get by fighting, immediately they spend unthriftily and wretchedly in riot. This people fighteth for the Utopians against all nations because they give them greater wages than any other nation will. For the Utopians like as they seek good men to use well, so they seek these evil and vicious men to abuse, whom, when need requireth, with promises of great rewards they put forth into great jeopardies, from whence the most part of them never cometh again to ask their rewards. But to them that remain alive they pay that which they promised faithfully that they may be the most willing to put themselves in like danger another time. Nor the Utopians pass not how many of them they bring to destruction, for they believe that they should do a very good deed for all mankind if they could rid out the world all that foul stinking den of that most wicked and cursed people.

Next unto these they use the soldiers of them for whom they fight; and then the help of their other friends; and, last of all, they join to their

---

[219] "Smack in covetousness" = "taste of their greed."

own citizens, among whom they give to one of tried virtue and prowess the rule, governance, and conduction[220] of the whole army. Under him they appoint two others, which, whiles he is safe, be both private and out of office. But if he be taken or slain, the one of the other two succeedeth him, as it were by inheritance. And if the second miscarry, then the third taketh his room, lest that (as the chance of battle is uncertain and doubtful) the jeopardy or death of the captain should bring the whole army in hazard.

They choose soldiers out of every city those which put forth themselves willingly, for they thrust no man forth into war against his will because they believe if any man is fearful and fainthearted of nature, he will not only do no manful[221] and hardy act himself, but also be occasion of cowardness to his fellows. But if any battle be made against their own country, then they put these cowards (so that they be strong-bodied) in ships among other bold-hearted men, or else they dispose of them upon the walls from whence they may not fly. Thus, what for shame that their enemies be at hand and what for because they be without hope of running away, they forget all fear. And many times extreme necessity turneth cowardness into prowess and manliness.

But as none of them is thrust forth of his country into war against his will, so women that be willing to accompany their husbands in times of war be not prohibited or letted. Yea, they provoke and exhort them to it with praises. And in set field[222] the wives do stand every one by their own husbands' side. Also every man is compassed next about with his own children, kinsfolks, and alliance,[223] that they, whom nature chiefly moveth to mutual succor, thus standing together may help one another. It is a great reproach and dishonesty for the husband to come home without his wife, or the wife without her husband, or the son without his father. And therefore, if the other part stick so hard by it that the battle come to their hands, it is fought with great slaughter and bloodshed, even to the utter destruction of both parts. For as they make all the means and shifts that may be to keep themselves from the necessity of fighting, or that they may dispatch the battle by their hired soldiers, so when there is no remedy but that they must needs fight themselves, they do as courageously fall to it as before, whiles they might, they did wisely avoid and refuse it. Nor they be not most fierce at the first brunt.[224] But

---

[220] "Conduction" = "command."
[221] "Manful" = "brave."
[222] "In set field" = "in the order of battle."
[223] "Alliance" = "relations by marriage."
[224] "First brunt" = "initial assault."

in continuance by little and little their fierce courage increaseth with so stubborn and obstinate minds that they will rather die than give back an inch. For that surety of living, which every man hath at home being joined with no careful anxiety or remembrance how their posterity shall live after them (for this pensiveness oftentimes breaketh and abateth courageous stomachs) maketh them stout and hardy and disdainful to be conquered. Moreover, their knowledge in chivalry[225] and feats of arms putteth them in a good hope. Finally, the wholesome and virtuous opinions, wherein they were brought up even from their childhood, partly through learning and partly through the good ordinances and laws of their weal public, augment and increase their manful courage. By reason whereof they neither set so little store by their lives that they will rashly and unadvisedly cast them away, nor they be not so far in lewd and fond love therewith that they will shamefully covet to keep them when honesty bids leave them.

When the battle is hottest and in all places most fierce and fervent, a band of chosen and picked young men, which be sworn to live and die together, take upon them to destroy their adversaries' captain, whom they invade now with privy wiles, now by open strength. At him they strike both near and far off. He is assailed with a long and a continual assault, fresh men still coming in the wearied men's places. And seldom it chanceth (unless he save himself by flying) that he is not either slain or else taken prisoner and yielded to his enemies alive.

> The captain is chiefly to be pursued to the intent the battle may the sooner be ended.

If they win the field, they persecute not their enemies with the violent rage of slaughter, for they had rather take them alive than kill them. Neither they do so follow the chase and pursuit of their enemies, but they leave behind them one part of their host in battle array under their standards.[226] Insomuch that if all their whole army be discomfitted[227] and overcome, saving the rearward, and that they therewith achieve the victory, then they had rather let all their enemies escape than to follow them out of array.[228] For they remember it hath chanced unto themselves more than once, the whole power and strength of their host being vanquished and put to flight, whiles their enemies rejoicing in the

---

[225]"Chivalry" = "martial art."

[226]"Neither they do so follow the chase and pursuit of their enemies, but they leave behind them one part of their host in battle array under their standards" = "they do not pursue their enemies without leaving behind a part of their force assembled under their standards ready for battle."

[227]"Discomfitted" = "defeated."

[228]"Out of array" = "out of formation."

victory have persecuted them, flying some one way and some another, a small company of their men lying in an ambush, there ready at all occasions, have suddenly risen upon them thus dispersed and scattered out of array, and through presumption of safety unadvisedly pursuing the chase, and have incontinent changed the fortune of the whole battle, and spite of their teeths wresting out of their hands the sure and undoubted victory,[229] being a little before conquered, have for their part conquered the conquerors. It is hard to say whether they be craftier in laying an ambush or wittier[230] in avoiding the same. You would think they intend to fly when they mean nothing less. And, contrariwise, when they go about that purpose, you would believe it were the least part of their thought. For if they perceive themselves either overmatched in number or closed in too narrow a place, then they remove their camp either in the night season with silence, or by some policy they deceive their enemies, or in the daytime they retire back so softly that it is no less jeopardy to meddle with them when they give back than when they press on.

They fence and fortify their camp surely[231] with a deep and a broad trench. The earth thereof is cast inward. Nor they do not set drudges and slaves a-work about it; it is done by the hands of the soldiers themselves. All the whole army worketh upon it, except them that keep watch and ward in harness[232] before the trench for sudden adventures.[233] Therefore, by the labor of so many a large trench closing in a great compass of ground is made in less time than any man would believe. Their armor and harness which they wear is sure Their armor. and strong to receive strokes and handsome[234] for all movings and gestures of the body, insomuch that it is not unwieldy to swim in, for, in the discipline of their warfare, among other feats they learn to swim in harness. Their weapons be arrows aloof,[235] which they shoot both strongly and surely, not only footmen but also horsemen. At handstrokes they use not swords but poleaxes, which be mortal as well in sharpness as in weight, both for foins[236] and downstrokes. Engines for

[229] "And spite of their teeths wresting out of their hands the sure and undoubted victory" = "and notwithstanding the resistance having wrested out of their enemies' hands the certain victory."

[230] "Wittier" = "cleverer."

[231] "Surely" = "securely."

[232] "Keep watch and ward in harness" = "keep guard fully armed."

[233] "For sudden adventures" = "against surprise attacks."

[234] "Handsome" = "well suited," "appropriate."

[235] "Arrows aloof" = "arrows shot from a distance," i.e., with a long bow, which was also the favored weapon of the English yeoman at arms.

[236] "Foins" = "thrusts."

war they devise and invent wondrous wittily, which, when they be made, they keep very secret lest, if they should be known before need require, they should be but laughed at and serve to no purpose. But in making them hereunto they have chief respect that they be both easy to be carried and handsome to be moved and turned about.

Truce taken with their enemies for a short time they *Of truces.* do so firmly and faithfully keep that they will not break it, no not though they be thereunto provoked. They do not waste nor destroy their enemy's land with foragings,[237] nor they burn not up their corn. Yea, they save it as much as may be from being overrun and trodden down either with men or horses, thinking that it groweth for their own use and profit. They hurt no man that is unarmed, unless he be an espial.[238] All cities that be yielded unto them they defend, and such as they win by force of assault they neither despoil nor sack, but them that withstood and dissuaded the yielding up of the same they put to death. The other soldiers they punish with bondage; all the weak multitude they leave untouched. If they know that any citizens counseled to yield and render up the city, to them they give part of the condemned men's goods. The residue they distribute and give freely among them whose help they had in the same war, for none of themselves taketh any portion of the prey. But when the battle is finished and ended, they put their friends to never a penny cost of all the charges that they were at, but lay it upon their necks that be conquered. Them they burden with the whole charge of their expenses, which they demand of them partly in money to be kept for the use of battle and partly in lands of great revenues to be paid unto them yearly forever. Such revenues they have now in many countries, which by little and little rising of divers and sundry causes be increased above seven hundred thousand ducats by the year.[239] Thither they send forth some of their citizens as lieutenants[240] to live there sumptuously like men of honor and renown. And yet, this not

---

[237] "Foragings" = "plundering," "pillaging."

[238] "Espial" = "spy.

[239] The ducat, in circulation in More's day in the Holy Roman Empire including the Netherlands, was a gold coin, issued originally in 1475 by Ferdinand and Isabella, which was exchanged for English currency at a little more than four to the pound sterling. It was recognized as legal tender in England by a royal proclamation in 1522, which fixed its value at 4 shillings and 6 pence, i.e., 22.5 percent of a pound. See *Tudor Royal Proclamations,* ed. Paul L. Hughes and James F. Larkin, 3 vols. (New Haven: Yale University Press, 1964–69), vol. 1, p. 136. On this basis, the Utopians' income of 700,000 ducats per year would have represented about £155,000–160,000 per year, which probably exceeded the annual income of the English king in 1515 by about £30,000–40,000; see p. 39.

[240] "Lieutenants" = "representatives."

withstanding, much money is saved which cometh to the common treasury, unless it so chance that they had rather trust the country with the money, which many times they do so long until they have need to occupy it. And it seldom happeneth that they demand all. Of these lands they assign part unto them, which at their request and exhortation put themselves in such jeopardies, as I spoke of before. If any prince stir up war against them, intending to invade their land, they meet him incontinent out of their own borders with great power and strength, for they never lightly make war in their own country, nor they be never brought into so extreme necessity as to take help out of foreign lands into their own island.

Of the Religions in Utopia

There be divers kinds of religion not only in sundry parts of the island, but also in divers places of every city. Some worship for god the sun; some the moon; some, some other of the planets. There be that give worship to a man that was once of excellent virtue or of famous glory, not only as a god, but also as the chiefest and highest god. But the most and the wisest part (rejecting all these) believe that there is a certain godly power unknown, everlasting, incomprehensible, inexplicable, far above the capacity and reach of man's wit, dispersed throughout all the world, not in bigness, but in virtue and power. Him they call the father of all. To him alone they attribute the beginnings, the increasings, the proceedings, the changes, and the ends of all things.[241] Neither they give any divine honors to any other than to him. Yea, all the others also, though they be in divers opinions, yet in this point they agree altogether with the wisest sort, in believing that there is one chief and principal god, the maker and ruler of the whole world, whom they all commonly in their country language call Mythra.[242] But in this they disagree, that among some he is counted one and among some another. For every one of them, whatsoever that is which he taketh for the chief god, thinketh it

---

[241]The belief among the majority of Utopians in a single god, who is the first cause and the final ending of all things, associates them with the theological views of those medieval philosophers, such as Aquinas, who, following Aristotle, sought to establish that the characteristics of the Christian God could be known solely through the use of human reason.

[242]Mythra, or Mithras, was the ancient Aryan god of light and truth, worshiped initially in Persia by the Zoroastrians. By the first century C.E., Mythra was worshiped throughout the Roman empire as the votive figure of a mystery cult that shared many features with early Christian practice, including baptism and the ceremonial meal, a subject noticed as early as the second century C.E. Note here the reputed affinity of the Utopian language with Persian (165).

to be the very same nature, to whose only divine might and majesty, the sum and sovereignty of all things by the consent of all people is attributed and given. Howbeit, they all begin by little and little to forsake and fall from this variety of superstitions and to agree together in that religion which seemeth by reason to pass and excel the residue. And it is not to be doubted, but all the others would long ago have been abolished, but that whatsoever unprosperous thing happened to any of them as he was minded to change his religion, the fearfulness of people did take it, not as a thing coming by chance, but as sent from God out of heaven. As though the god, whose honor he was forsaking, would revenge that wicked purpose against him.

But after they heard us speak of the name of Christ, of his doctrine, laws, miracles, and of the no less wonderful constancy of so many martyrs, whose blood willingly shed brought a great number of nations throughout all parts of the world into their sect, you will not believe with how glad minds they agreed unto the same, whether it were by the secret inspiration of God or else for that they thought it nighest unto that opinion which among them is counted the chiefest. Howbeit, I think this was no small help and furtherance in the matter that they heard us say that Christ instituted among his[243] all things common and that the same community does yet remain amongst the rightest Christian companies.

Verily, howsoever it came to pass, many of them consented together in our religion and were washed in the holy water of baptism. But because among us four (for no more of us was left alive, two of our company being dead) there was no priest, which I am right sorry for; they, being entered and instructed in all other points of our religion, lack only those sacraments which here none but priests do minister.[244] Howbeit, they understand and perceive them and are very desirous of the same. Yea, they reason and dispute the matter earnestly among themselves whether without the sending of a Christian bishop, one chosen out of their own people may receive the order of priesthood. And, truly, they were minded to choose one, but at my departure from them they had chosen none.

Religious houses.

They also which do not agree to Christ's religion fear no man from it,[245] nor speak against any man that hath received it, saving that one of our company in my presence was sharply punished. He, as soon as he

---

[243] "Among his" = "among his followers."

[244] In Catholic practice, baptism could be performed by a layperson if no priest was available and the child was in danger of dying before one could be found. The Eucharist, penance, and extreme unction required an ordained priest; confirmation and ordination required a bishop.

[245] "Fear no man from it" = "do not deter anyone from practicing it."

was baptized, began against our wills, with more earnest affection than wisdom, to reason of Christ's religion and began to wax so hot in this matter that he did not only prefer our religion before all others, but also did utterly despise and condemn all others, calling them profane and the followers of them wicked and devilish and the children of everlasting damnation. When he had thus long reasoned the matter, they laid hold on him, accused him, and condemned him into exile, not as a despiser of religion, but as a seditious person and a raiser-up of dissension among the people.

For this is one of the ancientest laws among them, that no man shall be blamed for reasoning in the maintenance of his own religion.[246] For King Utopus,[247] even at the first beginning, hearing that the inhabitants of the land were before his coming thither at a continual dissension and strife among themselves for their religions, perceiving also that this common dissension (whiles every several sect took several parts in fighting for their country) was the only occasion of his conquest over them all as soon as he had gotten the victory, first of all, he made a decree that it should be lawful for every man to favor and follow what religion he would, and that he might do the best he could to bring others to his opinion, so that he did it peaceably, gently, quietly, and soberly, without hasty and contentious rebuking and inveighing against others. If he could not by fair and gentle speech induce them unto his opinion, yet he should use no kind of violence and refrain from displeasant and seditious[248] words. To him that would *Seditious reasoners punished.* vehemently and fervently in this cause strive and contend was decreed banishment or bondage. This law did King Utopus[249] make not only for the maintenance of peace, which he saw through continual contention and mortal hatred utterly extinguished, but also because he thought this decree should make for the furtherance of religion. Whereof he durst define and determine nothing unadvisedly, as doubting whether God, desiring manifold and diverse sorts of honor, would inspire sundry men with sundry kinds of religion. And this, surely, he thought a very unmeet[250] and foolish thing, and a point of arrogant presumption, to compel all others by violence and threatenings to agree

---

[246] In his subsequent political and governmental career, More himself took a different view; he was a great scourge of heresy, especially during his service as Lord Chancellor. See p. 52.

[247] At this point, the original Latin text again has just the name Utopus without any title; CW 4, p. 218.

[248] "Displeasant and seditious" = "angry and factious."

[249] Once again, the original Latin text gives just the name Utopus; CW 4, p. 220.

[250] "Unmeet" = "excessive," "unfit," "improper."

to the same that thou believest to be true. Furthermore, though there be one religion which alone is true, and all other vain and superstitious, yet did he well foresee (so that the matter were handled with reason and sober modesty) that the truth of the own[251] power would at the last issue out and come to light. But if contention and debate in that behalf should continually be used, as the worst men be most obstinate and stubborn and in their evil opinion most constant, he perceived that then the best and holiest religion would be trodden underfoot and destroyed by most vain superstitions, even as good corn is by thorns and weeds overgrown and choked. Therefore, all this matter he left undiscussed and gave to every man free liberty and choice to believe what he would, saving that he earnestly and straightly charged them that no man should conceive so vile and base an opinion of the dignity of man's nature as to think that the souls do die and perish with the body or that the world runneth at all adventures governed by no divine providence.

No vile opinion to be conceived of man's worthy nature.

And, therefore, they believe that after this life vices be extremely punished and virtues bountifully rewarded. Him that is of a contrary opinion they count not in the number of men, as one that hath avaled[252] the high nature of his soul to the vileness of brute beasts' bodies, much less in the number of their citizens whose laws and ordinances, if it were not for fear, he would nothing at all esteem. For you may be sure that he will study either with craft privily to mock or else violently to break the common laws of his country, in whom remaineth no further fear than of the laws, nor no further hope than of the body. Wherefore, he that is thus minded is deprived of all honors, excluded from all offices, and rejected from all common administrations in the weal public. And thus he is of all sorts despised, as of an unprofitable and of a base and vile nature. Howbeit, they put him to no punishment, because they be persuaded that it is no man's power to believe what he list.[253] No nor they constrain him not with threatenings to dissemble his mind and show countenance contrary to his thought. For deceit and falsehood and all manner

Irreligious people secluded from all honors.

A very strange saying.

Deceit and falsehood detested.

---

[251] "The own" = "its own."

[252] "Avaled" = "sank from," "descended from," "lowered himself from."

[253] "It is no man's power to believe what he list" = "it is in no one's power to believe whatever he chooses." The marginal note at this point — "A very strange saying" — does not appear in the original Latin text; it was added by Robynson, who appears not to have understood the point. It turns on whether the person in question has been compelled, prior to any act of will, to accept an idea by its apparent credibility, something about which he or she could be in profound error.

of lies, as next unto fraud, they do marvelously detest and abhor. But they suffer him not to dispute in his opinion, and that only among the common people. For else apart among the priests and men of gravity they do not only suffer, but also exhort him to dispute and argue, hoping that at the last that madness will give place to reason.

There be also others, and of them no small number, which be not forbidden to speak their minds, as grounding their opinion upon some reason, being in their living neither evil nor vicious. Their heresy is much contrary to the others, for they believe that the souls of brute beasts be immortal and everlasting, but nothing to be compared with ours in dignity, neither ordained and predestinate to like felicity.[254] For all they believe certainly and surely that man's bless[255] shall be so great that they do mourn and lament every man's sickness but no man's death, unless it be one whom they see depart from his life carefully[256] and against his will. For this they take for a very evil token, as though the soul being in despair and vexed in conscience, through some privy and secret forefeeling of the punishment now at hand, were afraid to depart. And they think he shall not be welcome to God, which, when his is called, runneth not to him gladly, but is drawn by force and sore against his will. They, therefore, that see this kind of death do abhor it, and them that so die they bury with sorrow and silence. And when they have prayed God to be merciful to the soul and mercifully to pardon the infirmities thereof, they cover the dead corpse with earth.

A marvelous strange opinion touching the souls of brute beasts.

To die unwillingly, an evil token.

Contrariwise, all that depart merrily and full of good hope, for them no man mourneth but followeth the hearse with joyful singing, commending the souls to God with great affection. And, at the last, not with mourning sorrow but with great reverence, they burn the bodies. And in the same place they set up a pillar of stone with the dead man's titles therein graved. When they be come home, they rehearse his virtuous manners and his good deeds, but no part of his life is so oft or gladly talked of as his merry death. They think that this remembrance of the virtue and goodness of the dead doth vehemently provoke and enforce the living to virtue and that nothing can be more pleasant and acceptable to the dead, whom they suppose to be present among them when they talk of them, though

A willing and merry death, not to be lamented.

---

[254] Among ancient philosophers, Pythagoreans and Platonists held similar views. The original Latin text at this point speaks not of heresy, but only of error.

[255] "Bless" = "bliss," "blessing."

[256] "Carefully" = "full of grief or sorrow."

to the dull and feeble eyesight of mortal men they be invisible, for it were an inconvenient thing that the blessed should not be at liberty to go whither they would. And it were a point of great unkindness in them to have utterly cast away the desire of visiting and seeing their friends, to whom they were in their lifetime joined by mutual love and amity, which in good men after their death they count to be rather increased than diminished. They believe, therefore, that the dead are presently conversant among the quick as beholders and witnesses of all their words and deeds. Therefore, they go more courageously to their business as having a trust and affiance[257] in such overseers. And this same belief of the present conversation of their forefathers and ancestors among them feareth them from all secret dishonesty.

They utterly despise and mock soothsayings and divinations of things to come by the flight or voices of birds, and all other divinations of vain superstition, which in other countries be in great observation. But they highly esteem and worship miracles that come by no help of nature, as works and witnesses of the present power of God, and such, they say, do chance there very often. And sometimes in great and doubtful matters, by common intercession and prayers, they procure and obtain them with a sure hope and confidence and a steadfast belief.

Soothsayers not regarded nor credited.

Miracles.

They think that the contemplation of nature, and the praise thereof coming, is to God a very acceptable honor. Yet there be many so earnestly bent and affectioned to religion that they pass nothing for learning, nor give their minds to any knowledge of things.[258] But idleness they utterly forsake and eschew, thinking felicity after this life to be gotten and obtained by busy labors and good exercises. Some, therefore, of them attend upon the sick, some amend highways, cleanse ditches, repair bridges, dig turfs, gravel, and stones, fell and cleave wood, bring wood, corn, and other things into the cities in carts, and serve not only in common works, but also in private labors as servants, yea, more than bondmen. For whatsoever unpleasant, hard, and vile work is anywhere, from the which labor loathsomeness and desperation doth fray others, all that they take upon them willingly and gladly,

The life contemplative.

The life active.

---

257 "Affiance" = "confidence."
258 "Yet there be many so earnestly bent and affectioned to religion that they pass nothing for learning, nor give their minds to any knowledge of things" = "yet there are many that are so disposed and attached to their religion that they shun or disregard all forms of learning and knowledge of the everyday world."

procuring quiet and rest to other, remaining in continual work and labor themselves, not embraiding others therewith.[259] They neither reprove other men's lives nor glory in their own. These men, the more serviceable they behave themselves, the more they be honored of all men.

Yet they are divided into two sects. The one is of them that live single and chaste, abstaining not only from the company of women, but also from eating of flesh and some of them from all manner of beasts, which, utterly rejecting the pleasures of this present life as hurtful, be all wholly set upon the desire of the life to come by watching and sweating,[260] hoping shortly to obtain it, being in the mean season merry and lusty. The other sect is no less desirous of labor, but they embrace matrimony, not despising the solace thereof, thinking that they cannot be discharged of their bounden duties towards nature without labor and toil, nor towards their native country without procreation of children. They abstain from no pleasure that doth nothing hinder them from labor. They love the flesh of four-footed beasts because they believe that by that meat they be made hardier and stronger to work. The Utopians count this sect the wiser, but the other the holier, which in that they prefer single life before matrimony, and that sharp life before an easier life, if herein they grounded upon reason they would mock them, but now forasmuch as they say they be led to it by religion, they honor and worship them. And these be they whom in their language by a peculiar name they call Buthrescas,[261] the which word by interpretation signifieth to us men of religion or religious men.

It is not all one to be wise and good.

They have priests of exceeding holiness and, therefore, very few, for there be but thirteen in every city according to the number of their churches, saving when they go forth to battle, for then seven of them go forth with the army, in whose steads so many new be made at home. But the other, at their return home again, reenter every one into his own place, they that be above the number, until such time as they succeed into the places of the others at their dying, be in the mean season continually in company with the bishop, for he is the chief head of them all. They be chosen of the people, as the other magistrates be, by secret voices for the avoiding of strife.[262] After their election they be consecrate of their own company.

Priests.

---

[259] "Not embraiding others therewith" = "not criticizing others for failing to do the same."

[260] "Watching and sweating" = "keeping vigil and laboring."

[261] "Buthrescas" is another Greek compound, meaning literally "wonderously or extraordinarily religious."

[262] Relying on "secret voices," or secret balloting, would have been highly unusual in More's England, where virtually all elections were by publicly declared voice vote.

They be overseers of all divine matters, orderers of religions, and, as it were, judges and masters of manners. And it is a great dishonesty and shame to be rebuked or spoken to by any of them for dissolute and incontinent living. But as it is their office to give good exhortation and counsel, so is it the duty of the prince and the other magistrates to correct and punish offenders, saving that the priests whom they find exceeding vicious livers, them they excommunicate from having any interest in divine matters. Excommunication.
And there is almost no punishment among them more feared, for they run in very great infamy and be inwardly tormented with a secret fear of religion, and shall not long scape[263] free with their bodies, for unless they by quick repentance approve the amendment of their lives to the priests, they be taken and punished of the council as wicked and irreligious. Both childhood and youth is instructed and taught of them. Nor they be not more diligent to instruct them in learning than in virtue and good manners, for they use with very great endeavor and diligence to put into the heads of their children, whiles they be yet tender and pliant, good opinions and profitable for the conservation of their weal public, which when they be once rooted in children, do remain with them all their life after and be wondrous profitable for the defense and maintenance of the state of the commonwealth, which never decayeth but through vices rising of evil opinions.

The priests, unless they be women (for that kind is not excluded from priesthood, howbeit few be chosen and none but widows and old women), the men priests, I say, take to their wives the chiefest women in all their country, for to no office among the Utopians is more honor and prominence given. Insomuch that if they commit any offense, they be under no common judgment, but be left only to God and themselves, for they think it not lawful to touch him with man's hand, be he never so vicious, which after so singular a sort was dedicate and consecrate to God as a holy offering. Women priests.

The majesty and preeminence of priests.

This manner may they easily observe because they have so few priests and do choose them with such circumspection. For it scarcely ever chanceth that the most virtuous among virtuous, which in respect only of his virtue is advanced to so high a dignity, can fall to vice and wickedness. And if it should chance indeed (as man's nature is mutable and frail) yet by reason they be so few and promoted to no might nor power, but only to honor, it were not to be feared that any great damage by them should happen and ensue to the

[263] "Scape" = "escape."

commonwealth. They have so rare and few priests, lest if the honor were communicated to many, the dignity of the order, which among them now is so highly esteemed, should run in contempt, specially because they think it hard to find many so good as to be meet for that dignity, to the execution and discharge whereof it is not sufficient to be endued with mean virtues.

Furthermore, these priests be not more esteemed of their own countrymen than they be of foreign and strange countries, which thing may hereby plainly appear, and I think also that this is the cause of it. For whiles the armies be fighting together in open field, they a little beside, not far off, kneel upon their knees in their hallowed vestments, holding up their hands to heaven, praying first of all for peace, next for victory of their own part, but to neither part a bloody victory. If their host get the upper hand, they run into the main battle and restrain their own men from slaying and cruelly pursuing their vanquished enemies, which enemies, if they do but see them and speak to them, it is enough for the safeguard of their lives. And the touching of their clothes defendeth and saveth all their goods from ravin and spoil. This thing hath advanced them to so great worship and true majesty among all nations that many times they have as well preserved their own citizens from the cruel force of their enemies as they have their enemies from the furious rage of their own men. For it is well known that when their own army hath reculed[264] and in despair turned back and run away, their enemies fiercely pursuing with slaughter and spoil, then the priests, coming between, have stayed the murder and parted both the hosts, so that peace hath been made and concluded between both parts upon equal and indifferent conditions. For there was never any nation so fierce, so cruel, and rude[265] but they had them in such reverence that they counted their bodies hallowed and sanctified, and, therefore, not to be violently and unreverently touched.

They keep holy the first and the last day of every month and year, dividing the year into months, which they measure by the course of the moon as they do the year by the course of the sun. The first days they call in their language Cynemernes and the last Trapemernes,[266] the which words may

The observation of holy days among the Utopians.

---

[264] "Reculed" = "retreated."
[265] "Rude" = "barbarous."
[266] "Cynemernes" derives from Greek roots meaning literally "dog day"; "Trapemernes" means "turning day."

be interpreted primifest and finifest, or else, in our speech, first feast and last feast.[267]

Their churches be very gorgeous and not only of fine and curious workmanship, but also (which in the fewness of them was necessary) very wide and large and able to receive a great company of people. But they be all somewhat dark. Howbeit, that was not done through ignorance in building but, as they say, by the counsel of the priests because they thought that overmuch light doth disperse men's cogitations,[268] whereas in dim and doubtful light they are gathered together and more earnestly fixed upon religion and devotion, which, because it is not there of one sort among all men, and yet all the kinds and fashions of it, though they be sundry and manifold, agree together in the honor of the divine nature, as going divers ways to one end. Therefore, nothing is seen nor heard in the churches but that seemeth to agree indifferently with them all.

Their churches.

Churches of dim light and a reason why.

If there be a distinct kind of sacrifice peculiar to any several sect, that they execute at home in their own houses. The common sacrifices be so ordered that they be no derogation or prejudice to any of the private sacrifices and religions. Therefore, no image of any god is seen in the church to the intent it may be free for every man to conceive God by their religion after what likeness and similitude they will. They call upon no peculiar name of God, but only Mythra, in the which word they all agree together in one nature of the divine majesty whatsoever it be. No prayers be used but such as every man may boldly pronounce without the offending of any sect. They come, therefore, to the church the last day of every month and year, in the evening yet fasting, there to give thanks to God for that they have prosperously passed over the year or month, whereof that holy day is the last day. The next day they come to the church early in the morning to pray to God that they may have good fortune and success all the new year or month which they do begin of that same holy day.

But in the holy days that be the last days of the months and years, before they come to the church, the wives fall down prostrate before their husbands' feet at home, and the children before the feet of their parents, confessing and

The confession of the Utopians.

---

[267] Here Robynson carries over *primifest* and *finifest* directly from the original Latin text and then translates the terms into their English equivalents. See CW 4, p. 230.

[268] "Cogitations" = "meditations," "contemplations."

acknowledging themselves offenders either by some actual deed or by omission of their duty, and desire pardon for their offense. Thus if any cloud of privy displeasure was risen at home, by this satisfaction it is overblown, that they may be present at the sacrifices with pure and charitable minds, for they be afraid to come there with troubled consciences. Therefore, if they know themselves to bear any hatred or grudge towards any man, they presume not to come to the sacrifices before they have reconciled themselves and purged their consciences, for fear of great vengeance and punishment for their offense.

When they come thither, the men go into the right side of the church and the women into the left side. There they place themselves in such order that all they which be of the male kind in every household sit before the good-man [269] of the house, and they of the female kind before the goodwife. [270] Thus it is foreseen that all their gestures and behaviors be marked and observed abroad of them by whose authority and discipline they be governed at home. This also they diligently see unto, that the younger evermore be coupled with his elder, lest, children being joined together, they should pass over that time in childish wantonness [271] wherein they ought principally to conceive a religious and devout fear towards God, which is the chief and almost the only incitation to virtue.

An order for places in the church.

They kill no living beast in sacrifice, nor they think not that the merciful clemency of God hath delight in blood and slaughter, which hath given life to beasts to the intent they should live. They burn frankincense and other sweet savors, and light also a great number of wax candles and tapers, not supposing this gear to be anything available to the divine nature, as neither the prayers of men. But this unhurtful and harmless kind of worship pleaseth them, and by these sweet savors and lights, and other such ceremonies, men feel themselves secretly lifted up and encouraged to devotion with more willing and fervent hearts.

Ceremonies.

The people weareth in the church white apparel. The priest is clothed in changeable colors, which in workmanship be excellent, but in stuff not very precious, for their vestments be neither embroidered with gold nor set with precious stones, but they be wrought so finely and cunningly with divers feathers of fowls that the estimation of no costly stuff is able to countervail the price of the work. Furthermore, in these birds'

---

[269] "Goodman" = "master."
[270] "Goodwife" = "mistress."
[271] "Wantonness" = "foolishness," "frivolity."

feathers and in the due order of them, which is observed in their setting, they say, is contained certain divine mysteries, the interpretation
whereof known, which is diligently taught by the priests, they be put in
remembrance of the bountiful benefits of God toward them, and of the
love and honor which of their behalf is due to God, and also of their duties one toward another.

When the priest first cometh out of the vestry thus appareled, they fall
down incontinent every one reverently to the ground, with so still silence
on every part that the very fashion of the thing striketh into them a certain fear of God, as though he were there personally present. When they
have lain a little space on the ground, the priest giveth ————————
them a sign for to rise. Then they sing praises unto Their church music.
God, which they intermix with instruments of music, ————————
for the most part of other fashions than these that we use in this part of
the world. And like as some of ours be much sweeter than theirs, so
some of theirs do far pass ours. But in one thing doubtless they go exceeding far beyond us, for all their music, both that they play upon instruments and that they sing with man's voice, doth so resemble and express natural affections, the sound and tune is so applied and made
agreeable to the thing that whether it be a prayer or else a ditty[272] of glad-
ness, of patience, of trouble, of mourning, or of anger, the fashion of the
melody doth so represent the meaning of the thing that it doth wonder-
fully move, stir, pierce, and inflame the hearers' minds.

At the last the people and the priest together re- ————————
hearse solemn prayers in words expressly pronounced, Prayers.
so made that every man may privately apply to himself ————————
that which is commonly spoken of all. In these prayers every man rec-
ognizeth and knowledgeth God to be his maker, his governor, and the
principal cause of all other goodness, thanking him for so many benefits
received at his hand. But namely that through the favor of God he hath
chanced into that public weal which is most happy and wealthy and
hath chosen that religion which he hopeth to be most true. In the which
thing if he do anything err,[273] or if there be any other better than either
of them is, being more acceptable to God, he desireth him that he will
of his goodness let him have knowledge thereof, as one that is ready to
follow what way soever he will lead him. But if this form and fashion of
a commonwealth be best, and his own religion most true and perfect,
then he desireth God to give him a constant steadfastness in the same

---

[272] "Ditty" = "song," "hymn."
[273] "Do anything err" = "do err in anything."

and to bring all other people to the same order of living and to the same opinion of God, unless there is anything that in this diversity of religions doth delight his unsearchable pleasure. To be short, he prayeth him that after his death he may come to him, but how soon or late that he dare not assign or determine. Howbeit, if it might stand with his majesty's pleasure, he would be much gladder to die a painful death and so to go to God, than by long living in worldly prosperity to be away from him. When this prayer is said, they fall down to the ground again and a little after they rise up and go to dinner. And the residue of the day they pass over in plays and exercise of chivalry.[274]

Now I have declared and described unto you, as truly as I could, the form and order of that commonwealth, which, verily, in my judgment is not only the best, but also that which alone of good right may claim and take upon it the name of a commonwealth or public weal. For in other places they speak still of the commonwealth, but every man procureth his own private gain. Here, where nothing is private, the common affairs be earnestly looked upon. And, truly, on both parts they have good cause so to do as they do, for in other countries, who knoweth not that he shall starve for hunger unless he make some several provision for himself, though the commonwealth flourish never so much in riches? And, therefore, he is compelled even of very necessity to have regard to himself, rather than to the people, that is to say, to others. Contrariwise, there where all things be common to every man, it is not to be doubted that any man shall lack anything necessary for his private uses, so that the common storehouses and barns be sufficiently stored, for there nothing is distributed after a niggish sort, neither there is any poor man or beggar, and though no man has anything, yet every man is rich. For what can be more rich than to live joyfully and merrily, without all grief and pensiveness,[275] not caring for his own living, nor vexed or troubled with his wife's importunate complaints, nor dreading poverty to his son, nor sorrowing for his daughter's dowry? Yea, they take no care at all for the living and wealth of themselves and all theirs: of their wives, their children, their nephews, their children's children, and all the succession that ever shall follow in their posterity. And yet, besides this, there is no less provision for them that were once laborers and be now weak and impotent, than for them that do now labor and take pain.

Here now would I see if any man dare be so bold as to compare with this equity the justice of other nations, among whom, I forsake God, if I

---

[274] "In plays and exercise of chivalry" = "in pastimes and military exercises."
[275] "Pensiveness" = "melancholy."
[276] "Equity" = "principle of fairness and equal dealing."

can find any sign or token of equity[276] and justice. For what justice is this that a rich goldsmith or an usurer[277] or, to be short, any of them, which either do nothing at all or else that which they do is such that it is not very necessary to the commonwealth, should have a pleasant and a wealthy living either by idleness or by unnecessary business, when in the meantime poor laborers, carters, ironsmiths, carpenters, and plowmen by so great and continual toil as drawing and bearing beasts be scant able to sustain, and again so necessary toil, that without it no commonwealth were able to continue and endure one year, should yet get so hard and poor a living, and live so wretched and miserable a life, that the state and condition of the laboring beasts may seem much better and wealthier? For they be not put to so continual labor, nor their living is not much worse, yea, to them much pleasanter, taking no thought in the mean season for the time to come. But these silly poor wretches be presently tormented with barren and unfruitful labor, and the remembrance of their poor indigent and beggarly old age killeth them up.[278] For their daily wages is so little that it will not suffice for the same day, much less it yieldeth any overplus that may daily be laid up for the relief of old age. Is not this an unjust and an unkind public weal, which giveth great fees and rewards to gentlemen, as they call them, and to goldsmiths and to such others, which be either idle persons or else only flatterers and devisers of vain pleasures, and of the contrary part maketh no gentle provision for poor plowmen, colliers, laborers, carters, ironsmiths, and carpenters, without whom no commonwealth can continue? But after it hath abused the labors of their lusty and flowering age, at the last when they be oppressed with old age and sickness, being needy, poor, and indigent of all things, then, forgetting their so many painful watchings, not remembering their so many and so great benefits, recompenseth and acquiteth them most unkindly with miserable death. And yet besides this, the rich men not only by private fraud, but also by common laws do every day pluck and snatch away from the poor some part of their daily living, so whereas it seemed before unjust to recompense with unkindness their pains that have been beneficial to the public weal, now they have to this their wrong and unjust dealing (which is yet a much worse point) given the name of justice, yea, and that by force of a law.

Therefore, when I consider and weigh in my mind all these commonwealths which nowadays anywhere do flourish, so God help me, I can perceive nothing but a certain conspiracy of rich men procuring their

---

[277] "Usurer" = "greedy moneylender." Note that goldsmiths often also played the role of moneylenders.

[278] "Killeth them up" = "wears them out."

own commodities under the name and title of the commonwealth. They invent and devise all means and crafts, first how to keep safely, without fear of losing, that they have unjustly gathered together, and next how to hire and abuse the work and labor of the poor for as little money as may be. These devices, when the rich men have decreed to be kept and observed under color of the commonalty,[279] that is to say, also of the poor people, then they be made laws. But these most wicked and vicious men, when they have by their insatiable covetousness divided among themselves all those things which would have sufficed all men, yet how far be they from the wealth and felicity of the Utopian commonwealth?

Out of the which, in that all the desire of money with the use thereof is utterly secluded and banished, how great a heap of cares is cut away? How great an occa-

Contempt of money.

sion of wickedness and mischief is plucked up by the roots? For who knoweth not that fraud, theft, ravin, brawling, quarreling, brabbling,[280] strife, chiding, contention, murder, treason, poisoning, which by daily punishments are rather revenged than refrained, do die when money dieth? And also that fear, grief, care, labors, and watchings do perish even the very same moment that money perisheth? Yea, poverty itself, which only seemed to lack money, if money were gone, it also would decrease and vanish away.

And that you may perceive this more plainly, consider with yourselves some barren and unfruitful year wherein many thousands of people have starved for hunger, I dare be bold to say that in the end of that penury so much corn or grain might have been found in the rich men's barns if they had been searched as, being divided among them whom famine and pestilence then consumed, no man at all should have felt that plague and penury. So easily might men get their living, if that same worthy princess Lady Money did not alone stop up the way between us and our living, which, a God's name, was very excellently devised and invented, that by her the way thereto should be opened. I am sure the rich men perceive this, nor they be not ignorant how much better it were to lack no necessary thing than to abound with overmuch superfluity, to be rid out of innumerable cares and troubles than to be besieged and encumbered with great riches.

And I doubt not that either the respect of every man's private commodity or else the authority of our Savior Christ (which for His great wisdom could not but know what were best, and for His inestimable goodness could not but

A marvelous saying.

---

[279] "Under color of the commonalty" = "in the guise of supporting the commonwealth."
[280] "Brabbling" = "argumentative wrangling."

counsel to that which He knew to be best) would have brought all the
world long ago into the laws of this weal public if it were ————————
not that one only beast, the princess and mother of all <small>Pride.</small>
mischief Pride, doth withstand and let it. She mea- ————————
sureth not wealth and prosperity by her own commodities, but by the
misery and incommodities of others, she would not by her goodwill be
made a goddess if there were no wretches left over whom she might, like
a scornful lady, rule and triumph over, whose miseries her felicities
might shine, whose poverty she might vex, torment, and increase by
gorgeously setting forth her riches. This hellhound creepeth into men's
hearts and plucketh them back from entering the right path of life and
is so deeply rooted in men's breasts that she cannot be plucked out.

This form and fashion of a weal public, which I would gladly wish
unto all nations, I am glad yet that it hath chanced to the Utopians, which
have followed those institutions of life, whereby they have laid such
foundations of their commonwealth as shall continue and last not only
wealthily, but also, as far as man's wit may judge and conjecture, shall endure forever. For, seeing the chief causes of ambition and sedition with
other vices be plucked up by the roots and abandoned at home, there
can be no jeopardy of domestical dissension, which alone hath cast under foot and brought to naught the well-fortified and strongly defensed
wealth and riches of many cities. But forasmuch as perfect concord remaineth and wholesome laws be executed at home, the envy of all foreign princes be not able to shake or move the empire, though they have
many times long ago gone about to do it, being evermore driven back.

Thus when Raphael had made an end of his tale, though many things
came to my mind which in the manners and laws of that people seemed
to be instituted and founded of no good reason, not only in the fashion of
their chivalry, and in their sacrifices and religions, and in other of their
laws, but also, yea and chiefly, in that which is the principal foundation
of all their ordinances, that is to say, in the community of their life and
living, without any occupying of money, by the which thing only all nobility, magnificence, worship, honor, and majesty, the true ornaments
and honors, as the common opinion is, of a commonwealth, utterly be
overthrown and destroyed, yet because I knew that he was weary of talking and was not sure whether he could abide that anything should be
said against his mind, specially remembering that he had reprehended
this fault in others, which be afraid lest they should seem not to be wise
enough, unless they could find some fault in other men's inventions,
therefore, I, praising both their institutions and his communication, took
him by the hand and led him in to supper, saying that we would choose
another time to weigh and examine the same matters and to talk with

him more at large therein. Which would God it might once come to pass. In the meantime, as I cannot agree and consent to all things that he said, being else without doubt a man singularly well learned and also in all worldly matters exactly and profoundly experienced, so must I needs confess and grant that many things be in the Utopian weal public, which in our cities I may rather wish for than hope after.

Thus endeth the afternoon's talk of Raphael Hythloday concerning the laws and institutions of the island of Utopia.

TO THE RIGHT HONORABLE HIEROME BUSLIDE,

Provost of Arienn and Counselor to the Catholic King Charles,[1] Peter Giles, Citizen of Antwerp, wisheth health and felicity.

Thomas More, the singular ornament of this our age, as you yourself (right honorable Buslide) can witness, to whom he is perfectly well known, sent unto me this other day the *Island of Utopia*, to very few as yet known, but most worthy. Which, as far excelling Plato's *Commonwealth*,[2] all people should be willing to know specially of a man most eloquent, so finely set forth, so cunningly painted out,[3] and so evidently subject to the eye, that as oft as I read it, methinketh that I see somewhat more than when I heard Raphael Hythloday himself (for I was present at that talk as well as Master More) uttering and pronouncing his own words. Yea, though the same man, according to his pure eloquence, did so open and declare the matter that he might plainly enough appear to report not things which he had learned of others only by hearsay, but which he had with his own eyes presently seen and thoroughly viewed, and wherein he had no small time been conversant and abiding: a man truly, in mine opinion, as touching the knowledge of regions, peoples, and worldly experience, much passing, yea, even the very famous and

---

[1] Hierome Buslide is Jerome Busleyden, a noted patron of good letters in More's day. He was Provost of Saint Peter's Church at Aire (Arienn) in Artois and a counselor to Charles, who in 1516 inherited the throne of Aragon and along with it the title "the Catholic" from King Ferdinand, his grandfather; see pp. 88–89. More had met Busleyden in 1515 and devoted three of his *Epigrams* to him, celebrating his devotion to learning and virtue as well as his practical wisdom. Giles's letter to Busleyden appeared as front matter in the original 1516 Latin edition as did Busleyden's very generous letter to More commenting on the book. For the latter, see CW 4, pp. 32–37.

[2] "Plato's *Commonwealth*" = "Plato's *Republic*."

[3] "Painted out" = "depicted."

renowned traveler Ulysses; and, indeed, such a one, as for the space of these eight hundred years past I think nature into the world brought not forth his like, in comparison of whom Vespucci may be thought to have seen nothing. Moreover, whereas we be wont more effectually and pithily to declare and express things that we have seen than which we have but only heard, there was besides that in this man a certain peculiar grace and singular dexterity to describe and set forth a matter withal.

Yet the selfsame things as oft as I behold and consider them drawn and painted out with Master More's pencil, I am therewith so moved, so delighted, so inflamed, and so rapt that sometime methink I am presently conversant, even in the island of Utopia. And I promise you, I can scant believe that Raphael himself, by all that five years' space that he was in Utopia abiding, saw there so much as here in Master More's description is to be seen and perceived. Which description, with so many wonders and miraculous things is replenished,[4] that I stand in great doubt whereat first and chiefly to muse or marvel, whether at the excellency of his perfect and sure memory, which could wellnigh word by word rehearse so many things once only heard, or else at his singular prudence,[5] who so well and wittily marked and bare away all the original causes and fountains (to the vulgar people commonly most unknown) whereof both issueth and springeth the mortal confusion and utter decay of a commonwealth, and also the advancement and wealthy state of the same may rise and grow, or else at the efficacy and pith of his words, which, in so fine a Latin style, with such force of eloquence hath couched together and comprised so many and divers matters, specially being a man continually encumbered with so many busy and troublesome cares, both public and private, as he is. Howbeit, all these things cause you little to marvel (right honorable Buslide) for that you are familiarly and thoroughly acquainted with the notable, yea, almost divine wit of the man.

But now to proceed to other matters. I surely know nothing needful or requisite to be adjoined unto his writings, only a meter of four verses written in the Utopian tongue, which after Master More's departure Hythloday by chance showed me, that have I caused to be added thereto, with the alphabet of the same nation, and have also garnished the margin of the book with certain notes.[6] For, as touching the situation of the island, that is to say, in what part of the world Utopia standeth, the

---

[4] "Replenished" = "filled up."

[5] "Prudence" = "practical wisdom about matters of public importance."

[6] The four lines in the Utopian language, almost certainly created by Giles himself, follow this letter.

ignorance and lack whereof not a little troubleth and grieveth Master
More, indeed Raphael left not that unspoken of. Howbeit, with very few
words he lightly touched it, incidentally by the way passing it over, as
meaning of likelihood to keep and reserve that to another place. And the
same, I wot[7] not how, by a certain evil and unlucky chance escaped us
both. For when Raphael was speaking thereof, one of Master More's servants came to him and whispered in his ear. Wherefore, I being then of
purpose more earnestly addict[8] to hear, one of the company, by reason
of cold taken, I think, a-shipboard, coughed out so loud that he took from
my hearing certain of his words. But I will never stint[9] nor rest until I
have got the full and exact knowledge hereof, insomuch that I will be
able perfectly to instruct you, not only in the longitude or true meridian
of the island, but also in the just latitude thereof, that is to say, in the sublevation[10] or height of the pole in that region, if our friend Hythloday be
in safety and alive. For we hear very uncertain news of him. Some report
that he died in his journey homeward. Some again affirm that he returned into his country, but partly for that he could not away with the
fashions of his country folk,[11] and partly for that his mind and affection
were altogether set and fired upon Utopia, they say that he hath taken
his voyage thitherward again. Now as touching this, that the name of this
island is nowhere found among the old and ancient cosmographers, this
doubt Hythloday himself very well dissolved. For why, it is possible
enough (quoth he) that the name which it had in old time was afterward
changed or else that they never had knowledge of this island, forasmuch
as now in our time divers lands be found which to the old geographers
were unknown. Howbeit, what needeth it in this behalf to fortify the matter with arguments, seeing Master More is author hereof sufficient? But
whereas he doubteth of the edition or imprinting of the book, indeed
herein I both commend and also knowledge the man's modesty. Howbeit, unto me it seemeth a work most unworthy to be long suppressed
and most worthy to go abroad into the hands of men; yea, and under the
title of your name to be published to the world, either because the singular endowments and qualities of Master More be to no man better
known than to you or else because no man is more fit and meet than you
with good counsels to further and advance the commonwealth, wherein
you have many years already continued and travailed with great glory

[7]"Wot" = "know."
[8]"Addict" = "inclined."
[9]"Stint" = "cease."
[10]"Sublevation" = "elevation."
[11]"Could not away with the fashions of his country folk" = "could not put up with the
customs of his homeland."

and commendation, both of wisdom and knowledge and also of integrity and uprightness. Thus, O liberal supporter of good learning and flower of this our time, I bid you most heartily well to fare. At Antwerp, 1516, the first day of November.

A meter of four verses in the Utopian tongue,

briefly touching as well the strange beginning,

as also the happy and wealthy continuance,

of the same commonwealth.[1]

Utopos ha Boccas peula chama polta chamaan.
Bargol he maglomi Baccan soma gymnosophaon,
Agrama gymnosophon labarem bacha bodamilomin.
Volvala barchin heman la lavolvala dramme pagloni.

Which verses the translator, according

to his simple knowledge and mean

understanding in the Utopian
tongue hath thus rudely
Englished.

My king and conqueror Utopus by name,[2]
A prince of much renown and immortal fame,
Hath made me an isle that erst no island was,
Full fraught with worldly wealth, with pleasure and solace.
I one of all other without philosophy
Have shaped for man a philosophical city.
As mine I am nothing dangerous to impart,
So better to receive I am ready with all my heart.

[1] In the original Latin editions, this poem appeared as front matter. The Utopian tongue, created by Peter Giles for the 1516 Latin edition, is a pastiche of Greek and Latin roots. The printers supplied a Utopian "alphabet" to accompany the original Latin versions. However, the "printer" says to the reader at the very end of the volume (207) that it proved impossible for him to supply the letters of the alphabet for this English edition. For the alphabet as it appeared in Froben's 1518 edition, see Figure 11.

[2] In the original Latin version of this poem, Utopus is identified as *dux,* i.e., "leader" or "commander," not *rex,* i.e., "king."

A short meter of Utopia, written by Anemolius, poet laureate and nephew to Hythloday by his sister.[3]

Me Utopie cleped Antiquity,[4]
Void of haunt and herborough.[5]
Now am I like to Plato's city,
Whose fame flieth the world through.
Yea, like, or rather more likely,
Plato's plat to excel and pass.[6]
For what Plato's pen hath platted briefly
In naked words, as in a glass,
The same have I performed fully,
With law, with men, and treasure fitly.
Wherefore not Utopie, but rather rightly
My name is Eutopie: A place of felicity.[7]

Gerard Noviomage[8] of Utopia.

Does pleasure please? Then place thee here, and well thee rest,
Most pleasant pleasures thou shalt find here.
Does profit ease? Then here arrive, this isle is best.
For passing profits[9] do here appear.
Doth both thee tempt, and would thou grip both gain and pleasure?
This isle is fraught with both bounteously.
To still thy greedy intent, reap here incomparable treasure,
Both mind and tongue to garnish richly.
The hid wells and fountains both of vice and virtue

---

[3]The author of this poem is not known with certainty; it may have been supplied by More himself for the original Latin editions, where it appeared among the front matter. The name of the poet, Anemolius, derives from the Greek word meaning "windy."

[4]"Me Utopie cleped Antiquity" = "I am called Utopia in Antiquity (or among the ancients)."

[5]"Void of haunt and herborough" = "empty of society or people and of dwellings or buildings" (i.e., a "no place," which is the literal translation from the Greek of *Utopia*).

[6]"Plato's plat to excel and pass" = "surpassing Plato's model."

[7]"Eutopie," i.e., *Eutopia,* means "good place" in Greek.

[8]Gerard Noviomage, i.e., Gerard of Nijmegen, is Gerard Geldenhauer of Nijmegen (1482–1542) in the Netherlands, a Dutch humanist who assisted Dirk Martens, the Louvain printer, with the printing of the first edition of *Utopia.*

[9]"Passing profits" = "surpassing benefits."

Thou hast them here subject unto thine eye.
Be thankful now, and thanks where thanks be due
Give to Thomas More, London's immortal glory.

Cornelius Graphey[10] to the Reader

Wilt thou know what wonders strange
be in the land that late was found?
Wilt thou learn thy life to lead by divers ways that godly be?
Wilt thou of virtue and of vice understand the very ground?
Wilt thou see this wretched world, how full it is of vanity?
Then read and mark and bear in mind, for thy behoof,
     as thou may best.
All things that in this present work that worthy clerk Sir Thomas More,
With wit divine full learnedly, unto the world hath plain expressed,
In whom London well glory may, for wisdom and for godly lore.

The Printer to the Reader

The Utopian alphabet, good Reader, which in the above written Epistle is promised, hereunto I have not now adjoined because I have not as yet the true characters or forms of the Utopian letters. And no marvel, seeing it is a tongue to us much stranger than the Indian, the Persian, the Syrian, the Arabic, the Egyptian, the Macedonian, the Sclavonian,[11] the Cyprian, the Scythian, etc. Which tongues, though they be nothing so strange among us as the Utopian is, yet their characters we have not. But I trust, God willing, at the next impression hereof, to perform that which now I cannot: that is to say, to exhibit perfectly unto you, the Utopian alphabet. In the meantime, accept my goodwill. And so farewell.

Imprinted at London in Paul's
Churchyard, at the sign of the
Lamb, by Abraham Vele.
M.D.L.VI.

---

[10]Cornelius Graphey is Cornelis de Schrijver (1482–1558), a well-regarded Latin poet of his day, who settled in Antwerp in 1515, where he became a friend and colleague of Peter Giles.

[11]"Sclavonian" = "Slav."

¶ The Printer to the Reader.

THe Utopian Alpha
bete, good Reader, whiche in
the aboue wzitten Epistle is
pzomised, herunto I haue not
now adioyned, becauseI haue
not as yet the true characters
oz fourmes of the Utopiane
letters. And no maruell:se=
yng it is a tongue to vs muche straunger then the
Indian, the Persian, the Syziã, the Asiaticke, the
Egyptian, the Macedonian, the Sclauonian, the
cipziã, the Scythiã ꝛc. Which tõgues though they
be nothing so straunge among vs, as the Utopian
is, yet their characters we haue not. But I trust,
God willing, at the next impzession hereof, to per=
fourme that, whiche nowe I can not: that is
to saye: to exhibite perfectly vnto thee,
the Utopian Alphabete. In the
meane time accept my good
wyl. And so fare well.

¶ Impzinted at Londõ in Pau=
les Churche yarde, at the sygne of the
Lambe, by Abzaham Ueale.
M.D.LVI.

Figure 13. The final page of the 1556 edition of Robynson's translation of Utopia.

By permission of the Folger Shakespeare Library.

TO THE RIGHT HONORABLE

and his very singular good master, Master William Cecil, esquire, one of the two principal secretaries to the king his most excellent majesty,[1] Ralph Robynson wisheth continuance of health, with daily increase of virtue and honor.

Upon a time when tidings came to the city of Corinth that King Philip, father to Alexander surnamed the Great, was coming thitherward with an army royal to lay siege to the city, the Corinthians being forthwith stricken with great fear, began busily and earnestly to look about them and to fall to work of all hands. Some to scour and trim up harness, some to carry stones, some to amend and build higher the walls, some to rampire[2] and fortify the bulwarks and fortresses, some one thing and some another for the defending and strengthening of the city. The which busy labor and toil of theirs when Diogenes the philosopher saw, having no profitable business whereupon to set himself on work (neither any man required his labor and help as expedient for the commonwealth in that necessity) immediately girded about him his philosophical cloak and began to roll and tumble up and down hither and thither upon the hillside that lieth adjoining to the city, his great barrel or tun wherein he dwelled, for other dwelling place would he have none. This seeing one of his friends, and not a little musing thereat, came to him. And I pray thee Diogenes (quoth he) why dost thou thus or what meanest thou hereby?

---

[1] William Cecil (1520–1598), born into a well-connected gentry family in Northamptonshire, was educated in the liberal arts at the grammar schools of Stamford in that county and of Grantham in Lincolnshire and then at St. John's College, Cambridge; the latter was noted for the presence among its Fellows of the humanist educators Roger Ascham and John Cheke. Later Cecil was briefly a student at Grey's Inn in London. He sat in his first Parliament in 1542, and by 1547 he was in service as secretary to Protector Somerset. After Somerset's fall in 1549 and a short period out of office, he was sworn to the privy council and appointed one of the two secretaries of state under Edward VI. In this position he was responsible for handling the correspondence of the council in all its affairs, a post in which he continued until the end of Edward VI's reign in 1553. During Mary's reign, he served England on various diplomatic missions and sat for Stamford in Mary's first parliament in 1553 and for Lincolnshire in 1555. After being arrested and interrogated by Mary's royal councillors for his views during the 1555 session, he retired to Lincolnshire and only rarely appeared in London during the remainder of Mary's life. With the accession of Queen Elizabeth I in November 1558, he once again became a privy councillor and secretary of state, subsequently holding other important offices as one of Elizabeth's principal counselors until his death, as Lord Burghley, in 1598. He was knighted in October 1551. Since Robynson refers to him only by the honorific term "Master," this dedicatory letter must have been written sometime earlier in the year.

[2] "To rampire" = "to build ramparts."

Forsooth, I am tumbling my tub so (quoth he), because it were no reason that I only should be idle where so many be working.[3]

In semblable manner, right honorable sir, though I be, as I am indeed, of much less ability than Diogenes was to do anything that shall or may be for the advancement and commodity of the public wealth of my native country, yet I, seeing every sort and kind of people in their vocation and degree busily occupied about the commonwealth's affairs, and especially learned men daily putting forth in writing new inventions and devices to the furtherance of the same, thought it my bounden duty to God and to my country so to tumble my tub. I mean so to occupy and exercise meself in bestowing such spare hours as I, being at the beck and commandment of others, could conveniently win to meself, that though no commodity of that my labor and travail to the public weal should arise, yet it might by this appear that mine endeavor and goodwill hereunto was not lacking.

To the accomplishment, therefore, and fulfilling of this my mind and purpose, I took upon me to turn and translate out of Latin into our English tongue the fruitful and profitable book which Sir Thomas More, knight, compiled and made of the new isle Utopia, containing and setting forth the best state and form of a public weal, a work (as it appeareth) written almost forty years ago by the said Sir Thomas More, the author thereof. The which man, forasmuch as he was a man of late time, yea, almost of these our days, and for the excellent qualities, wherewith the great goodness of God had plentifully endowed him, and for the high place and room, whereunto his prince had most graciously called him, notably well known, not only among us his countrymen, but also in foreign countries and nations, therefore I have not much to speak of him. This only I say, that it is much to be lamented of all, and not only of us Englishmen, that a man of so incomparable wit, of so profound knowledge, of so absolute[4] learning, and of so fine eloquence was yet nevertheless so much blinded, rather with obstinacy than with ignorance, that he could not or rather would not see the shining light of God's holy truth in certain principal points of Christian religion, but did rather choose to

---

[3] Diogenes (c. 400–325 B.C.E.) was the founder of the sect of Cynics in Athens, a philosophical school that sought happiness and self-sufficiency by following the dictates of physical nature, limiting bodily needs, and satisfying them in the least costly and least complicated way; among other attributes, Diogenes was famous for living during summers in a tub. For the anecdote referred to by Robynson, see Lucian, "How to Write History," in *Lucian,* trans. A. M. Harmon, K. Kilburn, and M. D. Macleod, 8 vols. (London: William Heinemann, 1927–67), vol. 6, p. 5.

[4] "Absolute" = "consummate," "perfect."

persevere and continue in his willful and stubborn obstinacy even to the very death. This, I say, is a thing much to be lamented.

But letting this matter pass, I return again to *Utopia,* which (as I said before) is a work not only for the matter that it containeth fruitful and profitable, but also for the writer's eloquent Latin style, pleasant and delectable.[5] Which he that readeth in Latin as the author himself wrote it, perfectly understanding the same, doubtless he shall take great pleasure and delight both in the sweet eloquence of the writer and also in the witty invention and fine convenience[6] or disposition of the matter, but most of all in the good and wholesome lessons which be there in great plenty and abundance. But now I fear greatly that in this my simple translation through my rudeness and ignorance in our English tongue all the grace and pleasure of the eloquence, wherewith the matter in Latin is finely set forth may seem to be utterly excluded and lost, and therefore the fruitfulness of the matter itself much peradventure diminished and appaired. For who knoweth not, which knoweth anything, that an eloquent style setteth forth and highly commendeth a mean matter? Whereas on the other side rude and unlearned speech defaceth and disgraceth a very good matter. According, as I heard once a wise man say, a good tale evil told were better untold, and an evil tale well told needeth none other solicitor. This thing I, well pondering and weighing, in me felt and also knowing and knowledging the barbarous rudeness of my translation, was fully determined never to have put it forth in print had it not been for certain friends of mine, and especially one, whom above all other I regarded a man of sage and discreet wit and in wordly matters by long use well experienced, whose name is George Tadlowe, an honest citizen of London, and in the same city well accepted and of good reputation, at whose request and instance I first took upon my weak and feeble shoulders the heavy and weighty burden of this great enterprise.[7] This man with divers others, but this man chiefly (for he was able to do more with me than many others) after that I had once rudely brought the work to an end, ceased not by all means possible continually to assault me until he had the last, what by the force of his pithy arguments and strong reasons and what by his authority, so persuaded me that he caused me to agree and consent to the imprinting hereof. He, therefore, as the chief persuader must take upon him the danger which upon this bold and rash enterprise shall ensue. I, as I suppose, am herein clearly

---

[5]"Delectable" = "delightful."
[6]"Convenience" = "harmony."
[7]For Tadlowe, see pp. 61, 78*n*129.

acquit and discharged of all blame. Yet, honorable sir, for the better avoiding of envious and malicious tongues, I (knowing you to be a man not only profoundly learned and well affected towards all such as either can or will take pains in well bestowing of that poor talent which God hath endowed them with, but also for your godly disposition and virtuous qualities, not unworthily now placed in authority and called to honor) am the bolder humbly to offer and dedicate unto your good mastership this my simple work. Partly that under the safe conduct[8] of your protection it may the better be defended from the obloquy of them which can say well by nothing that pleaseth not their fond and corrupt judgments, though it be else both fruitful and godly, and partly that by the means of this homely present, I may the better renew and revive (which of late, as you know, I have already begun to do) that old acquaintance that was between you and me in the time of our childhood, being then schoolfellows together.[9] Not doubting that you for your native goodness and gentleness will accept in good part this poor gift as an argument, or token, that mine old goodwill and hearty affection towards you is not by reason of long tract of time and separation of our bodies anything at all quailed[10] and diminished, but rather (I assure you) much augmented and increased. This, verily, is the chief cause that hath encouraged me to be so bold with your mastership, else truly this my poor present is of such simple and mean sort that it is neither able to recompense the least portion of your great gentleness to me, of my part undeserved, both in the time of our old acquaintance, and also now laterly again bountifully showed, neither yet fit and meet for the very baseness of it to be offered to one so worth as you be. But almighty God (who therefore ever be thanked) hath advanced you to such fortune and dignity that you be of ability to accept thankfully as well a man's goodwill as his gift. The same God grant you and all yours long and joyfully to continue in all godliness and prosperity.

[8] In referring to Cecil's "safe conduct," Robynson is drawing an analogy with the granting, as a privilege usually conveyed in an official letter or document, of formal protection from interference or arrest while on a journey.

[9] Robynson attended the grammar schools at Stamford and Grantham with Cecil. He received his university education, however, at Corpus Christi College, Oxford, where he received his B.A. in 1540.

[10] "Quailed" = "withered."

Selected Bibliography

I. EDITIONS OF SIR THOMAS MORE'S WORKS

More, Thomas. *The Yale Edition of the Complete Works of St. Thomas More.* 15 vols. New Haven: Yale University Press, 1963–97.
———. *The Correspondence of Sir Thomas More.* Edited by Elizabeth Francis Rogers. Princeton: Princeton University Press, 1947.

II. ANCIENT AND EARLY MODERN TEXTS

A. Greek and Roman

Aristotle. *The Complete Works of Aristotle: The Revised Oxford Translation.* Edited by Jonathan Barnes. 2 vols. Princeton: Princeton University Press, 1984.
Augustinus, Saint Aurelius. *City of God.* Translated by Henry Bettenson, with an introduction by John O'Meara. Harmondsworth: Penguin, 1984.
Cicero, Marcus Tullius. *Cicero.* Translated by E. O. Winstedt et al. 28 vols. Loeb Classical Library. London: William Heinemann, 1912–79.
———. *On Duties.* Edited and translated by M. T. Griffin and E. M. Adkins. Cambridge: Cambridge University Press, 1991.
Epictetus. *The Discourse as Reported by Arrian, the Manual, and Fragments.* Translated by W. A. Oldfather. 2 vols. Loeb Classical Library. London: William Heinemann, 1926–28.
Homer. *The Odyssey.* Translated by A. T. Murray; revised by George E. Dimock. Loeb Classical Library. Cambridge, Mass.: Harvard University Press, 1995.
Livius, Titus. *Livy.* Translated by B. O. Foster et al. 14 vols. Loeb Classical Library. London: William Heinemann, 1919–59.
Lucan, Marcus Annaeus. *Lucan.* Translated by J. D. Duff. Loeb Classical Library. London: William Heinemann, 1928.
Lucian of Samosata. *Lucian.* Translated by A. M. Harmon, K. Kilburn, and M. D. Macleod. 8 vols. Loeb Classical Library. London: William Heinemann, 1927–67.

————. *Satirical Sketches.* Translated by Paul Turner. First Midland Book edition. Bloomington: Indiana University Press, 1990.

The Oxford Annotated Bible with the Apocrypha: Revised Standard Version. Edited by Herbert G. May and Bruce M. Metzger. New York: Oxford University Press, 1965.

Plato. *The Collected Dialogues of Plato, Including the Letters.* Edited by Edith Hamilton and Huntington Cairns. New York: Pantheon, 1961.

Plutarchus of Chaeronea. *Plutarch's Moralia.* Translated by Frank Cole Babbitt et al. 17 vols. Loeb Classical Library. London: William Heinemann, 1927–76.

Quintilianus, Marcus Fabius. *Institutio Oratoria.* Translated by H. E. Butler. 4 vols. Loeb Classical Library. Cambridge, Mass.: Harvard University Press, 1966–69.

Sallustius Crispus, Caius. *Sallust.* Translated by J. C. Rolfe. Loeb Classical Library. London: William Heinemann, 1931.

Terentius Afer, Publius. *Terence.* Translated by John Sergeant. Loeb Classical Library. London: William Heinemann, 1931.

Vergilius, Maro Publius. *Virgil.* Translated by H. R. Faircloth. 2 vols. Loeb Classical Library. Cambridge, Mass.: Harvard University Press, 1978–86.

B. Early Modern

Anghiera, Peter Martyr d'. *The Decades of the New Worlde or West India.* Translated by Richard Eden. London, 1555 (STC 645).

————. *De orbe novo.* Translated by F. M. McNutt. New York: G. P. Putnam's Sons, 1912.

Erasmus, Desiderius. *Collected Works of Erasmus.* Toronto: University of Toronto Press, 1974.

————. *Praise of Folly and Letter to Maarten van Dorp, 1515.* Edited by A. H. T. Levi; translated by Betty Radice. Harmondsworth: Penguin, 1971.

Fortescue, Sir John. *On the Laws and Governance of England.* Edited by Shelly Lockwood. Cambridge: Cambridge University Press. 1997.

Foxe, John. *The Acts and Monuments of John Foxe.* Edited by George Townsend. 8 vols. New York: AMS Press, 1965.

Saint Germain, Christopher. *St. Germain's Doctor and Student.* Edited by T. F. T. Plucknett and J. L. Barton. Publications of the Selden Society, vol. 91, 1974.

Sneyd, C. A., ed. *A Relation, or Rather a True Account, of the Island of England . . . about the Year 1500.* Camden Society, no. 37, 1847.

Vespucci, Amerigo. *The First Four Voyages of Amerigo Vespucci Reproduced in Facsimile and Translated from the Rare Original Edition (Florence, 1505–6).* London: Bernard Quartitch, 1893.

————. *Mundus novus: Letter to Lorenzo Pietro di Medici.* Translated by G. T. Northrup. Princeton: Princeton University Press, 1916.

III. USEFUL COMMENTARIES

A. Utopia

Baker-Smith, Dominic. *More's Utopia*. London: HarperCollins Academic, 1991.

Bradshaw, Brendan. "More on *Utopia*." *Historical Journal* 36 (1985): 1–27.

Hexter, J. H. "Intentions, Words, and Meaning: The Case of Thomas More's *Utopia*." *New Literary History* 6 (1975): 529–41.

———. "The Loom of Language and the Fabric of Imperatives: The Case of *Il Principe* and *Utopia*." *American Historical Review* 69 (1964): 945–68.

———. *More's Utopia: The Biography of an Idea*. Princeton: Princeton University Press, 1952.

———. "Thomas More: On the Margins of Modernity." *Journal of British Studies* 1 (1961): 20–37.

———. *The Vision of Politics on the Eve of the Reformation: More, Machiavelli, and Seyssel*. New York: Basic Books, 1973.

Keen, Ralph, and Daniel Kinney, eds. "Thomas More and the Classics." *Moreana*, no. 86 (1985).

Logan, George M. *The Meaning of More's Utopia*. Princeton: Princeton University Press, 1983.

Marc'hadour, Germain, and Richard S. Sylvester, eds. *Essential Articles for the Study of Thomas More*. Hamden, Conn.: Archon, 1977.

Skinner, Quentin. "More's *Utopia*." *Past and Present*, no. 38 (1967): 153–68.

———. "Sir Thomas More's *Utopia* and the Language of Renaissance Humanism." In *The Languages of Political Theory in Early Modern Europe*, edited by Anthony Pagden. Cambridge: Cambridge University Press, 1987, 123–57.

Surtz, Edward S. J. *The Praise of Pleasure: Philosophy, Education, and Communism in More's* Utopia. Cambridge, Mass.: Harvard University Press, 1957.

———. *The Praise of Wisdom: A Commentary on the Religious and Moral Problems and Backgrounds of St. Thomas More's* Utopia. Chicago: Loyola University Press, 1957.

Wootton, David. "Friendship Portrayed: A New Account of *Utopia*." *History Workshop*, no. 45 (1998): 29–47.

B. Ancient Philosophy and Literature

Annas, Julia. *An Introduction to Plato's Republic*. Oxford: Clarendon Press, 1981.

Barnes, Jonathan, ed. *The Cambridge Companion to Aristotle*. Cambridge: Cambridge University Press, 1995.

Irwin, Terence. *Aristotle's First Principles*. Oxford: Clarendon Press, 1988.

Keyt, David, and Fred D. Miller, eds. *A Companion to Aristotle's Politics*. Oxford: Blackwell, 1991.

Kraut, Richard, ed. *The Cambridge Companion to Plato.* Cambridge: Cambridge University Press, 1992.

Meikle, Scott. *Aristotle's Economic Thought.* Oxford: Clarendon Press, 1995.

Reeve, C. D. C. *Philosopher-Kings: The Argument of Plato's Republic.* Princeton: Princeton University Press, 1988.

Rorty, Amélie Oksenberg, ed. *Essay on Aristotle's Rhetoric.* Berkeley: University of California Press, 1996.

C. Medieval and Early Modern Philosophy and Literature

Adams, Robert P. *The Better Part of Valor: More, Erasmus, Colet, and Vives on Humanism, War, and Peace, 1496–1535.* Seattle: University of Washington Press, 1962.

Allen, J. W. *The History of Political Thought in the Sixteenth Century.* London: Methuen, 1941.

Burns, J. H., ed. *The Cambridge History of Medieval Political Thought, c. 350–c. 1450.* Cambridge: Cambridge University Press, 1988.

————, with Mark Goldie, eds. *The Cambridge History of Political Thought, 1450–1700.* Cambridge: Cambridge University Press, 1991.

Caspari, Fritz. *Humanism and the Social Order in Tudor England.* Chicago: University of Chicago Press, 1954.

Ferguson, A. B. *The Articulate Citizen and the English Renaissance.* Durham, N.C.: Duke University Press, 1965.

Fox, Alistair. *Politics and Literature in the Reigns of Henry VII and Henry VIII.* Oxford: Basil Blackwell, 1989.

Kraye, Jill. *The Cambridge Companion to Renaissance Humanism.* Cambridge: Cambridge University Press, 1998.

Lewis, C. S. *English Literature in the Sixteenth Century Excluding Drama.* Oxford: Clarendon Press, 1954.

McConica, James K. *English Humanists and Reformation Politics under Henry VIII and Edward VI.* Oxford: Oxford University Press, 1965.

Rabil, Albert, Jr. *Renaissance Humanism: Foundations, Forms, and Legacy.* 3 vols. Philadelphia: University of Pennsylvania Press, 1988.

Schmitt, Charles B. *Aristotle and the Renaissance.* Cambridge, Mass.: Harvard University Press, 1983.

————, Quentin Skinner, and Eckhard Kessler, with Jill Kraye, eds. *The Cambridge History of Renaissance Philosophy.* Cambridge: Cambridge University Press, 1988.

Screech, M. A. *Erasmus: Ecstasy and the Praise of Folly.* London: Penguin, 1988.

Skinner, Quentin. "Classical Eloquence in Renaissance England." In *Reason and Rhetoric in the Philosophy of Thomas Hobbes.* Cambridge: Cambridge University Press, 1966, 19–211.

———. *The Foundations of Modern Political Thought.* 2 vols. Cambridge: Cambridge University Press, 1978.

Tracy, James D. *The Politics of Erasmus: A Pacifist Intellectual and His Milieu.* Toronto: University of Toronto Press, 1978.

Trapp, J. B. *Erasmus, Colet, and More: The Early Humanists and Their Books.* London: British Library, 1991.

Vickers, Brian. *In Defense of Rhetoric.* Oxford: Clarendon Press, 1988.

Weiss, Roberto. *Humanism in England during the Fifteenth Century.* Oxford: Basil Blackwell, 1963.

Zeeveld, W. Gordon. *Foundations of Tudor Policy.* Cambridge, Mass.: Harvard University Press, 1948.

IV. BIOGRAPHIES

A. Sir Thomas More

1. EARLY MODERN

Ba., Ro. *The Lyfe of Syr Thomas More, Sometymes Lord Chancellor of England, by Ro: Ba:.* Edited by Elsie Vaughan Hitchcock and P. E. Hallett, with A. W. Reed. Early English Text Society, orig. ser., no. 222. London: Oxford University Press, 1950.

Harpsfield, Nicholas. *The Life and Death of Sir Thomas Moore, Knight, Sometimes Lord High Chancellor of England.* Edited by Elsie Vaughan Hitchcock. Early English Text Society, orig. ser., no. 186. London: Oxford University Press, 1932.

More, Cresacre. *D. O. M. S. the Life and Death of Sir Thomas Moore Lord High Chancellour of England Written by M. T. M. and Dedicated to the Queens Most Gracious Maiestie* (Douai, 1631?, STC 18066). In *English Recusant Literature, 1558–1640,* vol. 66, edited by D. M. Rogers. Menston, Yorks.: Scolar Press, 1971.

Roper, William. *The Life of Sir Thomas More.* In *Two Early Tudor Lives,* edited by Richard S. Sylvester and Davis P. Harding. New Haven: Yale University Press, 1962, 195–254.

Stapleton, Thomas. *The Life and Illustrious Martyrdom of Sir Thomas More.* Translated by Philip E. Hallett; edited by E. E. Reynolds. New York: Fordham University Press, 1966.

2. MODERN

Ackroyd, Peter. *The Life of Thomas More.* London: Chatto and Windus, 1998.

Ames, Russell. *Citizen More and His Utopia.* Princeton: Princeton University Press, 1949.

Bradshaw, Brendan. "The Controversial Sir Thomas More." *Journal of Ecclesiastical History* 36 (1985): 535–69.

Chambers, R. W. *Thomas More.* New York: Harcourt, Brace, 1935.

Elton, G. R. "The Real Thomas More?" In *Studies in Tudor and Stuart Politics and Government,* edited by G. R. Elton. 4 vols. Cambridge: Cambridge University Press, 1974–92, vol. 3, 344–55.

———. "Sir Thomas More and the Opposition to Henry VIII." In *Studies in Tudor and Stuart Politics and Government,* edited by G. R. Elton. 4 vols. Cambridge: Cambridge University Press, 1974–92, vol. 1, 155–72.

———. "Thomas More, Councillor." In *Studies in Tudor and Stuart Politics and Government,* edited by G. R. Elton. 4 vols. Cambridge: Cambridge University Press, 1974–92, vol. 1, 129–33.

Fox, Alistair. *Thomas More: History and Providence.* New Haven: Yale University Press, 1982.

Greenblatt, Stephen. "At the Table of the Great: More's Self-Fashioning and Self-Cancellation." In *Renaissance Self-Fashioning: From More to Shakespeare.* Chicago: University of Chicago Press, 1980, 11–73.

Guy, J. A. *The Public Career of Sir Thomas More.* New Haven: Yale University Press, 1980.

Marius, Richard C. *Thomas More: A Biography.* New York: Alfred A. Knopf, 1984.

Sylvester, Richard S., ed. *St. Thomas More: Action and Contemplation.* New Haven: Yale University Press, 1972.

B. Desiderius Erasmus

Bainton, Roland. *Erasmus of Christendom.* New York: Scribner, 1969.

Halkin, Léon-E. *Erasmus: A Critical Biography.* Translated by John Tonkin. Oxford: Blackwell, 1993.

Huizinga, Johan. *Erasmus of Rotterdam.* Translated by F. Hopman and Barbara Flower. London: Phaidon Press, 1952.

Jardine, Lisa. *Erasmus, Man of Letters: The Construction of Charisma in Print.* Princeton: Princeton University Press, 1993.

McConica, James K. *Erasmus.* Oxford: Oxford University Press, 1991.

Schoeck, Richard J. *Erasmus of Europe.* Edinburgh: Edinburgh University Press, 1990.

Tracy, James D. *Erasmus: The Growth of a Mind.* Geneva: Droz, 1972.

———. *Erasmus of the Low Countries.* Berkeley: University of California Press, 1996.

C. Other Contemporaries

Cavendish, George. *The Life and Death of Cardinal Wolsey.* In *Two Early Tudor Lives,* edited by Richard S. Sylvester and Davis P. Harding. New Haven: Yale University Press, 1962.

Gleason, John B. *John Colet.* Berkeley: University of California Press, 1989.

Gwyn, Peter. *The King's Cardinal: The Rise and Fall of Thomas Wolsey.* London: Barrie and Jenkins, 1990.

Hogrefe, Pearl. *The Sir Thomas More Circle.* Urbana: University of Illinois Press, 1959.

Jayne, Sears. *John Colet and Marsilio Ficino.* London: Oxford University Press, 1963.

Lupton, J. H. *A Life of John Colet, D.D., Dean of St. Paul's and Founder of St. Paul's School.* London: G. Bell and Sons, 1909.

Sturge, Charles. *Cuthbert Tunstall: Churchman, Scholar, Statesman, and Administrator.* London: Longmans, Green, 1938.

V. GENERAL AND POLITICAL HISTORY OF ENGLAND

Bacon, Francis. *The History of the Reign of King Henry VII and Selected Works.* Edited by Brian Vickers. Cambridge: Cambridge University Press, 1998.

Baker, J. H. *The Legal Profession and the Common Law: Historical Essays.* London: Hambledon Press, 1985.

Bush, M. L. *The Government Policy of Protector Somerset.* London: Edward Arnold, 1975.

Chrimes, S. B. *Henry VII.* Berkeley: University of California Press, 1972.

Coleman, Christopher, and David Starkey, eds. *Revolution Reassessed: Revisions in the History of Tudor Government and Administration.* Oxford: Clarendon Press, 1986.

Elton, G. R. *England under the Tudors.* 2d ed. London: Methuen, 1974.

———. *Reform and Reformation: England, 1509–1558.* Cambridge, Mass.: Harvard University Press, 1977.

———. "Tudor Government: The Points of Contact." In *Studies in Tudor and Stuart Politics and Government,* edited by G. R. Elton. 4 vols. Cambridge: Cambridge University Press, 1974–92, vol. 3, 3–57.

———. *The Tudor Revolution in Government: Administrative Changes in the Reign of Henry VIII.* Cambridge: Cambridge University Press, 1953.

———, ed. *The Tudor Constitution: Documents and Commentary.* 2d ed. Cambridge: Cambridge University Press, 1982.

Fox, Alistair, and John Guy. *Reassessing the Henrician Age: Humanism, Politics, and Reform, 1500–1550.* Oxford: Basil Blackwell, 1986.

Guy, John. *Tudor England.* Oxford: Oxford University Press, 1988.

———, ed. *The Tudor Monarchy.* London: Edward Arnold, 1998.

Jones, Whitney R. D. *The Mid-Tudor Crisis, 1539–1563.* London: Macmillan, 1973.

Jordan, W. K. *Edward VI: The Threshold of Power. The Protectorship of the Duke of Somerset.* Cambridge, Mass.: Harvard University Press, 1968.

———. *Edward VI: The Young King. The Dominance of the Duke of Northumberland.* Cambridge, Mass.: Harvard University Press, 1970.

Lehmberg, Stanford. *The Reformation Parliament, 1529–1536.* Cambridge: Cambridge University Press, 1970.

MacCulloch, Diarmaid, ed. *The Reign of Henry VIII: Politics, Policy, and Piety.* New York: St. Martin's Press, 1995.

Scarisbrick, J. J. *Henry VIII.* London: Eyre and Spottiswoode, 1968.

Tittler, Robert, and Jennifer Loach, eds. *The Mid-Tudor Polity, c. 1540–1560.* Totowa, N.J.: Rowman and Littlefield, 1980.

Wernham, R. B. *Before the Armada: The Emergence of the English Nation, 1485–1588.* New York: Harcourt, Brace and World, 1966.

Williams, Penry. *The Tudor Regime.* Oxford: Clarendon Press, 1979.

VI. SOCIAL AND ECONOMIC HISTORY

A. General

Amussen, Susan Dwyer. *An Ordered Society: Gender and Class in Early Modern England.* Oxford: Basil Blackwell, 1988.

Bridbury, A. R. *Economic Growth: England in the Later Middle Ages.* London: George Allen and Unwin, 1962.

Britnell, R. H. *The Commercialization of English Society, 1000–1500.* Cambridge: Cambridge University Press, 1993.

Clay, C. G. A. *Economic Expansion and Social Change: England, 1500–1700.* 2 vols. Cambridge: Cambridge University Press, 1984.

Cornwall, J. C. K. *Wealth and Society in Early Sixteenth-Century England.* London: Routledge and Kegan Paul, 1988.

Fletcher, Anthony. *Gender, Sex, and Subordination in England, 1500–1800.* New Haven: Yale University Press, 1995.

Heal, Felicity. *Hospitality in Early Modern England.* Oxford: Clarendon Press, 1990.

Hoskins, W. G. *The Age of Plunder: King Henry's England, 1500–1547.* London: Longman, 1976.

Houlbrooke, Ralph A. *The English Family, 1450–1700.* London: Longman, 1984.

McIntosh, Marjorie Kenniston. *Controlling Misbehavior in England, 1370–1600.* Cambridge: Cambridge University Press, 1998.

Palliser, David. *The Age of Elizabeth: England under the Later Tudors, 1547–1603.* London: Longman, 1983.

Slack, Paul. *Poverty and Policy in Tudor and Stuart England.* London: Longman, 1988.

Tawney, R. H. *Religion and the Rise of Capitalism: A Historical Study.* London: John Murray, 1926.

———, and Eileen Power, eds. *Tudor Economic Documents: Being Select Documents Illustrating the Economic and Social History of England.* 3 vols. London: Longmans, Green, 1924.

Wrigley, E. A., and Roger Schofield. *The Population History of England, 1541–1871: A Reconstruction.* London: Edward Arnold, 1981.

Youings, Joyce. *Sixteenth-Century England.* London: Penguin, 1984.

B. Education

Baldwin, T. W. *William Shakespeare's Small Latine & Lesse Greeke.* 2 vols. Urbana: University of Illinois Press, 1944.

Cressy, David. *Literacy and the Social Order: Reading and Writing in Tudor and Stuart England.* Cambridge: Cambridge University Press, 1980.

Hexter, J. H. "The Education of the Aristocracy in the Renaissance." In *Reappraisals in History: New Views on History and Society in Early Modern Europe.* 2d ed. Chicago: University of Chicago Press, 1979, 45–70.

Simon, Joan. *Education and Society in Tudor England.* Cambridge: Cambridge University Press, 1966.

C. Agrarian History and Rural Unrest

Beer, Barrett L. *Rebellion and Riot: Popular Disorder in England during the Reign of Edward VI.* Kent, Ohio: Kent State University Press, 1982.

Bindoff, S. T. *Ket's Rebellion, 1549.* Reprinted in *The Historical Association Book of the Tudors,* edited by Joel Hurstfield. London: Sidgwick and Jackson, 1973, 72–102.

Bridbury, A. R. "Sixteenth-Century Farming." *Economic History Review.* 2d ser., 27 (1974): 538–56.

Cornwall, J. C. K. *Revolt of the Peasantry, 1549.* London: Routledge & Kegan Paul, 1977.

Fletcher, Anthony, and Diarmaid MacCulloch. *Tudor Rebellions.* 4th ed. London: Longman, 1997.

Kerridge, Eric. *Agrarian Problems in the Sixteenth Century and After.* London: George Allen and Unwin, 1969.

Land, Stephen. *Kett's Rebellion: The Norfolk Rising of 1549.* Totowa, N.J.: Rowman and Littlefield, 1977.

Manning, Roger B. *Village Revolts: Social Protest and Popular Disturbance in England, 1509–1640.* Oxford: Clarendon Press, 1988.

Miller, Edward, ed. *The Agrarian History of England and Wales, 1348–1500.* Vol. 3. Cambridge: Cambridge University Press, 1991.

Rose-Troup, Frances J. *The Western Rebellion of 1549: An Account of the Insurrections in Devonshire and Cornwall against Religious Innovations in the Reign of Edward VI.* London: Smith, Elder, 1913.

Tawney, R. H. *The Agrarian Problem in the Sixteenth Century.* London: Longmans, Green, 1912.

Thirsk, Joan, ed. *The Agrarian History of England and Wales, 1500–1640.* Vol. 4. Cambridge: Cambridge University Press, 1967.

————. "Tudor Enclosures." In *The Rural Economy of England: Collected Essays*. London: Hambleton Press, 1984, 65–84.

D. Commercial and Urban Life

Beier, A. L., and Roger Finlay, eds. *London, 1500–1700: The Making of the Metropolis*. London: Longman, 1986.

Bridbury, A. R. "English Provincial Towns in the Later Middle Ages." *Economic History Review*. 2d ser., 34 (1981): 1–24.

Clark, Peter, and Paul Slack. *English Towns in Transition, 1500–1700*. London: Oxford University Press, 1976.

Dyer, Alan. *Decline and Growth in English Towns, 1400–1640*. Cambridge: Cambridge University Press, 1995.

Fisher, F. J. *London and the English Economy, 1500–1700*. Edited by P. J. Corfield and N. B. Harte. London and Ronceverte: Hambleton Press, 1990.

Patten, John. *English Towns, 1500–1700*. Hamden, Conn.: Archon, 1978.

Ramsay, G. D. *English Overseas Trade during the Centuries of Emergence: Studies in Some Modern Origins of the English-Speaking World*. London: Macmillan, 1957.

Sacks, David Harris. *The Widening Gate: Bristol and the Atlantic Economy, 1450–1700*. Berkeley: University of California Press, 1991.

Thomson, J. A. F., ed. *Towns and Townspeople in the Fifteenth Century*. Gloucester: Alan Sutton, 1988.

Wee, Herman van der. *The Growth of the Antwerp Market and the European Economy (Fourteenth–Sixteenth Centuries)*. 3 vols. The Hague: Martinus Nijhoff, 1963.

VII. RELIGIOUS AND ECCLESIASTICAL HISTORY

Aston, Margaret, and Colin Richmond, eds. *Lollardy and the Gentry in the Later Middle Ages*. New York: St. Martin's Press, 1997.

Bowker, Margaret. *The Henrician Reformation*. Cambridge: Cambridge University Press, 1981.

Brigden, Susan. *London and the Reformation*. Oxford: Clarendon Press, 1989.

Clebsch, William A. *England's Earliest Protestants, 1520–1535*. New Haven: Yale University Press, 1964.

Collinson, Patrick. *The Birthpangs of Protestant England: Religious and Cultural Change in the Sixteenth and Seventeenth Centuries*. New York: St. Martin's Press, 1988.

Cross, Claire. *Church and People, 1450–1660: The Triumph of the Laity in the English Church*. Hassocks: Harvester Press, 1976.

Dickens, A. G. *The English Reformation.* 2d ed. London: B. T. Batsford, 1989.

Duffy, Eamon. *The Stripping of the Altars: Traditional Religion in England, c. 1400 – c. 1580.* New Haven: Yale University Press, 1992.

Haigh, Christopher, ed. *The English Reformation Revised.* Cambridge: Cambridge University Press, 1987.

————. *English Reformations: Religion, Politics, and Society under the Tudors.* Oxford: Clarendon Press, 1993.

Heath, Peter. *The Parish Clergy on the Eve of the Reformation.* London: Routledge and Kegan Paul, 1969.

Hudson, Anne. *The Premature Reformation: Wycliffite Texts and Lollard History.* Oxford: Clarendon Press, 1988.

Knowles, David. *The Religious Orders in England.* 3 vols. Cambridge: Cambridge University Press, 1948 – 61.

Marshall, Peter, ed. *The Impact of the Reformation, 1500 – 1640.* London: Edward Arnold, 1998.

McFarlane, K. B. *Wycliffe and English Non-conformity.* Harmondsworth: Penguin, 1972.

O'Day, Rosemary, and Felicity Heal, eds. *Continuity and Change: Personnel and Administration of the Church of England, 1500 – 1642.* Leicester: Leicester University Press, 1976.

Rex, Richard. *Henry VIII and the English Reformation.* London: Macmillan, 1993.

Scarisbrick, J. J. *The Reformation and the English People.* Oxford: Basil Blackwell, 1984.

Swanson, R. N. *Church and Society in Late Medieval England.* Oxford: Basil Blackwell, 1989.

Thomson, J. A. F. *The Later Lollards, 1414 – 1520.* Oxford: Oxford University Press, 1965.

Index